"**W**hat a timely book for business managers and anyone who manages people. Most of the time people don't take responsibility because their responsibilities are not clear to them. *The Art of Constructive Confrontation* will be a valuable tool for my business and personal life. I have taken your advice and plan to put the principles described in the book to use next week."

— **Tina D'Aversa**
Publisher, *SportingKid* Magazine

"**A**s odd as it may seem, the subtitle of Hoover and DiSilvestro's book could be, 'Respecting and loving ourselves and our employees through a defined process of confrontation.' The ideas contained herein are psychologically and organizationally, to eyes that can see, a revolution in resolving practical-yet-difficult problems in employee and organizational motivation toward productive ends."

— **Richard Bruehl, PhD**
Diplomate of the American Association of Pastoral Counselors, Licensed Marriage and Family Therapist, Mediator

THE ART OF
CONSTRUCTIVE
CONFRONTATION

How to Achieve More
Accountability with Less Conflict

John Hoover
Roger P. DiSilvestro

WILEY

John Wiley & Sons, Inc.

Published by John Wiley & Sons, Inc., Hoboken, New Jersey.
Published simultaneously in Canada.

For general information on our other products and services please contact our Customer Care Department within the United States at (800) 762-2974, outside the United States at (317) 572-3993 or fax (317) 572-4002.

Wiley also publishes its books in a variety of electronic formats. Some content that appears in print may not be available in electronic books. For more information about Wiley products, visit our web site at www.Wiley.com.

Library of Congress Cataloging-in-Publication Data:

Hoover, John.
   The art of constructive confrontation : how to achieve more accountability with less conflict / John Hoover, Roger DiSilvestro.
      p. cm.
   ISBN-13 978-0-471-71853-6 (cloth : alk. paper)
   ISBN-10 0-471-71853-X (cloth : alk. paper)
   1. Communication in personnel management. 2. Interpersonal confrontation.
3. Conflict management. I. DiSilvestro, Roger, 1947– . II. Title.
   HF5549.5.C6H65 2005
   658.3'145—dc22
                                                        2004030896

10 9 8 7 6 5 4 3 2 1

Acknowledgments

With deep gratitude I thank the dozens of sales professionals, managers, and friends who demanded clarity from me so that our relationships might flourish. The dedication, energy, and compassion of Mr. Harry Moodie, my partner and boss for 25 years, set the standard for the constructive confrontation process in this book.

There are few words that could fully express my gratitude to my partner and mentor, Mr. Spencer Hays, who taught me to accept the hot seat of accountability. I'm likewise grateful to Ms. Janet McDonald, whose dignity and dedication under intense pressure taught me the importance of acting professionally under any condition.

The late Charles McBroom, my first mentor and boss, picked me up from career obscurity and showed me what I could become by giving others the opportunity to fulfill their personal and professional potentials. I am now and will forever be overwhelmed by the energy, talent, and patience of Dr. John Hoover, my co-author and dear friend. My gratitude would not be complete without acknowledging Norah Buikstra, whose love and faith encourages me to do the next right thing, and my son, Paul, the dearest blessing in my life.

ACKNOWLEDGMENTS

With heart-felt contrition, this book is dedicated to all the people I have attacked, confronted unfairly, and misled as I was learning a better way.

—*Roger DiSilvestro*

Matthew Holt, our editor at John Wiley & Sons, understood the tremendous value of increasing accountability and decreasing conflict in organizations and made this platform available to us from which we can preach the gospel of *constructive confrontation*. We are also grateful to Peter Miller of PMA Literary & Film Associates in New York City for making all the necessary arrangements with Matt. Finally, I appreciate Charles McBroom, Harry Moodie, Janet McDonald, and Spencer Hays, each of whom had a hand in preparing Roger to be a mentor and inspiration to me and everyone who has the privileged of working with him.

—*John Hoover*

Contents

Introduction   *ix*

PART I: Commitment

  1. The Case for Confrontation   3

  2. The Conversation   23

  3. The Commitment   63

  4. The Covenant   83

PART II: Confrontation

  5. Confrontation   119

  6. Staying Positive   149

  7. Changes and Challenges   169

  8. Cementing the Bond   185

PART III: Celebration

  9. Celebrating the Right Things   205

 10. Plan for the Peaks   223

 11. Rewards that Resonate   237

 12. Building Others   249

    Index   *265*

Introduction

The constructive confrontation system is a course of action that shows leaders how to use confrontation constructively to increase accountability and decrease conflict in their departments, divisions, and organizations. Confrontation is like fire or water. Properly used, it can save your life. It can also destroy. The difference emerges when confrontation is confused with conflict. Negative or conflictual confrontation is the explosion of pent-up frustration — frustration that wouldn't have existed had the course of action been followed to the end. The presence of anger and hostility in the workplace usually indicates that there has not been *enough* confrontation — specifically, *constructive* confrontation — to prevent friction and the frustration that inevitably follows. People in positions of leadership have the choice to confront constructively now or confront negatively later.

Do you have the courage to hold people accountable for the performance they agreed to deliver? If you were taught that accountability can only be enforced through conflict, there is good news ahead. Raw courage in the form of an iron fist is not what it takes to hold people accountable. Roaring like a lion and flashing a set of brass knuckles are more likely to produce acute anxiety than actual accountability.

If you follow the circle of constructive confrontation, courage becomes less necessary as the system takes over. By definition, confrontation merely means to communicate face-to-face. Sales professionals are keenly aware that the best way to influence other human beings is with face time. Why would the people within your sphere of influence at work be any different?

Constructive confrontation is a structured, systematic approach that *decreases* conflict and *increases* accountability by connecting the dots between what people want and what organizations need. Constructive confrontation reduces conflict in the same way it increases accountability through clear and well-articulated expectations, follow-up, and recognition. Increased accountability with less conflict requires consistent, constructive confrontation that establishes the course, makes course corrections, and reaffirms the course.

Confrontation is the weakest link in executive leadership because it is frequently mistaken for the tantrums of unskilled managers who reach the end of their ropes and blow up at those around them, especially those reporting to them. The following are two of the primary reasons for this behavior:

1. Confrontation is misunderstood, avoided, and not applied as soon, or as often, as needed.
2. When it *is* applied, it's usually an expression of frustration instead of skilled leadership.

There is nothing complicated about constructive confrontation as a road map for accountability. Supervisors, managers, and executives can successfully hold their direct reports (and themselves) accountable for their performance by using this three-step cycle:

Constructive confrontation is not a practice reserved for leaders to apply to subordinates. As you can see in Figure I.1, there is nothing complicated about constructive confrontation as a road map for accountability. Anyone, at any level, can, and should be encouraged to, engage in

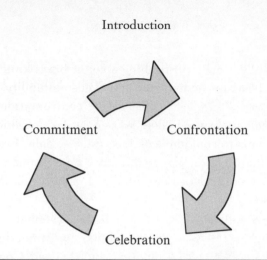

Commitment   Confrontation

Celebration

FIGURE I.1. Circle of confrontation

constructive confrontation. The conditions are simple: (1) There must be a covenant between the parties outlining the commitment, including expectations, methods, and measures; (2) All parties must confront one another to ensure that progress and performance are what they should be. This means peer-to-peer confrontation as well as team member-to-team leader confrontation. The rules and principles are the same for everybody, the only difference being range of institutional responsibility; (3) All parties to the covenant must celebrate the successful completion of each designated step in the process.

COMMITMENT TO EMOTIONAL PURPOSE

The process of securing true commitment is based on emotional purpose. Each team member must be able to clearly articulate his or her personal and professional ambitions in real and certain terms and how his or her current employment helps fulfill those ambitions. The supervisor, manager, or executive must also disclose his or her emotional purpose and relate them to his or her role in the organization. The discussion of emotional purpose helps team members internalize the context of the job.

Job functions are not typically tailored to suit what the individual wants and needs. But aligning the team member's wants and needs as closely as possible to what the organization needs sets the stage for enthusiastic and productive performance. Without this piece of the commitment conversation, both team leader and team member might operate from assumptions that can sabotage a working agreement.

COMMITMENT TO ONE ANOTHER

The commitment stage of the process eliminates the mind reading that so many supervisors, managers, and executives expect will fill in the gaps when their team members aren't adequately briefed. During the commitment stage, the team leader and team member discuss specific goals, the schedule for reaching the goals, and the process for achievement. The commitment consists of more than ethereal goals that sound good in motivational meetings or in the optimistic glow of goal-setting sessions or change management seminars.

The team member and team leader must commit to one another to fulfill their agreed-upon roles and responsibilities. One of the leader's responsibilities is confrontation. Team leaders must also be willing to be confronted by team members. If there is no clear, written covenant between the team leader and team member, there is no basis for confrontation by anyone, except by pulling rank.

THE TEAM LEADER/TEAM MEMBER COVENANT

Formation of a written covenant completes the commitment arc in a skilled leader's circle of confrontation. If expectations are created by one party without agreement from the other, if elements such as the time table remain ambiguous, or if the terms of the commitment are not recorded and communicated, there is no reason to expect compliance. Without a written road map of expectations for the performance of individual team members, there is no target to aim for. Nor is there a confirmed criterion or foundation for constructive confrontation.

If the commitment to action isn't cleansed of all ambiguity, the entire agenda is likely to be derailed. Tasks and objectives must be specific, concrete components individual team members can complete in a measurable manner. And they must be written down. The circle of confrontation begins with each team member's commitment to the required actions, in real time, to achieve real results. The covenant between the team member and team leader must be realistic, complete, and meaningful before it can be enforceable.

CONFRONTATION

Confrontation is course confirmation and, when needed, correction. In business and organizational life, as in many other aspects of human behavior, people set out to achieve predetermined goals and don't revisit the goal until it has been achieved, not been achieved, or the effort has been abandoned along the way. Any pilot or navigator knows that, although the aircraft or ship departs for a specific destination, course corrections en route are essential to reaching the destination.

Individuals and those responsible for the performance of others must check regularly for deviations from the course and make corrections as necessary. Waiting until the deadline is too late. Once-per-year performance reviews aren't nearly enough. Daily, weekly, and monthly constructive confrontation is a team leader's most fundamental responsibility to him- or herself, to team members, and to the well-being of the entire organization. Confrontation, as course correction, comes in a variety of packages, including the following:

1. *Rewriting or reaffirming goals and expectations.* As progress and performance are regularly monitored and evaluated, the original goals might need to be reevaluated. Internal or external changes to the organization might call for modification of the original goals. Other unforeseen influences might also require adjustments.
2. *Communicating what might have not been initially expressed and/or understood.* Thanks to a continuous refinement process of monitoring performance and progress, lack of adequate information or misunderstandings need not rear their ugly heads. Things can't be said once

and be expected to remain in the front of anyone's consciousness. Confrontation is reminding, reminding, and reminding again.

3. *Exposing intentional or unintentional misrepresentations.* People can innocently commit to more than they're capable of delivering. They can also *intentionally* misrepresent what they're capable of delivering, figuring that no one will confront them on it later. Windows can open for conflict to creep in when team leader or team member intentionally misrepresents him- or herself during the commitment stage. Consistent constructive confrontation deals with this issue sooner rather than later and provides everyone with an opportunity to come clean before too many opportunities are lost and too much damage is done.

Confrontation, based on the covenant the team leader and team member agreed to, is constructive and nonthreatening. It's not a personal attack because there is nothing personal about progress or lack of progress on a predetermined agenda. With a clear road map for progress, the discussion immediately focuses on whether the team member is on course. If not, the conversation can immediately segue into what is causing the disruption or disconnect and how it can best be addressed.

When little or no clarity exists about expectations, roles, and responsibilities, confrontation is almost always a negative and unproductive experience. The commitment stage must be fully completed before the confrontation stage can reach full value. Flexibility in course corrections or acquiring new information is always helpful. But "changing the rules as we go" is never a confidence builder in team members' minds and often results in cynicism. When supervisors, managers, and executives don't work the program, team members start bailing out.

CELEBRATION SETS THE TONE

Rewarded behavior is repeated behavior. Celebration helps keep confrontation *constructive.* If the only ongoing dialogue that team leaders offer team members deals with course correction and compensating for shortcomings, the long-term effect will be dampening. Constant recognition of achievement, appropriate for the size of the accomplishment, helps perk up the confrontation conversation. Nevertheless, celebration is unfamiliar to many.

Armed with recognition for the team members' successes, the team leader consistently and constructively confronts each team member as he or she guides the team member's personal and professional growth — all of which were included in the original covenant with an eye toward reaching and exceeding personal and organizational goals. When it works, however, many people are surprised and don't know what to do. For many, completely meeting a challenge is a new experience. It is part of the team leader's responsibility to help team members learn to lighten up. The team leader and team member alike must become good at celebrating, through recognition and reward, and not discount celebration as frivolous or irresponsible behavior.

Celebration is the consistent and continuous reinforcement of the little things *and* big things that make goal attainment possible, *especially* the little things. Celebration starts with the smallest achievements upon which the larger accomplishments are built. Just as monitoring progress and performance are essential elements of the process, *recognizing* successful completion of tasks and other process elements outlined in the commitment stage is also critical to successful completion of the circle of confrontation as a whole.

Without celebration, commitment and confrontation are meaningless. But what should be celebrated? The circle of confrontation is based in part on the achievement and acquisition of the things team members have identified as the possessions, moments, and memories they seek most in their lives. Life achievements outside the workplace need to be celebrated as much as milestones in the internal process. The act of celebrating is an excellent opportunity to reaffirm the connection between internal and external agendas and how they compliment each other.

If commitment and constructive confrontation result in successful completion of the covenant, celebration is essential to renew the cycle. The celebration component of the constructive confrontation process provides fuel for the continued effort. It marks the end of one cycle and the beginning of another. From celebration comes increased confidence and renewed commitment as the cycle begins again. Each new cycle of success begins with a newly energized person as a result of how well the team leader facilitated the team member's growth and development throughout the process. The ultimate cycle is fulfilled when the team member is able to step up and lead another person through the process of commitment, confrontation, and celebration. That's cause for *real* celebration.

DON'T QUIT NEAR THE END

If enterprise leadership lacks a spine about anything, it's the willingness to confront. A well-crafted covenant between team leaders and team members is only as good as the team leader's commitment to support each team member through consistent and constructive confrontation and celebration. To give executives, managers, and supervisors the benefit of the doubt, no one probably taught them how badly they are cheating themselves, their direct reports, and their organizations as a whole when they fail to confront in a thoughtful, methodical, systematic, and strategic manner.

Although confrontation in the form of coaching, encouragement, and accountability is an essential tool in a team leader's skill set, the craft of constructive confrontation is so rare that few have seen enough of it to imitate. It's not taught in master of business administration (MBA) programs. Typically, once goals and objectives are set in most organizations, many team members and team leaders look the other direction, aware at some level that there will be no follow-through. If team leaders fail to confront constructively, team members not only have the opportunity to disconnect from their commitments, but they also have a person to blame — the leader.

In practical terms, it's universally accepted that organizational performance suffers from lost productivity. Specifically, performance is lost as it falls through the cracks between what organizations need people to do and what actually gets done. That gap can only be bridged by constructive confrontation. The art of constructive confrontation is a commonsense cycle of individual *and* organizational success that explodes myths that would have you believe that performance can be enhanced by the following:

- Berating direct reports into submission to their leader's will
- Dangling diamond-crusted carrots in front of their faces
- Exposing them to a continuous stream of motivational propaganda
- Threatening to fire them

ACTION DRIVES THINKING

One of the core concepts supervisors, managers, and executives need to learn is that appropriate action drives right thinking, not the other way around. Training, education, hype, or fearmongering won't produce high performance over time. Even when eliminating hype, false promises, and fearmongering and staying with positive practices like training and education, the active follow-through of constructive confrontation is still vital to genuine performance enhancement. Once the three steps of constructive confrontation are understood, the necessary instruction and encouragement can be applied and measured evenly across the organization. Using constructive confrontation to map a course of action is the best assurance that you'll experience many victories in your organization's future.

PART 1
Commitment

The Case for Confrontation

We've all heard cynics say, "If you want to know how much difference you make in the grand scheme of things, put your hand in a bucket of water, pull it out, and see the impression you leave behind." That's true of water. Unless your hand is dirty enough to change the color of the water, there is no trace left behind. But the cynic's attempt to make a wet hand analogous to life in general — and your impact upon it — breaks down where the rubber meets the road: relationships.

Sure, if you back out to a wide shot of life, the impact individuals make in each other's lives and careers appears smaller. If you back out to a wide enough shot of our planet, say from the moon, Mount Saint Helens in full eruption is barely noticeable. Planet gazing won't accomplish much when professional success or failure is tied so directly to an immediate relationship. It's a matter of scale, perspective, and proportion. Although interpersonal confrontation is a factor in all relationships, *this* book deals with the scale, perspective, and proportion of *working* relationships between team members and team leaders. The relationships dealt with through the circle of confrontation involve people between whom there is a direct line of reporting.

The human psyche doesn't heal its wounds as easily and effortlessly as water does as it conforms to the shape of its container. Nor does the human psyche forget the most elevating and fulfilling moments in life. Unlike water, the human psyche *resists conforming* to the shape of its container. That makes working with human beings a trickier proposition, more unpredictable and wrought with potential peril than filling buckets with water. It also holds more promise for growth and development. When's the last time water learned a new trick?

CONFRONTATION'S BAD RAP

The term *confrontation* is considered by some to be synonymous with *conflict*. Other pejorative terms associated with confrontation include *battle, contest, crisis, dispute, showdown,* or *strife.* It's true that opposing ideas or beliefs, when trying to occupy the same space in the universe, can (and probably will) lead to a conflictual confrontation inspiring diversity advocates to plaintively plead, "Can't we all just get along?"

Perhaps we can. But people with diverse ideas and beliefs must successfully *confront* their differences, not merely deny they exist, if there is to be any hope of acceptance, inclusion, and co-existence. Despite attempts by ever-optimistic and naïve souls to wish the differences away, people with diverse ideas, beliefs, and opinions must consciously choose peaceful and productive coexistence over combative alternatives. If people of diverse ideas, beliefs, and opinions are to live and work together, they must confront their differences instead of each other. It's not unlike the old slogan: "Attack the problem, not the person."

One enormous difference between conflictual versus constructive confrontation is timing. Confrontation, as most people have come to use the term, means addressing divisive issues *after* they have caused dissonance, discord, disconnects, and disputes. Diverse ideas, beliefs, and opinions, if not confronted sooner, will surely become conflicts later. Diverse ideas, beliefs, and opinions can be so extreme and polarizing that they will never reside peacefully in the same vicinity.

If there is any hope of "getting along," it will only be made possible by the sooner-rather-than-later confrontation of the issues. This book is not about avoiding confrontation; it's about using confrontation constructively.

NEGATIVE CONFRONTATIONS NO MORE

The best way to avoid negative confrontations is to confront. More accurately, the best way to avoid negative confrontations is to purposefully and skillfully engage in constructive confrontation. Conversely, the best way to *guarantee* negative confrontations is to avoid confrontation and hope the negativity will just go away. Sorry. Sooner or later, confrontation will become inevitable. All of the energy and resources used up by avoiding confrontation will more than likely ensure confrontation. The art of constructive confrontation will either work *for* you, or you'll be doomed to the type of negative confrontations that most human beings will do anything to avoid.

Confrontation, the way the term is used here, is neutral. Confrontation, in and of itself, is not positive *or* negative. It becomes positive or negative depending on whether it's used proactively and preemptively or whether it becomes a consequence of neglect. Almost any unfortunate, unpleasant, after-the-fact confrontation could be described as "something that should have been confronted a long time ago."

In light of the negative synonyms for confrontation already listed, there are positive terms associated with confrontation, words that include *meeting, encounter, face down, face up to, stand up to, meet eyeball-to-eyeball,* or *withstand*. Problems in organizational life are dealt with faster, cheaper, and better when they are anticipated and prepared for. The best use of meetings also includes planning and preparing to meet what lies ahead. Every great plan has at least one contingency, so problems that will potentially be encountered won't derail the plan.

Negative influences need to be *faced down*, or neutralized. Realities of the internal and external marketplace need to be *faced up to*, or recognized.

Undue criticisms must be *stood up to,* lest they become debilitating. Any influence that threatens or contradicts the health and well-being of the organization and its internal and external stakeholders must be *faced eyeball-to-eyeball.* Shouldn't anything that needs facing be *faced straight on?* Doesn't any worthwhile task, assignment, project, or initiative potentially encounter hazards and challenges that need to be *withstood?*

That's what constructive confrontation is all about. It doesn't mean chatting about something, shooting the breeze, kibitzing, or navel-gazing. Constructive confrontation means premeditated, methodical, systematic, and well-orchestrated efforts to do the following:

- Get after something before it gets after you.
- Position yourself and your team members for maximum productivity and performance with minimal margin for error.
- Minimize exposure by confronting contingencies in advance.
- Shed excess baggage and burden before the seas get stormy.
- Decrease conflict while increasing accountability.

There are a wide variety of benefits the circle of confrontation will afford you. As conversations lead to commitment, commitment leads to covenant, and covenant becomes the basis for constructive confrontation, the stage is set to get the most from what you have. That beats the heck out of paying more and getting less. Your team members are *begging* for responsible, organized, and effective leadership. They won't come right out and ask for it. But when you ask what went wrong or why their performance tanked, you can bet your bottom dollar that they'll blame the failure on the absence of responsible, organized, and effective leadership.

Don't hold your breath waiting for them to blame themselves. To do so would be painful and possibly even humiliating; except for the masochist, who wants to beat him- or herself up. Despite the fact that they'll accept responsibility for any bad thing that happens, whether or not they have anything to do with it, who really wants to work with masochists? Even small children have a natural tendency to avoid self-indictment.

When provided complete indemnification and assurances that there will be no punishment, youngsters will still answer the question, "Who did this?" with, "I dunno," "The dog," "The monster," "My sister," "A burglar," or "President (fill in the blank)."

Constructive confrontation will focus and inspire your team members like nothing else, whoever is on your bus. When people bemoan a lack of leadership, this is what they're truly asking for:

- Someone to listen and understand their issues, even help them identify issues they might not know they have
- Someone who will stand beside them and fight the good fight shoulder-to-shoulder
- Someone who has their personal and professional growth and development at heart
- Someone who will provide guidance, instruction, and encouragement whenever needed
- Someone who will provide support and backup when others question the team member's motives and methods
- Someone to set boundaries, blow through barriers, and commit to staying the course alongside the team member, beginning to end

WHAT IF?

Constructive confrontation differs from conventional confrontation in that it's anticipatory, or pro-active, rather than reactive. It can spell the difference between coming off as a hero or an idiot. When problems arise, the hero says, "Have no fear, we've planned for this contingency." The idiot says, "Gee, I never thought *that* would happen." The truth is that the idiot never gave *any* thought to potential hazards and obstacles. He *assumed,* and we all know the story about the donkey.

More than any other distinguishing feature, constructive confrontation is grounded in careful planning and preparation, considering all options and anticipating as many potential problems as possible. Socially, a lot of hip folks make fun of Boy Scouts and Girl Scouts, preferring instead to party with their idiot friends. Why not? Idiots are predictably unpredictable and largely spontaneous, always looking for a good time. Meanwhile the scouts are carefully planning — always prepared.

Next time you get stuck in a blizzard on the turnpike, with whom would you rather be carpooling — idiots or scouts? Next time you veer off the ski slope into the woods and twist your ankle, who do you want to rescue you — a ski patrol person who was a scout or a ski patrol person still hung over from last night's idiot-fest at the lodge? We all ride trains or drive our cars over dozens of bridges, large and small, every day. Do you want to drive or ride over bridges built by architects, engineers, and construction contractors who anticipate potential problems and design solutions into the structures, or do you want to have the bridge collapse beneath you?

This isn't a far-fetched analogy. If a bridge collapses beneath a train or automobile traffic or if the wings fall off of a commercial jetliner, confrontation will follow. But by then, it's conventional, conflict-oriented, accusatory, negative, blame-placing, find-a-scapegoat, search-for-the-guilty, and punish-the-innocent confrontation. No thanks.

Wouldn't you prefer the confrontation to have taken place *before* things started to fall apart . . . literally? Like granny used to say, "A stitch in time saves nine." As the old industrial maxim teaches us, "There never seems to be enough time or money to do it right the first time, but there's always enough time and money to do it *over again.*" Proper planning almost always makes things turn out more pleasantly, and proper planning always includes constructive confrontation.

Some use the term *constructive confrontation* to describe a positive approach to after-the-fact confrontation. No matter when confrontation takes place, you should attempt to go through positive steps, like defining the problem, expressing how you feel about the situation, reflect to the other party what you understand his or her position to be, and find a compromise, if possible. None of this removes or diminishes the fact that postponing or neglecting regular, conscious, constructive confrontation allowed things to tank in the first place. None of the aforementioned positive behaviors, if applied after the fact, will make up for the time, productivity, resources, and money lost by not staying on top of the game.

Given what you've learned so far about constructive confrontation, you can begin considering a wide range of *what ifs:*

- What if structural and aeronautical architects, engineers, and construction contractors didn't anticipate problems? What if they didn't preemptively confront the challenges and potential perils of construction from conception through completion?

- What if teachers and coaches didn't make lesson plans and game plans before class or the big game? How valued would you feel if your teacher passed out a test before giving an assignment or teaching?

- What if teachers didn't confront students who are not performing up to their capabilities? Who's getting cheated? The student and the society that will be forced to subsidize what the student is unable to contribute later in life.

- What if your athletic coach expected you to show up for the game without holding any practices or running you through any drills or exercises? What if athletic coaches didn't confront athletes who settle for performance below their capabilities? What if vocal coaches, acting coaches, or executive coaches didn't confront the people who are counting on them to confront lackluster performance?

- What if executives committed enormous physical, financial, and human resources to projects without a well-thought-out strategic plan? What if they flew strictly by the seat of their wardrobe? That's simply some peoples' style. But the risks they take jeopardize more than their own success. The more that rides on your decisions and execution, the more you owe it to the organization you work for and the people (internal and external) who are affected by your actions to take well-thought-out strategic actions.

- What if project managers, supervisors, managers, and executives

9

engaged their team members regularly with *what ifs?* Inquisitiveness is a big part of constructive confrontation. We should never stop asking "What if?" or acting "As if."

TALK SHOW SHRINKS

Dr. Laura Schlessinger, Dr. Phil McGraw, and other media therapists make a habit of compressing therapy that ordinarily takes months or years into minutes. In other words, they deal more in headlines than details. Call it compressed therapy. After a four-alarm diagnosis, they immediately cut to the chase and begin confronting their callers and guests. That's where the rubber meets the road. When time is constrained, musing about problems gives way to the confrontation. People who call in or otherwise agree to be on the show are seeking confrontation because nothing else seems to be working.

Unless the on-air diagnosis is an epiphany of epic proportions, the solutions are found in simple behavior modification. Simple to *describe,* that is. If the appropriate behaviors, healthy habits, and productive activities were easy, or resonated with the caller's essential nature, they wouldn't need confrontation. If the radio or television therapist *called the callers* daily with reminders and encouragement about the right thinking and behavior, there wouldn't be as many fires to put out on the air. As a practitioner of constructive confrontation, think of yourself as a preemptive talk show shrink.

Anyone in the mental health field knows the road to recovery is difficult and requires new ways of thinking and behaving. For some it's easier than it is for others. Some people face mountains of problems while others face molehills. In any case, getting from where you are now to where you want to be requires change, even if it's only more effort. More anything is a change. Meaningful, purposeful change isn't going to happen without constructive confrontation. More specifically, change won't be *sustained* without constructive confrontation to keep goals and purpose in the front seat of our consciences.

THE COURAGE TO CONFRONT

Confrontation becomes a negative and potentially frightening proposition when it's not engaged early enough. Confrontation is often postponed, neglected, or avoided altogether because of the *perception* that it requires great courage. Confrontation *after* the fact, *after* things have gone sour, or *after* it's too late to do it right the first time requires courage because you know it's not going to be pretty. The need to act courageously is dispelled by caring enough to confront constructively and consistently on the front end. If "caring" sounds too *Kum-by-ya* for your tastes, just think of it as working smart.

What is courage all about if you're facing down a problem that never should have been allowed to fester in the first place? Sometimes you're called upon to clean up a catastrophe you had no culpability in creating. That's why you earn the big bucks. So keep your courage handy. You might be called upon to rise above the crowd. Generally speaking, when it comes to confrontation, consistency diminishes the need for courage.

As a matter of faith, confrontation among believers in certain religions is encouraged and even welcomed when the common principles are forgotten or violated. The key is common principles. Confronting someone over an agenda that person didn't sign onto in the first place won't produce positive results unless the agenda is imposed to preserve social order and the common good. If people share common principles and commit to holding one another accountable, confrontation ranges from a preventative measure to an immediate remedy applied soon enough to make a positive difference.

For Christians who profess love for all God's children as a principle of faith, confronting must be done lovingly lest it impeach the believers' core principles. Similarly, confrontation that upholds and reinforces positive principles is a hedge against hypocrisy. It's one thing to give lip service to a belief. But actively participating in its preservation is proof of commitment. Despite the fact that actions speak louder than words, the cycle of confrontation, with its conversation, commitment, covenant, and

11

continuous confrontation followed by celebration, consciously and deliberately transforms words into action.

HISTORICAL CONFRONTATION

Some of the most famous examples of constructive confrontation demonstrate how perseverance and commitment to the long haul have spread inspiration around the world. Unfortunately, fewer and fewer young people recognize the name Annie Sullivan. Thankfully, there are some who can still tell you who Helen Keller was. Annie Mansfield Sullivan overcame a difficult childhood, including life in the county orphanage (circa 1880), separation from her siblings following her mother's and her brother's deaths. She overcame the sight–stealing disease of trachoma, eventually regaining much of her eyesight, to become an advocate for and a teacher of the blind.

Annie Sullivan is remembered most for leading a seven-year-old youngster named Helen Keller out of the darkness and isolation of Helen's deafness and blindness. It was one of the most incredible feats ever accomplished by a teacher and student. Despite Keller's deafness, Sullivan taught her to speak. Despite Keller's blindness, Sullivan taught her to read and write. Helen Keller became one of the world's most celebrated authors and lecturers of her time. It could not have been done without consistent, virtually relentless, constructive confrontation.

Sullivan had to teach Keller fundamental discipline before ever approaching reading, writing, or speaking skills. Helen Keller, used to overprotection and pampering from her parents, was uncooperative to say the least. Things were so physically rough at times that Sullivan had to move Keller out of her parents' house because they couldn't stand the constant confrontation between teacher and student. In the end, it was Sullivan's commitment over the years to confronting Helen Keller's continued progress that produced what many people proclaim was nothing short of a miracle in human transformation.

Helen Keller would never have been able to realize her full potential, and possibly none of it, were it not for the incredible commitment made by Annie Sullivan. That's what leaders do in the circle of confrontation. They use an organized, systematic approach to help their team members realize their full potential in the context of the professional challenge to be met. In the most difficult constructive confrontation scenarios, 99.9 percent of all organizational leaders never face anything even resembling the challenge Annie Sullivan overcame. If Sullivan had not been willing to continuously confront her pupil and stick with it for as long as it took, very few people, if any, would remember the name Helen Keller.

What if more parents were willing to invest even a fraction of the effort into their children's lives that Sullivan invested in Helen Keller's life? If all else remained equal, teachers, schools, the economy, and so on, it's safe to predict that scholastic performance and discipline in schools would improve exponentially and social issues like teen pregnancy, adolescent alcohol consumption, and drug use would diminish significantly—perhaps to near extinction. Such improvements would transcend gender, ethnicity, sexual preference, and religious affiliation. Human beings are either challenged to excel, then consistently confronted to ensure success, or they're not.

Constructive confrontation is an investment in the future. How different would the world be today if Gandhi, Martin Luther King Jr., and Margaret Sanger had not confronted prejudice? How many business owners; community leaders; senators; congressional representatives; municipal, state, and federal judges; public agency heads; and presidential cabinet members would be African Americans, females, Hispanics, or other historically disenfranchised populations? What if John Adams, Thomas Jefferson, and Benjamin Franklin hadn't confronted taxation without representation in the name of liberty? What if free men and women throughout the world had not been willing to confront forces of oppression throughout the nineteenth and twentieth centuries? Without their sacrifices, world maps would be drawn very differently from how they are drawn today.

THE DESPERATE SALESMAN

Bring it back into the workplace. Consider, if you will, the salesman who was too burned out to continue. He was young and, like most young men, was confused about his direction in life and doubtful as to whether all of his hard would ever pay dividends. Wracked with self-doubt and emotional fatigue, a wise mentor took the young salesman under his wing and offered hope. The young man didn't know how to respond to a mentor. No one, including his own parents, had ever encouraged him before.

The mentor started confronting the young man on a regular basis, setting goals and building the *skills, habits, attitudes,* and *activities* the young man would need to succeed. Even with all of the encouragement, the young man wavered and faltered. He knew what he had agreed to do but couldn't seem to complete his mission. His mentor continued to confront him. When the young man pushed back and complained of his emotional exhaustion, the wise mentor told him, "I can't help how you feel. But I can teach you what you need to do to succeed."

The conversations continued. The young man committed to try again, and again, and again. Covenants were drafted, and the mentor confronted his mentee again, and again, and again. It took years, but the constructive confrontation took hold and became anchored deep in the young man's consciousness. Because a wise man cared enough to step into the path of the young man's self-doubt, because he cared enough to confront before and during the progress of the young man's career, their story had a happy ending. The young man is now a corporate chief executive officer (CEO), a figurative million years and miles from that time and place where he nearly threw in the towel. If you ask the CEO today the secret of his success, he'll point directly at his mentor and say, "I'm a success today because that person cared enough to confront me, and I had enough functioning brain cells left to respond."

Confrontation on the Court

Legendary athletes will almost always point to legendary coaches as the reason for their success. Raw talent, no matter how good it is, won't go very far if it's not molded, focused, and applied properly. It certainly won't be fully realized. This is true of *any* talent: business, musical, literary, visual, surgical, athletic, and so on. What great molders of talent do is confront, early and often. It's not uncommon for the talented ones to resist and even resent the confrontations while confrontation is occurring. With greater maturity, they invariably look back and thank the God of their understanding that someone cared enough to confront, and step into the path of apathy, complacency, and self-doubt.

Basketball fans know Bill Walton as a legendary athlete, from his days as a student athlete at the University of California, Los Angeles (UCLA) throughout his National Basketball Association (NBA) career. Walton points to legendary coach John Wooden, not only as a motivator, but also as a teacher. But it was Wooden's relentless constructive confrontation that shaped Walton's life and career.

True to form, Walton didn't fully understand or appreciate it at the time that it was going on. Writing about Wooden later, Walton spoke for himself and his former teammates, "Of course we didn't understand or realize any of this while we were doing it. We thought he was nuts, crazy." Such is the nature of youth and ignorance. Unfortunately, those with age and wisdom can't slam dunk like they used to. Could you imagine what would happen if John Wooden's mind could be transplanted into Kobe Bryant's body?

Almost three decades after John Wooden ceased to coach Walton in an official capacity, the player still fondly describes how his former coach took him and his teammates to "places we didn't want to go," driving them in "directions that we weren't aware of," and teaching invaluable life lessons through "explanation, demonstration, correction, and repetition." Earning the "privilege of becoming a member of the UCLA basketball team" under Wooden required "living up to your responsibilities."

Through it all Walton describes Wooden's confrontation as "always constructive."

These are the essential elements in the circle of constructive confrontation: *conversation* (explanation and exploration), *commitment* (living up to responsibilities), *covenant* (memorializing what's been committed to), *confrontation* (correction and repetition), and *celebration*. Using constructive confrontation as a premeditated, systematic approach to increasing accountability and reducing conflict is consistent with what Wooden describes as the "triumph of executing an organized plan over hoping that you'll be lucky." Leading people in the workplace without taking full advantage of all constructive confrontation components is trading on luck. Without "an organized plan," you'll be lucky to see your team members meet anything that resembles your expectations.

CONFRONTATION IN THE RED ZONE

When asked about turning around poorly performing football franchises, Bill Parcells, who has done it a few times, has some philosophies that further illustrate the value of constructive confrontation in workplace relationships. Parcells believes that holding frank conversations with everyone in the organization is essential to success and that those frank conversations include a full explanation of what the organization can and will do for the player and what the player will contribute to the team to help it reach its goals.

When performance is the problem, confrontation is the only way out. Constructive confrontation is the best way to ensure that performance won't *become* a problem.

This is all part of constructive confrontation. The process is not unique to any individual or application. If you're wondering where the celebration is in all of this, wait until the next touchdown.

The road map for constructive confrontation, just like Bill Purcell's turnaround philosophy, is not complicated. It merely requires the effort that you're already being paid to make. Before you start thinking constructive confrontation is some kind of manipulation or punitive ploy on the part of upper management to get you to work harder, be advised that following the constructive confrontation process makes your life easier by *reducing wasted effort*. Parcells wouldn't do the things he does if the effort was wasted. If his philosophy didn't work, he'd be the first to admit and abandon it.

WRITE FIRST, CONFRONT LATER

The conversation phase of the circle of confrontation is critical to the process. The commitment phase is equally important. But, for heaven's sake, *write it down*. The horror stories that follow verbal contracts are legion. It doesn't matter how chummy a leader and his or her team members are, write down the commitment in the form of a covenant. Friends don't always stay friends. Bickering over loosely interpreted verbal agreements will end a friendship faster than borrowing money.

There was once a corporate communications consultant who was called in by an old buddy to nail down a new corporate client for his buddy's emerging video production company. The communications consultant had the reputation and track record to meet the high standards demanded by the prospective client. As a result of the consultant's affiliation with the project and a parade of his previously published works, his buddy received the contract. The quid pro quo was simple; the consultant would write the scripts for the corporate media productions at his standard fee. It all looked rosy. The client liked the first production, and it appeared to be the start of a long and beautiful friendship.

When the communications consultant ran into the new client at a charity golf tournament a few months later, he was surprised to hear that the subsequent productions were "okay," despite the consultant's lack of involvement. "I sure wish you had stayed on the project; I nearly cancelled everything when I heard you quit," said the client. "Quit?" the communications consultant thought to himself. "Subsequent productions?" The consultant immediately confronted his "buddy," the production company owner.

He went to the production company offices and took his "buddy" out to lunch to politely move the conversation off-campus. The consultant, after all, was a communications expert. He went through all the sharing and caring stuff about "I hear you saying . . . blah, blah, blah," in an attempt to have a *pleasant confrontation.* But pleasant or not, it was too late. The communications "expert" hadn't written down the agreement in the form of a covenant nor bothered to have the handshake agreement witnessed. His "buddy" invoked selective memory to renegotiate.

Admitting that he didn't want to pay the consultant his going rate for scripting the corporate videos, the production company owner had hired a less-expensive writer without bothering to discuss it with the consultant. When the client noticed deterioration in the quality of writing, the production company owner told him that the consultant had quit the project and was no longer available. He had to spring for a couple of expensive golf resort weekends for the client, but he hung on to the contract.

By not drafting a covenant up front, the communications consultant created an impossible situation, impossible to get out of gracefully, that is. With no witnesses to the verbal agreement, there was no way to enforce it after it was violated, which the consultant *assumed* would never happen. This is when some people hire the law firm of Louie and Guido to collect. Fortunately, the communications consultant was too classy for that. With all avenues for legitimate remedy closed to him, he smarted over the loss of tens of thousands of dollars in income over the life of the project but chalked it up as an expensive lesson.

The moral of this story: write it down. No matter how warm and fuzzy you feel when you make the commitment, write it down. You might innocently forget exactly what you committed to, the other party might innocently forget what he or she committed to, or there might be nothing innocent about the amnesia when it happens. There might be misunderstandings or misinterpretation. It won't matter. The only thing worse than an after-the-fact, too-late-to-be-anything-but-ugly confrontation is confronting after the fact with no document to operate from. Little good can come out of an after-the-fact confrontation when the majority of the damage has already been done. Without a covenant, the process will break down long before there is anything to celebrate.

EXPECTATIONS

Any relationship is vulnerable to unrealized expectations. Virtually any conflict or hostility in the workplace can be traced to someone's disappointment over the failure of someone else to accomplish what he or she was expected to do. This works up *or* down the organizational food chain. The wild card: who was expecting whom to do what and why? How many times have you heard it said that *assuming* makes an ass out of "u" and "me"? Virtually any conflict or hostility in the workplace means somebody assumed something. There are occasions when someone simply blows off his or her responsibilities. But those are rare and quickly remedied.

Having an expectation is not necessarily a bad thing. The critical factor is how realistic the expectation is. In the absence of a competent approach to constructive confrontation, it is difficult to form a foundation for an expectation. Constructive confrontation begins with a conversation about the expectation and includes a full dialogue about what's real and relevant to the job, task, assignment, project, or initiative. The circle of confrontation virtually assures that expectations are realistic.

Constructive confrontation is, by design, self-correcting. If you discover later that something has not been accounted for or has been misdiagnosed, the cyclical nature of constructive confrontation will accommodate the course correction. There's no vice in admitting a mistake has been made and correcting it as soon as possible. The vice occurs when you operate under false assumptions and unrealistic expectations for a long period of time incurring expensive and possibly irreversible damage.

CHAPTER 1 SUMMARY

It's important to establish the role a leader plays in the growth and development of every person in his or her sphere of influence. Although
constructive confrontation works both ways, leader to team member and
vice versa, guiding the performance of every team member is a core leadership responsibility. Some of the highlights to keep in mind as you read
this book include the following:

- High performance is everybody's business. The future career options of every person in the organization depend on the ability to get
  things done. More than that, career success depends on a documented track record of accomplishment. Constructive confrontation not only gives leaders an easy-to-follow road map for maximizing accountability while minimizing conflict, it keeps a detailed
  written record of the process.
- Think of it as 20/20 foresight leadership. The memoirs of successful
  men and women in business, education, medicine, science, sports,
  and public service are filled with tributes to their coaches, mentors,
  teachers, and trusted advisors — the people who saw more potential
  in them than they saw in themselves. Constructive confrontation is
  a road map for leadership.
- Looking back upon their lives and careers, people whose names
  have become household words and whose accomplishments have
  become legendary invariably give credit to the people who encouraged them and, more importantly, patiently taught them the
  processes and disciplines that made extraordinary achievements
  possible.
- These successful and grateful people, who, like their mentors before
  them, now enjoy the view from atop a mountain of experience, pay
  tribute to those who tried to share that view and *cared enough to
  confront them.*
- With its commitment and celebration components, constructive
  confrontation is a premeditated, methodical, and systematic ap-

proach to leveling the leadership playing field. Premeditated, systematic confrontation stands the best chance of being constructive. After-the-fact, reactive confrontation will most likely be negative.

- Constructive confrontation is a tactical *pass-it-foreword* tool in any organizational leadership system. The simple-yet-profound leadership mantra, *Lead the way you like to be led*, makes confrontation inevitable. It's your choice to make it constructive. Every aspect of clear direction, support, and recognition leaders want from those they report to is equally important to those reporting to *them*.

- Constructive confrontation could be called leadership engineering. Without it, direction and proper course corrections will be coincidental at best. It's a road map that can be easily followed and applied consistently across organizations, between clients and vendors, and with customers.

Let the cynics say, "If you want to know how much difference you make in the grand scheme of things, put your hand in a bucket of water, pull it out, and see the impression you leave behind." Ask Helen Keller, Bill Walton, the desperate salesman-turned-CEO, or Bill Parcells . . . using constructive confrontation *will* leave an impression behind. Not using constructive confrontation will also leave an impression behind. But those are the impressions you'll likely try to forget. It all begins with the next stop: the conversation.

CHAPTER 2

The Conversation

During the 1980s, business people read or heard about an effective leadership technique called "Management by Walking Around" (MBWA). Management by Walking Around was pioneered at Hewlett-Packard (HP) by Bill Hewlett and Dave Packard themselves. *That's* endorsement of a leadership principle from the highest level in the organization. The value of engaging employees in regular and meaningful conversation about their work (MBWA style) was chronicled in Tom Peters and Robert Waterman's *In Search of Excellence* (New York: Harper & Row, 1982).

It's even more impressive to hear 30-year HP veterans, like George Zering, talk about how Management by Walking Around changed their lives. Retired since 1986, George remains a tireless, almost evangelical, advocate of MBWA and how Bill and Dave practiced it. Genuine regard between team members and team leaders is *that* powerful. Will the people who report to you now still be extolling your leadership virtues 20 years after they retire?

Public service advertisements (and the research that supports them) claim that the most powerful antidrug programs are regular and meaningful conversations between parents and children. Such premeditated and purposeful conversations are the essence of constructive confrontation. When things are talked about openly and honestly, they're much less likely to result in conflict and *destructive* confrontation. In the cycle of commitment, confrontation, and celebration, regular and meaningful conversations between working people (not to mention family members) can practically *eliminate* confrontation as the negative and pejorative experience we commonly associate with the word. Regular and meaningful conversations increase accountability and decrease conflict.

MBWA LOST

Despite the fact that MBWA is probably the closest thing to a universal leadership solution to come out of the twentieth century, MBWA, unlike Total Quality Management (TQM) or Six Sigma, was never documented, packaged, and sold by thousands of business consultants as a panacea. International Organization for Standardization (ISO) 9000, 9001, 9002, 9003, and other iterations of the standardization initiative, are heralded from huge banners strung across sides of corporate buildings. There were no banners suspended from buildings or corporate water towers proclaiming, "We Practice Management by Walking Around Here." Although it was tried far and wide, the concept of MBWA outside of HP eventually deteriorated, for the most part, into a loose parody of meaningful workplace dialogues.

Over time, MBWA became increasingly characterized as corporate muckety-mucks reluctantly walking out of their offices every day promptly at 3:00 P.M., spending the next 10 to 15 minutes glad-handing the troops, asking things like, "How're you doing?" (without slowing down long enough to hear the answer), and generally patting people on the back. This behavior lasted anywhere from three to six months before the muckety-mucks decided that MBWA wasn't significantly improving organizational performance, productivity, or profits.

Duh. If practiced incorrectly or disingenuously, MBWA ceases to be a means of encouraging team member buy-in, productivity, performance, and profitability. Disingenuous MBWA makes team members feel as if they're being mocked, which is the fastest way to *discourage* buy-in, productivity, performance, and profitability. Most team members would rather endure a bellowing *bosshole* (thanks to authors Will Douglas, Robert Nicholson, and Carol Lynne) than a smiling Philistine.

The following are three of the most prominent reasons why MBWA is not more widely and enthusiastically practiced:

1. *No style.* Meaningful workplace conversations were never management's style to begin with. If they were, they would've been happening all over the place. If a supervisor or manager has the institutional power to chew somebody out with impunity, why bother to be delicate about it, right? If meaningful conversations *do* occur in the workplace, they're usually only by coincidence or if muckety-mucks accidentally stumble upon a topic of mutual interest with subordinates, like professional sports, golf, softball, bowling, or bass fishing. Management by Walking Around is not a major emphasis in mainstream MBA programs. As more and more MBAs explode onto the scene and propagate, most lingering hope of structured, intentional, purposeful, and meaningful conversations between team members and corporate muckety-mucks continues to fade away.

2. *No time.* It takes a long time to build a trusting relationship between team members and team leaders. One of the many lessons the demise of the World Trade Center illustrates is that which takes years and a nearly indescribable amount of effort to build can be turned to ashes in less than an hour. Detroit or Tokyo can manufacture a beautiful automobile in an hour, but it can be destroyed in a second. Commitment and dedication will sustain effort over time. But anger, misunderstanding, and hatred can quickly take out what takes commitment and dedication a long time to build. Even if emotions are removed from the equation, most managers and supervisors just don't have the patience to invest the time necessary to engage in regular, meaningful conversations. Even if they *have* the

patience, pressure from upper management and stockholders subverts their efforts to build and sustain meaningful relationships with team members.

3. *No support.* Hewlett-Packard MBWA proponent, George Zering, also pointed out that no productivity or performance initiative is worth a flip if it's not supported, yea verily *lived,* from the top. (Any consultant can tell you that organizational initiatives and interventions not supported or modeled by top management are generally dead on arrival (DOA). Of course, each failed intervention opens the door for consultants to pitch new ones. There's plenty of motivation all around to do the dance of denial.) At HP, MBWA had a commitment from the top. That's why it worked there. More than that, HP veterans report that Bill Hewlett and Dave Packard *cared about them.* But, consultants and training modules can't teach people to care. Here's your leadership panacea right here: *Instead of trying to convince leaders to care, make people who care leaders.* As wonderful as that might sound, it's easier said than done, especially given who you might already have, as Jim Collins might say, on your bus.

MBWA REBORN

Assuming you can't empty your bus, level the playing field, and start all over again with an entirely new organization chart from supervisors on up, constructive confrontation might be your best answer. A major part of constructive confrontation is the art of teaching and using meaningful conversation related to corporate initiatives *as a skill.* As lovely as a chat about our children might be, meaningful workplace conversations discussed in this book ultimately serve the purpose of building the business. Even if someone's heart is not totally in it, properly executed constructive confrontation will produce results and improve workplace relationships.

Conversation is the first component in the commitment, confrontation, and celebration cycle. Without consistent, purposeful, and skilled conversation, commitment will be meaningless, confrontation will be reduced to venting frustration over unmet expectations that were never realistically defined to begin with, and there will be nothing to celebrate. The conversations will flow downhill to the gutter where all you talk about with your team members are your common enemies.

Superficial conversations about golf, softball, bowling, or bass fishing are not a problem in and of themselves. But *meaningful* conversations are rare. Consistent, premeditated, and skillfully executed meaningful conversations in the workplace are about as rare as Mega Lotto winners. In fact, over a year's time, there might be *more* Mega Lotto winners in the United States than there are premeditated and skillfully executed meaningful conversations in the workplace, at least ones that produce meaningful results.

This dismal portrait is being painted to let muckety-mucks off the hook, at least partially. Your supervisors, managers, or executives are probably not bad people. But the odds are about 1:1 that your muckety-mucks, especially MBA muckety-mucks, don't know *how* to have meaningful conversations with their team members. Most people in positions of authority have no core training in meaningful communications. Where would they have picked it up? In childhood? In school? While studying for their MBAs?

The reason the concept of regular, meaningful conversations went the way of MBWA was only *partially* because people in positions of authority didn't know how to do it. Outside of Hewlett and Packard's direct influence on people like HP Midwest employee #14, George Zering, and the Svengali influence Tom Peters has over Public Television viewers, few people came to realize the immense value of MBWA for all the aforementioned reasons. Where were they supposed to learn the art and craft of facilitating meaningful conversations? They were probably promoted into positions of authority because they demonstrated aptitude in exercising institutional authority over others, not by earning popular authority.

Any contact with your team members, aside from yelling, accusing, beating, torture, and other old-school management practices, is good. You might even stumble into some knowledge of which you would not have otherwise become aware. The Western Electric Hawthorne Plant studies of the 1920s made us aware of how much employees appreciate even the *appearance* of interest from corporate muckety-mucks.

This means the stage is set for making an immediate, positive improvement in organizational communication, productivity, and performance. As mental health professionals often say, "As long as we're not doing others harm, we're all better off for the conversation." There once was a boss who worked with a team member for 25 years before he ever knew his team member was an orphan. That's a fairly important piece of background to find out two and one-half decades into a relationship.

CRITICAL COMPONENTS: CONVERSATION, COMMITMENT, AND COVENANT

Constructive confrontation must come from covenant. Covenant comes from commitment. Commitment comes from conversation. Not only does the cycle of commitment, confrontation, and celebration begin with conversation but the conversation never ceases. This means the flow of information is continuous. The opportunities to promote and extend understanding are increased, and the chances for misinformation, misunderstanding, disconnect, and conflicts are proportionately decreased.

You're about to find out what a *craft* quality conversation can be. As you become an increasingly skilled person of the craft, several things will happen to you. First, as a master of meaningful conversation you won't experience a diminished sense of power, the way controlling personalities fear. You'll quickly sense increased power. Lest you think that skilled conversation is a manipulative, controlling tactic, the experience can be more accurately described as increased effectiveness. Skilled conversation improves relationships and performance in others very differently than invoking institutional authority.

You will also discover a heightened sense of awareness and a reduced sense of anxiety. There won't necessarily be any more going on around you than before, but you will be better tuned into it. Your team members won't tend to cloak information as much as they did before — when you were relying on your institutional authority to manage them. Last, as you become more open to sharing big-picture information with your team members, they'll feel more comfortable bringing valuable information to *you* in the form of their small-picture observations at the flashpoints where your enterprise thrives. As soon as you become more revealing, they'll become more revealing.

Conversation is information exchange, and, as the leader, you go first. Because the conversation sets the stage for the commitment (Chapter 3) and the covenant (Chapter 4), getting it right is all-important. It's not a step that can be skipped or rushed. Don't think of the conversation as something to finish before moving on to commitment and covenant. Think instead of establishing the concept of conversation, collecting enough information, then moving on to the commitment and covenant with the understanding that the conversation will continue indefinitely.

WHEN TO CONVERSE

Winston Churchill said, "Never flinch, never weary, never despair." Effective leaders never grow weary of talking to their team members. If you are truly adverse to regular, meaningful conversations with your team members, you can skip straight to conflict. It works every time it's tried. Organizations, organizational populations, marketplaces, and economic environments are never static. They're dynamic. An absence of effective communications will ultimately lead to conflict.

If conversations are rare and need to be started from scratch every time, they get put off or avoided altogether. Unfortunately, putting off constructive confrontation in hopes that situations will magically correct themselves is the rule in organizational life more than the exception. Procrastination invariably gives problems time to abscess and even spread their infection. It's much easier to address important issues, and keep infections from spreading, if the conversation is *continuous*. Although sooner is always better than later, don't take your team member by surprise. Catching someone off guard produces instant defensiveness.

A former National Broadcasting Company (NBC) network programming vice president (VP) recalls standing at the men's room urinal, on more than one occasion, when the network president came in, stood at the next urinal, and asked what changes were being considered for the primetime line up. The slightly embarrassed programming veep outlined the programming strategy as best he could under the circumstances and also remembered how more than one major program shift in the prime-time line up was made before they zipped up their pants. The network president no doubt called the VP into his office or visited the VP's office much more often than convening at the urinals. But the urinal summits made a more entertaining story to tell for the next 20 years and illustrate that conversation can take place anywhere.

Surprising your team members for an impromptu conversation, especially about something as important as laying the groundwork for a commitment, puts everybody at a disadvantage and compromises the circle of confrontation. Your team member will be unprepared and defensive, and you won't get the quantity or quality of information you want and need. Cold turkey conversations can reveal what a person is in the middle of mentally at that moment, which can be interesting. But it doesn't tell you a whole lot about his or her long-term *habits, skills, attitudes,* and *activities.* For that you'll need to examine results over time.

No Surprises

Respect their time. What someone is doing from moment to moment is not as important as what they're *getting done.* As you'll learn more about in the confrontation section of this book, there is a practical link between how a person uses his or her time and the results he or she can show. For now, consider time a part of personal space. You don't like anybody dropping in on you and demanding an explanation of your activities and accomplishments to the minute. Neither do they.

If you make a habit of surprising your team members with cold turkey inquiries, they will develop a nervous twitch, never knowing when you'll pounce. The nervous twitch will eventually start to bother their spouses and frighten their children and small pets. They'll seek medical treatment for anxiety disorder and, before you know it, you've single-handedly driven up organizational health care costs by 7 percent. Nice going, Ace.

Your *element of surprise* tactics now have your otherwise alert team members heavily medicated to the point of dulling their senses, slowing their reactions, and slurring their speech. But never mind all of that. Aside from the fact that lives and careers have been ruined by your need for tactical superiority, you've probably driven the stronger of the species, those who try to tough it out without drinking at lunch or otherwise medicating their anxiety, underground. The last thing you want is a paranoid team that shares nothing with you. Worse yet, intentionally keeping your team members off balance might cause them to develop the unpleasant habit of lying.

When you don't act deliberately and intentionally proactive, what you *don't* want to happen tends to happen. Without a system like constructive confrontation that promotes and encourages continuous conversation, you're most likely to blow up, or someone's likely to blow up in *your* face, in the name of confronting the problems that will inevitably crop up and bite your backside. There will *always* be problems. As a practitioner of constructive confrontation, you will always have the next conversation scheduled, dooming the problems, no matter how inevitable, to an early demise.

You will intentionally schedule future conversations during your commitment and covenant-building conversations. Team members will not be surprised that they're obligated to report in on schedule. Conversation is a two-way street. How they report in and the form the reports take will vary depending on what least disrupts their important work and what's most appropriate for their circumstances and yours. But they won't be surprised that you expect information on a scheduled basis. The details of such reporting will be discussed further in Chapter 4.

HELLO AND GOOD-BYE

Quick conversations are reminders of larger conversations. A greeting and a compliment is a greeting and a compliment. Even though a conversation that takes only 10 seconds might seem of little consequence, the timing, location, and method of your delivery still matter. Taking the time to say "good morning" to everyone in your area is a lot less burdensome than paying the consequences of a staff that feels you don't care if they're there. How hard is it to hit "reply" on an informative e-mail and write, "Thanks, Ed," "This is great news, Sally. Keep it up," or "Good work, Marge"? It's so-o-o-o easy, takes so little, and means so much.

Timing is important all of the time. Don't interrupt a conversation in the hallway to deliver an "atta girl" *unless* you have determined in advance that doing so in front of your team member's peers will be particularly beneficial. It might be convenient for you to pull rank and clumsily interrupt a conversation among your team members to deliver a compliment, but if the interruption embarrasses your complimentee, your compliment has done more harm than good. Think through your selection of place and time *ahead of time.* The gesture of complimenting folks is important. Enhance and maximize the gesture by timing it correctly.

Interrupting a hallway conversation to demonstrate respect for your team member's time is a good maneuver when well-timed and executed. "Excuse me, folks. Fred, I need five minutes to check in on the Bigsby matter today. Let me know when is best for you." What just took place was a strategic conversation, loaded with good things:

- "Excuse me, folks . . .": This is a way to express respect for your team members and not invoke your disparity of power through rude behavior *because you can.* It's sort of like asking permission when, in fact, you're going to say what you're going to say anyway. However, modeling courtesy to team members, who know a boss can invoke institutional authority and even get away with being rude, also establishes a standard of behavior and sets the bar for how you expect them to behave, at least on your watch.
- "Fred . . .": This is more than identifying the person with whom you need to connect. Fred suddenly becomes the man of the moment in that little group. Be aware that people will feel valued when treated

courteously, especially in front of an audience. You want to seize every opportunity to make people feel good.

- "I need five minutes . . .": You could have said, "Be in my office in five minutes, gawl darn it." But, you wouldn't do that. The implication in your enlightened choice of words is that Fred has something you value, important information that you, the team leader, need. This again makes him an important citizen. You're purposely not delivering an ominous, "I want to see you" kind of thing that might make his peers say, "You're in trouble now, buddy," as you disappear into the restroom. You're also extending Fred the courtesy of advance notice on the amount of interruption you plan to make in his day. Become known as a person who sticks to five minutes if you promise five minutes. Too often people say, "This will only take five minutes," when it typically runs into 30, 60, or 90 minutes.

- "to check in on the Bigsby matter . . .": By telling Fred, and his fellow team members, *what's* on your agenda, you give him advance warning of what to prepare for. You also provide him time to catch up on what might be lagging behind on the Bigsby matter.

- "today.": This issue will be addressed before Fred goes home. Have no doubt about it. If necessary, you could have said "this morning," which means this issue will be addressed before Fred goes to Taco Bell for lunch. This is solid information, and people like being given parameters. Unless something is not very important at all, you don't want to say apologetically, "whenever you get around to it." That means it's not important to *you*. In which case, why did you bother interrupting their conversation in the first place?

- "Let me know when is best for you.": This is another command-courtesy combo. You've set the larger parameter in terms of "today" or "this morning." But you left Fred with some measure of control and self-respect. He can call the time and the place by designating that he'll come see you. He won't command you to come see him, unless there's something nontransportable you need to view in his work place, like the full-scale mock-up of the Bigsby Suburban

Assault Vehicle. If Fred doesn't designate where, you will — before you apologize for the interruption and disappear into the restroom.

This is a classic example of *leading the way you like to be led*. Extending courtesy at the same time you're delivering clear and explicit instructions. That's how you become a leader *in fact* (i.e., popular authority). A leader in *name* has institutional authority vis-à-vis his or her position on the organizational food chain. A leader in *fact* is someone people choose to follow. Your people are much more likely to consider you a stand-up boss when you treat them the way *you* like to be treated. No double standard. If you had rudely interrupted their conversation, that would have slapped them in the face with your superior versus subordinate double standard. You might as well have gone the distance and said, "Get back to work, you lazy bums, before I outsource your jobs to Senegal."

This is one of the reasons constructive confrontation is called an *art*. As you just read, the little comment about needing to see Fred was loaded with opportunities to continue shaping your organization's culture, moving a project forward, winning the loyalty and appreciation of your team members, making someone feel important, sending a message that you expect work to get done, and generally establishing yourself as an effective leader, in name and in fact, with institutional *and* popular authority.

Although this brief conversation with Fred took place in *less than seven seconds*, you had to first be aware of how powerful your words and actions would be and intentionally use them in a purposeful and strategic manner. When to hold a conversation is an important facet of the circle of confrontation for many reasons above and beyond you and your team members simply finding a hole in your collective schedules or you arbitrarily poking a hole in theirs.

WHERE TO CONVERSE

Where a conversation takes place has a dramatic impact on how well it serves a positive purpose. Sitting down at a table full of team members in the cafeteria or at Taco Bell and trying to discuss the emotional purpose in a single team member's career would be embarrassing and will, more than likely, waste everybody's time, except to confirm their suspicions that their boss is an idiot. Be careful when trying to behave outside your bun and act like an open and accessible person. There is a best time and place for everything, and it's probably not at Taco Bell with the whole gang present. Embarrassing your team members won't make you a popular boss. Embarrassing *yourself* in front of your team members won't make you a popular boss, either. Save your embarrassing moments for when you're out of town, alone.

The emotional purpose discussion (more to come shortly) at the core of the commitment conversation, essential to helping focus the team member's energies and to internalize his or her essential motivations for doing good work, is best held privately in your office, in his or her office (if it's private), or off-campus, during a private Taco Bell lunch or dinner. The benefits of privacy obviously encourage candor.

Beware — even in the sanctity of your inner sanctum. Another faux pas or two can still spoil it. One mistake is sitting in your own desk chair. Conversing across the great expanse of your desk is intimidating to the visitor and reeks of that superior versus subordinate thing. If you're meeting in your office, get out from behind your desk to chat. That opens you up and removes a major physical barrier. If the only place you're comfortable is behind the great expanse of your desk, it's time to conduct some self-inventory and see what all that insecurity is about.

It's better to hold such conversations in your team member's office, if she or he has a private one. Let him or her have the security of sitting behind the desk, with you in the more vulnerable, subordinate position. You have the institutional authority, if not the popular authority, of a leader in fact. Diminishing the symbols of your status and leveling the playing field will lend license and encourage your team member to be more honest and disclosing. If the team member doesn't have a private place, use a conference room or off-site location.

WHAT TO COVER IN THE CONVERSATION

What's important to you as a representative of the organization? What's important to you as an individual? Where those interests intersect, you'll find the emotional purpose in your work. Inasmuch as your working fulfills essential and emotional needs in your life, you have an emotional investment in the work you do, in protecting the interests of the organization that employs you, and in working to promote resonance between the two. If the organization that pays you has a larger investment in you than you have in the organization, there's something wrong, *terribly* wrong.

The same holds true of everyone within your sphere of leadership influence, inside and outside of the organization. Everyone has an emotional purpose. Whether that emotional purpose in any way resonates with the job they're being paid to do is another matter. As a leader, committed to the circle of constructive confrontation, the emotional purpose that simmers within each individual is the most powerful point of connection possible between you, your team members, and the needs of Mother Organization.

Emotional purpose will become part of your lexicon before you're finished with this chapter, much less this book. It's a critical component of the commitment, confrontation, and celebration cycle, otherwise known as the circle of confrontation. As a leader, you can't afford to be afraid of the emotional purpose in your life or in the lives of those in your area of authority. More importantly, the prospect of commanding a rudderless ship in stormy seas, which is roughly the same thing as leading without the skill sets required to confront in a constructive way, should scare the bejeebers out of you. When it comes to *not* engaging in regular and meaningful conversations — and the commitment, confrontation, and celebration that come with them — be afraid. Be *very* afraid.

TRIANGULATING INFORMATION

Three sources — one understanding. Learning all you can about others is a deliberate, intentional, pro-active behavior. To conduct effective conversations and reach the type of consensus just discussed, it's vital to know your people as well as you possibly can. Getting to know them and the emotional purposes that drive them takes time and effort. But the amount of time and effort can be reduced by learning smart. There are three ways to become more enlightened about people:

1. Observe them from afar.
2. Gather feedback from others about them.
3. Talk to them directly.

You must pay attention to the details you gather. There are lots of good uses for them. You will use the information you gather by observing from afar to *triangulate*. In the context of constructive confrontation, triangulation compares your discrete observations with third-party peer or customer feedback data and information you gather from direct contact. Triangulation serves to confirm the information or reliability of your sources. Nobody said being a great leader would be easy.

TRIANGULATION PART ONE: OBSERVING FROM AFAR

Conjure the classic image of factory management staring down at the assembly line from elevated offices overlooking the factory floor. The architecture itself implied an important versus less important, powerful versus less powerful, and superior versus subordinate relationship between those in the elevated offices and those toiling below. Wall Street power brokers gazing down on the frenetic activity on the floor of the Exchange from their perches, like Randolph and Mortimer Duke in the Eddie Murphy and Dan Akroyd film *Trading Places*, gives a similar impression.

Observing from afar isn't necessarily that sinister. There is good reason to collect some of your information about people from afar. Hopefully, if they don't know you're watching, then they're not putting on a performance. When your team members observe *you* from afar, they're looking for your real behavior, not the company line stuff.

They don't necessarily want to catch you being phony. They hope to confirm you're a stand-up boss. They want to ensure you really are an authentic person. If you're not, they want to know that, too. When it comes to trust, your people *want* to trust you more than they want to *distrust* you. However, they're not going to be damn fools about it. If you demonstrate any suspicious behavior or reason for them not to trust you, the team will consider the threat level to be elevated. Team members who don't trust their leaders won't focus their energies on efficiency, productivity, and high performance. Their behavior will become defensive.

Knowing who people really are is important because your expectations regarding their performance and productivity potential depend on it. This doesn't mean hiding around corners or eavesdropping from the next bathroom stall or the next cubicle. Even though you're likely to hear some interesting things that way, the discovery will be purely coincidental. The last thing you want to do is get caught and discredit yourself in the eyes of the very people with whom you're trying to build trust.

Observing from afar means paying attention to what's already around you, like a detective or archaeologist. As a team leader, you can study people when they're not around. You have access to personnel files, employee records, reports, and correspondences that contain volumes of data about people and how they think and behave. How about asking probing questions in meetings and brainstorming sessions, then sitting back and *listening?* UCLA studies have taught us that only 7 percent of face-to-face communication results from words people speak. That leaves 93 percent of the communicating to be done with vocal inflection, volume, body language, gestures, and the other senses; smell, taste, and touch.

Listen to the questions your team members ask of you and of their peers. What do they want to know? Maybe they're not curious at all. That tells you they're probably disinterested, undermotivated, shy, cynical, or burned out. Maybe they're shy and insecure and don't feel they know enough to ask questions without appearing foolish. Maybe they feel they know it all and don't *need* to interact with others or ask questions. The more information you gather, the more reliable your conclusions.

Pay attention when opportunities arise to observe people interacting with peers or customers. Don't be oblivious to how people lead themselves. The more you can rely on people to uphold the principles and practices of your organization without supervision, the less you will need to intervene. When observing a team member making a formal presentation, interacting informally with a coworker, or working in isolation, note the following things:

- How does your team member interact with others on the phone or in person?
  - Does your team member respect personal space and privacy?
  - Does your team member waste other people's time?
  - Does your team member encourage others?
  - Does your team member criticize others?
  - Is your team member friendly? Unfriendly? Abrasive? Helpful? Threatening?
- How does your team member present him- or herself cosmetically?
  - What style of clothes does your team member wear?
  - What is the condition of your team member's clothes?
  - What are your team member's personal grooming habits?
- How does your team member work in isolation?
  - Does your team member show respect for his or her work space?
  - Does your team member show respect for property other than his or her own?
  - Does your team member ask for help if needed?
  - Does your team member make efficient use of time?
- Is your team member strong in *habits*, like punctuality, documenting, and researching?
  - Does your team member consistently demonstrate positive personal and professional habits?
  - Does your team member consistently demonstrate negative personal and professional habits?
  - Is your team member inconsistent when it comes to *habits*?
- Is your team member strong in *skills*, like problem solving, selling, and designing?

- Does your team member possess valuable personal and professional skill sets?
  - Does your team member lack valuable personal and professional skill sets?
  - Is your team member inconsistent when it comes to skills?
- Does your team member demonstrate a positive or negative attitude?
  - Is your team member easily irritated?
  - Is your team member a fence-mender or peacemaker?
  - Is your team member withdrawn?
  - Is your team member eager to participate?
  - Is your team member unpredictable when it comes to mood?
- How well does your team member communicate?
  - How do you rate your team member's verbal skills? Vocabulary? Grammar?
  - Is your team member comfortable or uncomfortable making presentations?
  - Is your team member a better communicator on the telephone, face-to-face, or in writing?

Use this list as a guide and add observations that are more relevant or specific to the challenges you and your team face at work. You're noting these kinds of things in order to reference them in future constructive confrontation conversations. Can you describe your team members' energy levels? Interest or disinterest in their jobs? Do your team members arrive alert and ready to work in the morning? There's nothing wrong with complimenting someone on his or her professionalism. So gather ammunition. Constructive confrontation is up close and personal. Be prepared. Be careful. Be positive. Hopefully, HR has you trained well enough not to get *too* personal, especially with opposite-sex compliments or criticisms. If you can't keep your sensibilities or decorum intact, go to the index and look up "corporate counsel."

Triangulation Part Two: Gathering Feedback from Others

Feedback from others is the second point in your emerging triangulation process. Does the way others describe the team member you're trying to get to know validate or contradict your observations? If it's a contradiction, is it because you're unwilling to face facts about the team member or yourself? Is it because the people providing third-party observations are conspiring against you, the team member, or all of the preceding? If everybody around you says you look like a duck, walk like a duck, quack like a duck, you're, in all likelihood, a duck. So is the team member they describe in the same way.

Self-image can be a far cry from the way others see you. This is true for everyone. If you're in a position of institutional authority seeking popular authority, you must be willing to reconcile any difference between who you really are, as evidenced by your words and deeds, and who you present yourself to be. Acting as a true leader in fact, you should be the first one willing to submit yourself to 360-degree feedback from your peers and superiors and, especially, from your team members. The leader goes in first, remember?

The more feedback you gather, the richer the data pool. The richer the data pool, the more willing you should be to toss your contradictory opinions out the window. If the data is accurate, going against it is unlikely to bring about the results you want. Never mind the stories of how one person, against all odds, proved the rest of the world wrong. Those things happen about as often as people are struck by lightening while cashing in their winning Mega Lotto tickets. It's possible, in the rarest and most extreme cases, that there *is* a conspiracy against you or the person you're trying to get to know. If that's true, you have some major confronting to do, and it's way *overdue*.

No matter how bad you've allowed things to become on your watch, it's doubtful that anyone is out in the parking lot wiring your car for explosives. The bigger issue here is validation. As you begin the circle of confrontation, intentionally seeking out solid information and validating that information against other information, you will gain confidence in your own analytic ability and have a more solid foundation from which to engage your people in positive and productive ways. The better your data, the more realistic your expectations for accountability.

TRIANGULATION PART THREE: TALKING TO THEM DIRECTLY

Cinch up your socks and buckle your boots. All three sources of information and knowledge are important, but the one that will require you to sharpen your saw the most is number three: talking to your team members directly. Engaging in what we refer to as *the conversation* is part of a well-planned and orchestrated approach to staying ahead of the curve with your team members, bosses, customers, and other important players in your success — not behind the eight ball. The conversation you have with the people whose performance you are responsible for is extremely important to you in the fulfillment of your professional commitments and responsibilities, and it's extremely important to them as they fulfill *their* responsibilities.

The importance of observation might seem obvious. Yet its benefits are often ignored because supervisors, managers, and executives aren't sufficiently coached in how to make positive use of the information. That and the very thought of confronting someone on the basis of personal and professional observations just plain scares whatever bejeebers they have left right out of them. For example, you want to pay particular attention to *inconsistencies* in thinking and behavior.

Orchestrating a commitment conversation, or the apex of your information-gathering triangle, begins with the purpose of the information exchange. Once the circle of confrontation is under way, you might have multiple types of conversations rolling up on one another. One project, or circle of confrontation, might just be getting under way while another is winding down or transitioning into another phase. There are four basic motivations for conversation:

1. To gather new information for the purpose of forming a commitment

2. To disseminate important information your team members need to know
3. To assess and confront productivity and performance progress
4. To recognize and reward achievements

Is a person on your team frustrated because he or she doesn't receive much respect from other team members? Is it because he or she doesn't command respect, which is to say that his or her peers don't feel he or she has earned it? This might be a real situation, but, without the skill set to confront it, many bosses look the other way rather than skillfully say, "It doesn't appear to me that your fellow team members treat you respectfully. With your help, I think we can change that."

Many people in organizations avoid talking to one another. Unfortunately, many people who avoid talking to one another are the people that need to be engaged in conversation the most. You don't need to be someone's best friend to have a conversation. If you're someone's boss, it's a bad idea to be, or to try to be, his or her best friend. For a constructive conversation to take place, you should remain role appropriate and help your team members to do the same. Acting like you're someone's best buddy makes constructive confrontation harder, not easier.

ASSESSING AND CONFRONTING PROGRESS AND PERFORMANCE

These very important conversations take place down the road a piece. However, the constructive confrontations to reconnoiter where things stand and current movement (Chapters 5 through 8) are based on the early conversations that align the emotional purpose of the team member's career and the practical and tactical needs of the organization as a whole. The quality and quantity of the information you collect about your team members has everything to do with the quality and quantity of work you can expect over time.

As the leader, the quality and quantity of the information you share with your team members will directly impact the level of their trust, loyalty, and motivation over time. The constructive confrontations you schedule and promise during the commitment stage (Chapter 3) and write into the covenant (Chapter 4) are grounded in the resonance you achieve with your team members early on. Just because things are going well is no reason to stop or slow down the conversations at any stage of the cycle. You simply become a more fervent encourager. You owe it to your team members to confront them consistently and constructively. It's amazing how, when things start going well, people tend to stop doing the good things.

Each confrontation conversation will enrich your data about your team members. Your keen, observing eye should never dim or look away, assuming everything is under control and nothing will change. Observation from afar, peer review, and direct dialogue with your team members will give you plenty of ammunition to compliment them on consistency and effort. You will also be positioned to remind team members of the commitments they made, the emotional purposes upon which they made the commitments, and hold them accountable for their results.

If adjustments are called for, you and your team members have a database of information and knowledge to fall back on in order to ensure that any revisions are, in fact, competent course corrections. If course adjustments are being made within the context of a confrontational conversation and an initial commitment conversation is taking place on *another project* or another matter, you and your team member have a chance to improve the initial conversation as the learning loops back on itself. Every conversation, if skillfully executed, makes the next conversation better.

RECOGNIZING AND REWARDING ACHIEVEMENTS

The celebration conversation (Chapters 9 through 12) is as important to the complete circle of confrontation as the initial commitment conversation. As the leader, you must pay close attention to results *and* effort. Of course, you must pay attention, period. How demotivating will it be if your team members knock themselves out to live up to their commitments only to find you asleep at the switch? When a team member rushes in and says, "I did it!" Don't say, "Did what?" Say, "Fantastic, give me *who, what, when, where,* and *how.*" Otherwise, you can forget about any significant effort on his or her part again. Make sure you note everything. Never let your pen stop moving for long when a team member is bragging *or making excuses.*

Assuming you're paying attention, if someone is demonstrating good habits in the execution of your mutually agreed on strategy but not getting results, several things could be happening: you and the team member might have (1) set up the wrong strategy, (2) embarked on the wrong initiative, or (3) broken it down into the wrong tasks. Bear in mind than not getting results will break a team member's heart faster than anything else. More observation, peer input, and conversation will help.

In gathering new information, you might discover that it's none of the preceding. It might be that your team member has good *habits,* that is, punctuality and prompt and thorough attention to details, processes, and proven work practices. Still, the results aren't there. It could be that certain *skills* are called for, and the team member, despite his or her good habits, might lack enough of them to generate desired results.

In gathering yet more information, you might discover that it's not lack of necessary *habits* or *skills.* Don't start tearing your hair out . . . yet. It could be that, despite good habits and skills, your team member might be having an *attitude* problem. Attitude problems aren't necessarily as obvious as, say, someone gluing the lid to the photocopier shut with 3M spray adhesive. Sometimes, team members, just like their team leaders, are affected by miniscule attitude blocks that slow things down or bring them to a halt altogether.

Dealing with attitudes in the workplace is a sticky wicket. Depending on the severity of the issue, you might need to consult HR, or Dr. Phil. As a supervisor, manager, or executive, the best you can do is create that environment of honest disclosure, intentionally seek out all of the information and knowledge you can to create resonance between your team member's emotional purpose and the realities of the organization's needs, and consistently apply the circle of confrontation. With that, you've done the best you can.

But unless you've maintained the priority of monitoring effort and results and have provided the appropriate recognition and rewards, you can never claim to have done your best. If you continue to deal with a habits, skills, or attitude issue, it might be time to cycle the circle of confrontation back to the initial conversation and dig deeper. Putting all the right pieces together is a greater challenge with some people than it is with others. The worst thing for a team leader *and* a team member is to not come up with anything to celebrate.

How to Begin a Conversation

In the course of publishing works of Ken Blanchard and Dr. Norman Vincent Peale in the mid-80s, John Hoover attended many lectures by both men. Blanchard often referred to the Sea World San Diego killer whale, Shamu. He told the story of how Sea World trainers jump into the tanks with the killer whales, or any other marine mammal they're training, and play for at least 30 minutes before any training begins. According to Blanchard, this puts the animal at ease and sends the message that the trainers mean them no harm. The same thing applies to humans, especially when there is a disparity of power between boss and subordinate. If you've worked hard at achieving a popular leader in fact status, this safety zone has already been established.

This isn't to say that the first thing out of your mouth should be, "I'm not going to hurt you, Fred." When Fred arrives at your office, or vice versa, asking a general "How are you?" can start things on a friendly note. Making an effort to be friendly and courteous is a way of demonstrating respect for your team members. Some supervisors, managers, and executives are too anxious to get to the point and don't strive to make their team members feel safe. You'll get to the point soon enough.

Others launch into stand up comedy routines with jokes so old and bad that team members wish they had a facts-and-nothing-but-the-facts manager. You need to use your best judgment with each of your team members. Their moods have a lot to do with how much settling-in time you should allow before getting down to business. The more conversations you have, the smoother these openings become.

BE SPECIFIC

Commitment can't come from vagueness. The commitment and covenant you're working toward can't be any stronger than the conversation. Commitment and the future cause for celebration will come from the resonance between your team members' emotional purposes and the work they do.

Being specific requires being prepared. If you don't intentionally script the conversation with specific, clear, and unambiguous questions and statements, you invite your team member to wiggle. When that happens, you're doing a disservice to your team member and to your organization. Ultimately, you're letting yourself down because your team's performance is a reflection on you and your leadership abilities. Those above you on the organizational food chain hold you accountable for your team's performance, no matter how much you might try to blame your team.

You're getting paid for the work your team does, not how pretty you look trying to get them to do it. Dressing yourself and decorating your office in all the trappings of success won't keep you from eventually stepping into a steel-jawed trap. The more evident you make it that you're a leader in name only, with nothing more than institutional authority, the more traps your team members will set for you, intentionally and unintentionally. The odds are against you on this. There are more team members than there are of you. The time to realize all of this is not after you feel the big pinch around your ankle.

If the goal, task, or milestone is not specified in the conversation, complete with the timing and methods for measurement, it can't be specific in the covenant. This leaves the commitment between you and your team member fuzzy, and you diminish the chances of meaningful and productive conversations in the future. Nonspecific and ambiguous initial conversations disqualify you, as a leader, a team member, or a family member, to confront specifics of an agreement later. If there are no specifics, there can be no constructive confrontation later, except perhaps to confess that you booted the initial conversation, commitment, and covenant stages.

That's your fault, bucko, because you have the power to deal with the details in the initial conversations. Without specific targets to discuss and specific questions about the targets, a conversation will be the waste of time your team members leave your office grumbling about. Wasting your team members' time is a sure ticket to lose their respect, loyalty, cooperation, and decrease collaboration among them, except to complain about you.

REACHING AGREEMENT

Your conversations are intended to reach agreement about the next steps in the commitment, covenant, confrontation, and celebration cycle. This is so, even if the agreement is to disagree. What can't be disagreed about is what the specific goals are, how they'll be measured, and what the rewards or consequences will be for making or not making them. Five of the basic ways to reach agreement include the following:

1. *Expertise.* If what you need most to make a decision is expertise (as in "what are the chemical components of rocket fuel?"), it's up to you to either possess that expertise or defer to someone who does, either inside or outside of the organization. In many cases, individual team members have more expertise than a team leader. This is a great opportunity for the team leader to boost morale by maximizing team member buy-in and a sense of participation and ownership. But it remains the leader's responsibility to set up parameters for achievement, measurement, and reward.

2. *Compromise.* Take a group average. There can be multiple opinions about what should or shouldn't be done on a project. Although the team leader still bears ultimate responsibility, averaging the options is sometimes the best and most inclusive solution. At other times, when everyone compromises, nobody wins. If it takes somebody giving up a little bit so everyone can gain a lot, it's probably worth it. You might get some serious attitude from those you ask to give

up a lot so that everyone can gain a little. In that case, it pays to keep searching for a solution.

3. *Majority rule.* This is where a few might be asked to give up a lot so the many can benefit a little. Sometimes that's the way it must be. But the tyranny of the majority is always a threat. As a leader, it's up to you to make sure members of your team who do not share the majority opinion are not disenfranchised by what the majority wants to do. Leadership requires judgment and a sense of what serves the greater good for the most people.

4. *Minority rule.* When it's you, the leader, versus your entire team, you might need to exercise minority rule. Hopefully, you can keep the emotional purpose for the work you and your team members do in resonance with the organization's needs enough that this won't be the case. When the needs of the organization can only be served by the exploitation of its organizational population, minority rule becomes an exercise in institutional authority. When the squeaky wheel squeaks so loud it's unbearable, the minority might be flexing their muscles. As the leader, you need to bring that behavior back into balance as well.

5. *Consensus.* Sometimes it's not possible for everyone to have their way. But that doesn't mean they can't support the ultimate decision. Reaching a consensus can be difficult and time consuming, but, unless all team members are sold on the underlying and overarching principles guiding the decision, your new problem will be compliance. You can either invest the time and effort to achieve consensus in the initial conversations or you can invest much *more* time and effort trying to get the project supported later. It's your choice. Make it wisely.

Scripts: Outlining Conversations

The references to and examples of scripting here and throughout this book are not intended to put words in your mouth. They're intended to illustrate how important it is to prethink your conversations and confrontations (which are conversations) and to choose your words wisely. It might be more accurate to call scripted conversations "guided" conversations. Writing out what you want to say and then reciting the words verbatim would be a stiff delivery at best and a comedy at worst. Either way, you'll diminish your own effectiveness and compromise constructive confrontation outcomes.

Some supervisors, managers, and executives script their remarks and then deliver them in no uncertain terms, with no room for discussion and no room for learning or making adjustments. When things don't work out as strictly scripted, the supervisor, manager, or executive gets frustrated and repeats the inflexible script — *louder*. The cycle repeats itself. The script is recited again, louder still, regardless of feedback or response, and frustration builds until something or someone explodes. In the meantime, precious human and capital resources have been squandered, and the team member's attitude, if it was good to begin with, is as flat as a pancake.

Remaining flexible but on point is the key to effective conversations. Allowing distractions or intentional diversions to get you off topic will result in frustration on your part and confusion, even conflict, later when things are done as you thought they were agreed to be done. Working from an outline is better than working from an exact script when engaging team members in conversation. It's up to you to set the agenda, or allow the team member to express his or her agenda (if that's the agenda), or a combination of both. You can have the greatest game plan in the world, but if your team members don't feel there is any room for their input or concerns, buy-in will be low.

No matter what emerges in a conversation, everything that needs to be covered needs to be *thought out in advance* and not left to chance in the moment. Everyone must emerge from conversations with a clear sense that something good was accomplished. As you walk away from a conversation, or someone leaves your office following a conversation, the constructive confrontation angel sitting on your right shoulder will ask, "Did you accomplish what you set out to accomplish?" A hard "yes" indicates your conversation was well-prepared and executed. The softer the "yes," the more likely preparation, execution, or both were lacking.

If the little confusion devil sitting on your left shoulder is smirking, you probably allowed your own insecurities to muddy the waters and make your conversation fuzzy and inconclusive. You might have allowed your team member to muddy the waters and make your conversation fuzzy and inconclusive. That's natural. The little devil on your left shoulder likes muddy water and general confusion because it inevitably leads to conflict.

People have all kinds of reasons to avoid concise and conclusive conversations. A clear and concise understanding of expectations places a demand on performance, which many of us tend to shy away from. With greater clarity and concision, constructive confrontation becomes a stronger and more effective tool. Any confrontation that begins with, "I should have told you a long time ago that there's no budget for this," or "Did I forget to mention the gas leak in the warehouse when I asked you to send in the welders?" is bound to turn out badly.

A successful constructive commitment or confrontation conversation will leave that little devil sitting with its arms folded, pouting. You and your team member should know *why* you're having the conversation, *who* the key players are, *what* the issues are, *where* the action is required, *when* and how often action is required, *how* the job is to be done (including how results will be measured), and how much will be required in terms of time, effort, and resources.

The old *who, what, when, where, why,* and *how* routine is as old as the hills. Yet, in most organizations its regular application in conversation is as rare as the supervisor, executive, or manager who actually makes it a priority to actively engage team members in regular, well-orchestrated, and meaningful MBWA. *Who, what, when, where, why,* and *how* can be addressed in various orders, depending on the nature of the conversation and the commitment being made to a task, assignment, project, or initiative. The important thing is to cover them all and document what's been discussed as you'll deal with specifically in Chapter 4 on the covenant.

WHO?

This is the statement of personnel, a role call if you prefer. It's important to make clear who the key participants are in the topic being discussed. There are inclusive and omissive reasons for this. Inclusively speaking, there are people the team member could work with, should work with, or must work with for the successful completion of the task, assignment, project, or initiative. It must be understood and documented who these people are. By omitting nonessential people, you block potential disconnects during later confrontations when excuses are likely to emerge.

You should never hear, "You never told me I could ask for help." You should never say, "Why didn't you ask so-and-so for information or assistance?" Asking such questions later without a comprehensive *who* discussion up front will virtually guarantee the "You never told me . . ." bit.

Omissively speaking, you want to avoid the future blaming of other people for lack of success. You don't want your team member to dump his or her responsibility on someone else and then blame that person when it doesn't get done. "This is your ball to carry or to drop." "We're depending on you to see that this gets done." Whatever words you use, there should be no ambiguity about *who* is responsible.

In that same vein, *you* are ultimately responsible. "If you have any questions outside of our regular conversations or if you find anyone to be uncooperative or not helpful is some way, let me know. I don't want someone else's performance or lack of performance to reflect badly on you." This establishes very succinctly *who* is responsible and *who* will be held accountable.

Just because you've thought out *who* "this" and *who* "that" before initiating the conversation doesn't mean your team member doesn't have other ideas. The second of the four basic motivations for conversations mentioned earlier is to gather *new* information. If your team member has a problem taking on responsibility, this is the time to discuss it. In many cases, your team member has a more educated and realistic understanding of *who* does what well around the office, the department, or the organization. This is why you listen as much as you talk. You could learn something important that will enhance what you're trying to accomplish. *Who* is best qualified to do the things you need done? If you ask your team members, they might have very different ideas than you do, based on exposure to and experiences with people you don't have or aren't aware of. There's a lot to learn and consider about *who* during your conversations.

WHAT?

This is a statement of outcome. *What* is this thing you're trying to accomplish? *What* will it look like? This is an extremely important aspect of the conversation because your team member must buy into the outcome the way you describe it. This puts the pressure on you to be a good storyteller and evangelist. You need to clearly articulate your vision as you interpret the organization's vision.

Good listening skills are called for here, just as they are in every other aspect of the conversation. You need to monitor your team member's feedback. Remember that your pen should seldom stop moving. Is your team member able to restate in his or her own words an accurate description of what you've described? Is the outcome your team member describes the same as yours? If not, you need to sharpen your communication skills.

Giving only the rosy picture of a task, assignment, project, or initiative is manipulative and ultimately bites you in the backside. If the project is generally innocuous, except for the part where your team member has to sacrifice his or her firstborn child, leaving out the part about the child in the initial conversation will disqualify you as a leader and render you impotent to confront your team member later. Either your team member buys-in to everything, or your team member will likely accomplish nothing.

It's tempting to pitch and switch your team member. It reduces pushback and arguments in the initial conversation. Ending an initial conversation with a limited and intentionally incomplete picture of the task, assignment, project, or initiative might make everything seem warm, fuzzy, and copacetic. But if that little devil on your left shoulder is smirking, you know in your gut that you've just postponed, and probably amplified, the eventual conflict.

What isn't resolved now will be harder to resolve later. If your team members aren't engaged with you in continuous conversations and constructive confrontations about what they're doing, you might feel smug about the absence of conflict and tension in your area of responsibility. But precious time, talent, and resources are still being wasted. Honesty is the best policy. What you and your team members are trying to accomplish, including all of the positive and negative ramifications, needs to be on the table. If anyone sweeps them under the table, and that someone had better not be *you*, it's your job to put them back on display.

WHEN?

Timing is the topic here. As conversations establish realistic expectations for *who* is involved, *what* the outcome should be, and logistics, it's also important to establish a realistic, doable schedule. You don't want to be the poster child for the universal truth mentioned earlier: There never seems to be enough time or money to do it right the first time, but there's always time and money to do it over again. You don't want to cast your team member in the role of poster child either.

There are many factors that inform a task, assignment, project, or initiative timetable. *When* does the customer want it? *When* does the customer *need* it? *When* can we realistically get it done? Does doing it fast make it too expensive considering the final price tag? Will you need to hire additional staff only to lay them off again after the project is delivered? Is taking the time to do it right too expensive considering the final price tag?

Timing needs to be relative. You can have an effective conversation regarding all other aspects of a constructive confrontation commitment and covenant only to put a completely unreasonable time frame on the task, assignment, project, or initiative. You might as well set your team members up to fail. Every time they fail because they were burdened with unreasonable expectations, the more cynical and unwilling they become to invest emotionally in new tasks, assignments, projects, or initiatives.

Timing mustn't be too loose either. Think Goldilocks theory. The timing of a task, assignment, project, or initiative should be optimally balanced between do-ability and the necessary urgency. In other words, the schedule shouldn't be too tight or too loose. It should be just right. Value your team members' time and your organization's needs by not wasting time, effort, or resources, making people do things over again that could have been done right the first time.

Any time you find yourself or people in your sphere of influence doing things over again, ponder how much time you're stealing from progress and new efforts. Don't ponder so much as to inconsolably depress yourself or lay a guilt trip on your people from which they'll never recover. But never kid yourself that time isn't money. If you're tempted to think that way, dock *yourself* for all the time spent redoing something.

WHERE?

What are the logistics involved? Geography might be all-important to the task, assignment, project, or initiative, or it might be incidental. This all-important issue should also be considered in your preconversation planning *and* be subject to reconsideration based on your team member's learned feedback.

Is it better to build a single large processing plant for frozen potatoes in Idaho where the potatoes are grown? This would mean shipping the frozen Idaho Fries in refrigerated trucks across country to market. Or do we ship raw potatoes to smaller regional plants where the frozen Idaho Fries need only be transported short distances to market, and even then in a distributor's refrigerated truck, eliminating a need for our own fleet of refrigerated trucks. "Hm-m-m-m," you think. "There is a larger labor pool for plant staffing in metropolitan areas."

"Labor is cheaper in Idaho than it is in Chicago," your team member points out. "Fewer unions and *hidden expenses*, if you know what I mean."

"Hadn't thought of that," you reply, still rubbing your chin. The back-and-forth exchange of information about how *who* affects *where* is extremely valuable. When not engaged in structured conversation or intentional dialogue, things like important logistics might be left to chance. Such negligence can cost you and your organization plenty. Asking your team member, "Why didn't you think of that sooner?" doesn't make you look like an organized and effective leader.

WHY?

This is a statement or restatement of the problem or challenge. Sometimes it's obvious *why* certain tasks, assignments, projects, or initiatives need to be executed. Sometimes it's not. Sometimes there's more to it than meets the eye. There are often complex and layered reasons to do things. It's your job as a leader to make sure all the various needs are brought out into the open. There are few things more aggravating than being asked to do something without being told *why*. Being only given part of the truth is not the same as being told the truth.

If your team members are expected to invest themselves enthusiastically, they must know *why* they're doing it. This is critical to aligning the all-important emotional purpose driving the team member's involvement with the needs of the organization. To find out later that there are aspects of the organization's agenda that don't align with the team member's emotional purpose will make the team member feel used.

This doesn't mean you should disclose everything in the universe to your team members. Certain things are classified. If so, tell them so. Avoid the smug and privileged position that your team members are on a need-to-know basis, and you'll be the arbiter of what they need to know. You represent the organization. Your team members should be told that you're sharing everything you know about the task, assignment, project, or initiative and that if you're withholding something, it's not your decision.

They should trust that you would never withhold anything for the purpose of misleading or manipulating them. You should share everything you're at liberty to share. Sometimes you're not at liberty to share everything. In such cases, you need to make the case that you're being as disclosing as you can be under the circumstances and you need to proceed with your commitment conversation based on what you know.

The reasons for doing things must resonate with your team members' emotional purposes. If they don't, expect dissonance and less than a hearty effort. Depending on how out of phase organizational needs are with personal emotional purposes, you might even be inviting anything from disinterest and lethargy to outright sabotage. It just doesn't make sense to ask people to operate against their essential natures. If it comes down to the chicken and egg question, the team member is there to serve the organization's needs first.

On a positive note, seeking the best alignment possible between your organization's agenda and your team member's emotional purposes is the fastest way to maximize interest and enthusiasm for the work to be done. These are all components of the constructive confrontation process. This knowledge and these operating principles are part of your emerging skill set as an increasingly effective leader. If you expect to use constructive confrontation in a productive manner, you need to be operating on the most solid and resonant platform possible.

How?

This is about methodology and measurement. This is another great opportunity to engage your team members' expertise. By discussing methodology, you're seeking input based on your team members' experience. By deferring to your team members' experience and expertise, you're honoring the value they bring to the table. Don't think that won't have an immense motivational benefit that will increase energy, enthusiasm, and sense of ownership.

Your expertise and experience as the team leader should only come up in the conversation to confirm or affirm your team members' expertise and experience. It's not important for you to be the most talented, the wisest, and the most powerful creature in the Black Lagoon. If you're in a position of leadership, you're there to serve. You don't do that from a pedestal.

You are, however, ultimately responsible for the success of the task, assignment, project, or initiative. That means a productive conversation will lead to a meeting of the minds on the best ways to *execute* the task, assignment, project, or initiative. Because the *how* involves use of resources, scheduling, coordination, deadlines, and other considerations, it's critical that the conclusions and agreements that transform commitment into covenant be realistic and achievable. That's ultimately your call as leader. The more your team members play a functional role in those decisions, vis-à-vis the conversation, the more solid the foundation for the circle of confrontation.

HOW MUCH?

This is the bonus question about resources *required;* cash, raw materials, sweat, whatever it takes, and resources *returned,* cash, sweat, raw materials, whatever is needed. More conventional business people talk about return on investment, income versus expenses, or cost-return ratios. The price tag business discussed earlier has two dimensions: the cost to you and what a customer will pay for it.

Like every other component of the conversation, there will be much you can learn from your team member about *how much* is too little, too much, or just right. The Goldilocks theory applies again. You're always trying to price your products and services in such a way as to maximize sales and minimize costs. The conversation you're having with a team member might involve an overall pricing strategy or merely involve the internal expense of a project component.

Departmental budgets are generally components of the larger project, which is *running a profitable enterprise.* Hello. Asking "How much?" is *always* important. Just because costs are buried and obscured by the macrobudgeting practices of your organization doesn't mean they don't mean anything. Whether you're a small enterprise where every dollar spent or saved noticeably hits the bottom line or you're part of a large organization in which your department's financial performance is practically indistinguishable in the annual report figures, *how much* is still an important issue.

If for no other reason, asking and establishing *how much* something costs or *how much* will be returned to the organization in revenues, good will, or in-kind services begins the all-important discussion of measurement. As another old saying goes, "What can't be measured can't be managed." A commitment and covenant that will be the basis for constructive confrontation must have metrics.

Just what to measure and how to measure it will, like most aspects of constructive confrontation, come from organizationally imposed realities *and* feedback from experienced and involved team members. This also involves the question of *"How* and *how much* will the team member benefit from the successful execution of this task, assignment, project, or initiative?"* Salaried employees obviously differ from commissioned salespeople in how directly their financial fortunes are tied to their performance.

Regardless of your team member's compensation scheme, the direct and indirect benefits for the team member need to be specifically spelled out during initial conversations leading to commitment. Even if the reward for successful completion of the task, assignment, project, or initiative is a smile and a hearty handshake, so be it. Without making promises you can't keep, you might want to point out that promotions, when they're available, tend to be based on accumulated smiles and handshakes more than upon reprimands and write-ups.

How much your team member will benefit from his or her successful involvement is extremely important. If there is no significant benefit, don't expect much enthusiastic involvement. However, research indicates that job satisfaction from engaging in rewarding activities (i.e., the kinds of things people like to do) is high on the list of employee motivations. Nobody ever does something worthwhile without deriving some sort of tangible or intangible benefit. That benefit, and how much of it your team member can expect, needs to be discussed in the conversation — *not left to the imagination.*

Chapter 2 Summary

- No apology is necessary.
  - Gone are the days when leaders could command obedience out of their direct reports and receive anything that resembled top performance. But that doesn't mean the conversation between the constructively confrontational, career-building leader and the person whose career is being built becomes apologetic. You set the agenda and guide the conversation. However, a big part of your agenda is encouraging your team members' contribution of ideas and information.
  - The most effective leadership resembles a circle, not a ladder. Lead the way you like to be led and be amazed at how cooperative your team members become. When decreasing conflict and increasing accountability are your twin targets, say things to people that you know would motivate *you,* and say them in a way you know will help them hear and understand the message. Be as clear and consistent with your team members as you want your boss to be with you. Accountability starts with unambiguous expectations and willing disclosure.
- Put the emotional purpose to good use.
  - The conversation must begin with the most essential issue in professional development: the emotional purpose that drives work. Leaders must engage their long-time team members as well as new hires in a well-focused discussion about why the team member works, why he or she works in this particular field and this particular organization, and how this particular job resonates with the team member's emotional purpose.
  - Through the team leader-team member dialogue, opportunities for resonance between the team members' emotional purpose

and the organization's needs are identified. This fuels the circle of confrontation. The intersection of the team member's emotional purpose and organizational needs is the reference point for ongoing constructive confrontation conversations. This resonance transforms a sense of burdensome obligation to a sense of willing accountability.

- Control the conversation with *who, what, when, where, why,* and *how.*
  - The team member whose career is being built, like so many successful people in the past, doesn't know at this point what questions to ask, which direction to go, or where to best focus his or her energies. This is why the constructive confrontation conversation, and the direction so many successful people attribute to their coaches, mentors, teachers, and trusted advisors, is so vital. Here, the team leader shares the view from atop a mountain of experience *and* invites experience from team members.
  - One of the ways you can become a leader in fact, as well as in name, is by acknowledging the mountain of experience your team members have to offer. That makes listening as important as sharing. As you script out conversations, consider the outcome you want and work backwards from there. In doing so, consider what to say, how best to say it, and build in time to *listen*. Reference the information and knowledge you've accumulated, and then seek even more.
- Be a Stand-Up Boss
  - The conversation is more than just a time to triangulate information gathered from observation, research, and conversation. Conversations are the time for disclosure from supervisors, managers, and executives about the leader's emotional purpose and his or her job. These are opportunities to model the behavior you want in your area, to live it out. In constructive confrontation, team leaders don't ask team members to do anything they're not willing to do themselves. How can you teach what you don't know? You can't lead someone where you won't go.

Decreased conflict and increased accountability are natural by-products of the circle of confrontation. Do yourself, your team members, and the organization that employs you a huge favor and become good at it. Mastering the conversation component of constructive confrontation is a great place to start. Next, the conversation turns to commitment.

CHAPTER 3

The Commitment

In the circle of confrontation, commitment means binding together and pledging to one another with an obligation to support a doctrine or cause. Those might not be the kind of words you hear bandied about in your organization on a regular basis, but they describe the concepts you need to master if you're going to turn confrontation into a constructive tool for success. Your organization stands for something. Whether you have ever paused to contemplate it, your team members, your peers, your bosses, and the community you serve can all describe their piece of the organizational identity if asked. In other words, they can all tell you what the organization means to them and how it fits into their lives.

So can you. As a leader, you need to have a solid image of the organization and what it means in your life. You must understand why you're committed to the doctrines and principles that guide your organization. Before you can expect a commitment from your team members, you need to clearly articulate how the emotional purpose in your life matches the emotional purpose in your work.

In the circle of confrontation, nothing creates a sense of ownership and propriety more than a personal and professional commitment based upon a sense of purpose. The sense of purpose revealed in the conversation is not entirely couched in terms of material possessions but in *achievements that bring meaning to the team member's life*. In your early conversations you find out what's important to your team members, both personally and professionally. How can they be expected to commit to the organizational agenda if the agenda doesn't resonate with their own?

The foundation for commitment must be the fulfillment of emotional purpose more than a mere paycheck. Material possessions are important rewards to be sure. However, they're strengthened and become more meaningful when considered in terms of the joy and happiness they will bring to the achiever's family and significant others. This is the rubber-meets-the-road stuff.

On a higher level, although commitment involves submission to the guiding principles and mission of the organization, *surrender* is a term we are socialized to avoid. It implies loss of freedom. In reality, what many consider freedom in professional pursuits can bind them up, mired in the minutiae of running a business. For intrapreneurial people, surrender to a successful process of achievement, like the circle of confrontation, provides the greatest opportunity for personal and professional self-actualization.

LEADERSHIP: A TWO-WAY STREET

Leaders must make it clear that they are as willing to hold up their end of the bargain as their team members, or all bets are off. Without equal commitment from supervisors, managers, and executives and their team members, the motivation for compliance falls back on the leader's institutional authority. You want commitment from your team members. You want them to buy into your agenda. You want them to work enthusiastically and tirelessly to meet or exceed organizational expectations for your area. You want them to carry you off the field on their shoulders after the big win.

Too bad it's not all about you. Although MBWA has not become a household word in most organizations, any MBA student should be able to tell you that, nowadays, leaders carry team members off the field on their shoulders after the big win. After a major defeat, leaders ideally carry team members back to safety draped over their shoulders.

It's definitely about *them*. That's why commitment is so important. Not just their commitment to you, but also your commitment to them. Do you think that the extra pay and perks you receive for being the boss come with the privilege of walking around acting like a boss and annoying everybody's socks off? Sorry. The big bucks are for those who will subordinate their will to the greater good of the organization and the internal and external populations it serves. It's in the fine print of that executive agreement you never signed.

That sort of takes the butter off your popcorn, doesn't it? It's no joke though. The greatest qualifications for leadership are not competency or even intelligence. The fastest and most efficient software code writer, even if he or she *has* the highest IQ in the organization, is not necessarily (nor likely to be) the best leader of people. Those most qualified to lead are those who care enough to serve the needs of others with integrity, enthusiasm, and pride. Those are the folks who deserve the big bucks. Research indicates that those are also the folks who inspire their team members to achieve big results. There *should* be some sort of alignment there; don't you agree? If the person who supports and encourages his or her team members to achieve great things *also* writes great software code, well all-righty then.

If you're going to expect your team members to do what they're being paid to do, it begins with you doing what you're paid to do. Fair is fair. Except that you might not have received formal preparation for leadership any more than first-time parents receive intensive training for raising their first child. Go ahead and put some butter on your popcorn. You deserve it. We're all in service of the bottom line because the bottom line pays for the popcorn to begin with. At the end of the day, just like at the beginning of the day, and at midday, it's not about you *or* them as much as it's about *all of us*. If you're not clear about what it is you're being paid to do, it's time to engage the circle of confrontation with those above you on the organizational food chain.

WHAT'S IN IT FOR ME?

If you're in a position of institutional authority, you probably know exactly what's in it for you. You can probably describe to the penny the extent of your benefits package and what your contribution is versus the organization's contribution on your behalf. You know exactly what you earn and the most intricate details of your bonus or stock option plan. Why not? You *should* know. Benefits and compensation are very important, especially to your family.

On the other side of the street, do the people who report to you at work (1) have the same benefits and compensation package you do, and (2) know the details of theirs as well as you know yours? Do you spend as much time reviewing your team members' benefits and compensation packages as you do your own? Probably not. It wouldn't be a realistic or efficient use of your time. But what makes you think that they don't worry about what's in it for them as much as you ponder what's in it for you?

Many supervisors, managers, and executives consider an employee's compensation and benefits issues secondary to on-the-job performance. The classic comeback when a team member asks his or her boss about benefits is, "Call Human Resources." We won't argue with that, except to warn you that there are no unimportant people in your organization, as the "Call Human Resources" brush-off would indicate. Less money doesn't mean less important. It means the issue of what's in it for them must be important to you. After all, their level of motivation, performance, and productivity are all part of how you earn what's in it for you.

Motivating your team members for high performance and productivity when there's less in it for them than there is for you makes your job an even bigger challenge. If your organization has any integrity at all, their success and your success are interdependent. Even if they're not — even if your organization allows you to screw up with impunity, sacrificing all of your team members to save your own skin, leaving you the last one standing amidst the rubble of what was once your department or division — taking an active interest in what's in it for them is still in your best interest. Being sincerely concerned with the health and well-being of your team members and the people they care about is your best foothold in their hearts and minds.

Know What's Important

As you develop your conversational skills around commitment, the good news is that money is not a primary motivator for your team members. If it is, they're a statistical anomaly. Research indicates that workers are more concerned with security, longevity, and lifestyle fulfillment than they are with actual dollars. The actual dollars have much to do with supply and demand in the employee versus employer market tug-of-war. Employee market — bucks go up. Employer market — bucks go down. Yet there's much more than money at stake.

Employers that exploit an employer's market to chisel a few bucks off the salary of incoming team members are losing sight of the big-picture benefits of secure and committed people, which means they are committed because they feel secure. Even at top market salaries, it would be hard to keep good people on the job for long if all they did was carry rocks from one side of the field to the other, then, when all the rocks had been relocated, move them back again. Is the last person left moving rocks the person you want on your staff? He or she might be loyal, dedicated, and hard-working, but he or she will also be, in all likelihood, clueless.

What's in it for you, just like what's in it for them, must be the total package, the complete deal, the whole enchilada. What's in it for me (WIFM) is, at its very core, about emotional purpose as a basis for commitment. As a leader, you not only have a license to engage your people in these types of discussions, but it's also your obligation to stay on top of what motivates them the most.

If you avoid issues like compensation, benefits, and job satisfaction, or deal with them reluctantly only when Human Resources (HR) forces you to, you're doing yourself, your team members, and the organization that pays you a disservice. Everything discussed in this book so far points to how important it is for leaders to be skilled conversationalists. The circle of constructive confrontation is one conversation after another, after another, after another, and every conversation builds commitment.

FORMING A COMMITMENT

Everything that follows in the circle of confrontation is based on commitment. Unless a documented commitment exists between you and your team members (i.e., the covenant described in chapter 4), you abdicate your right to complain later. "I said/you said" doesn't cut it because the only place for you to fall is, "I have the institutional authority; therefore, what I say goes." One way to define cruelty is to expect someone to do something without teaching them how or at least confirming that they already know how. Only someone intoxicated with institutional authority would complain about people not doing what they didn't commit to do in the first place. Someone who abuses institutional authority like that deserves to get tangled up in all of those double negatives.

It's doubly cruel to punish somebody for not doing something they never agreed to do because you never discussed it. This "punish the innocent" technique is popular among sadistic bosses who tortured small animals as children. (Relax, you wouldn't be reading this book if you were that psychotic.) Sadists usually know they're sadists. But, on average, people don't know what they don't know.

You can end the cruelty by committing to make sure your team members possess the necessary *habits, skills, attitudes,* and *activities* to do what they're committing to do. Or you will commit to helping them get it. What you *won't* do is *assume* that they have what they need. One of the first things you and your team member will commit to (and it will be in the covenant) is asking each other questions in a continuous free-flow exchange of information. If Fred asks you every five minutes, "How am I doing, Boss? How am I doing, Boss?" you might have to slap him. It's the employee version of micromanaging, otherwise known as *subordinates' revenge.*

What keeps the free-flow exchange of information from becoming micromanaging is that you both agree to it in advance. Part of your discussion is coming to consensus on how often informal contact should be made and how often formal contact should be made. What needs to be documented and what doesn't? The fact that your exchange of information is likely to leave an information trail is good. Not only are you covering each other's backsides and forcing focus on progress, but you're also leaving a trail of crumbs through the forest that you can re-trace to diagnose what went wrong if something does.

Now that you have a more complete picture of your team members, by triangulating information gathered through observation, research, and conversation, the issue becomes context and conditions for commitment from team members to the organization and the organization to the team members. The initial conversation about a commitment needs to deal with the team member's expectations, the organization's formal expectations, *your* expectations, and what the team member's peers expect.

It will be tough to make a commitment hold up if the conditions and expectations are forced down someone's throat. That would be tyranny of the minority. Keeping the initial conversation open-ended will curb the team member's impulse to push back against your institutional authority. Holding the reins loosely at first will also help you avoid committing to rules you won't want to enforce later.

You really want to have your facts straight during the commitment phase of the commitment, confrontation, and celebration cycle. When setting up the commitment conversation, it's important to recognize the weight of the outcome up front. You don't want to have a confrontation conversation where Fred says, "Gee, boss, I didn't know you were really *serious* about getting all this done. I thought we were just shooting the breeze, flapping our gums, chewing the fat . . ." Wink. Wink. You'll have trouble keeping a simple slap from becoming a compound fracture.

Thanks to observing from afar, peer review, and direct conversations, you'll know enough about your team members, and they'll know enough about you, to tell if everyone is serious and on board. Don't be overconfident. When new hires arrive, or you're newly inserted as boss, it's best to take it slow. That doesn't mean delaying observation, peer review, and direct conversation. You will just want to ease up on your firm expectations until their behavior settles out over time.

People can pull muscles in odd places trying to impress their new boss. They can also appear more aloof and recalcitrant when trying to show you who is *really* boss. That's okay; the constructive confrontation you're practicing is going to eventually align what they do best with what the organization needs most. If you believe in the process, the process will pull you through.

Scripts: Mixing It Up/Straightening It Out

You've heard Stephen Covey's notion about beginning with the ending in mind. So do it. When forming a commitment, the conversation must cover all significant aspects of the expectations being set forth, as in *who, what, when, where, why,* and *how.* However, you don't have to structure your commitment conversation so rigidly that you sound like you're programming a computer. Conversations that form commitments should be, in a word, conversational.

When engaging a team member in the commitment-forming conversation, combine elements of *who, what, when, where, why,* and *how* in a natural way, knowing all the while you're going to recap at the end. Specific and accurate descriptions of the task, assignment, project, or initiative — and the responsibilities that go with it — are blended with who's involved and why:

"The company is looking to increase sales revenues by 15 percent, Francine. As I understand it, the objective is to increase *actual dollars collected* by 15 percent, not necessarily 15 percent more transactions. You're a skilled researcher, and we don't want to get stuck or slowed down by what we don't know, what we don't know we don't know, or what we think we know but really don't know. The CEO wants the sales division to have all the leverage they can get. Even though we're Training and Development, she wants us to support them with objective research. Based on your research experience, what kind of information can we get our hands on that they can put to use?"

WHO?

You get that all-important extra point for using Francine's name. But, that's just part of the *who* issue. Francine, the company, the CEO, the sales team, and *you* are all part of the *who* coalition. By intentionally mentioning all of these folks, you're putting pictures in Francine's head and in your own head. By engaging the visual, you're starting a sort of mental movie that will play out over the course of the initiative.

Be sure to ask her if there are any other people who should be part of the mix. Depending on how well you know Francine, she might assume that you will only allow the people you named to be involved. By asking if anyone else should be included you (1) remind her that there might be a need for more people, in case it didn't occur to her, (2) give her permission to suggest casting changes or additions, and (3) increase her sense of buy-in by empowering her in the casting decision.

Who is an important decision and part of your overall responsibility to handle correctly. The right assignment for the right reasons, at the right time, and with the right game plan can nonetheless get screwed up royally if the wrong people are on the job. This doesn't imply that some people are better than others in general. It's a matter of aligning the right people with the right activities. The best National Football League game plan would be poorly executed if a team from the Women's National Basketball Association showed up in Soldier's Field to execute it against the Bears. Before you start crying "sexist," it would be equally as implausible to expect the Chicago Bears to compete in the Women's NBA. They would no doubt get their lights shot out. *Who* is a very important part of the complete picture.

What?

The company needs to increase revenue from sales. Cutting costs in operations and generating funds from other activities like rent or leasing might also be going on, but *what* you've been given to deal with is the revenue increase. It's important to be specific. That's why you made it clear that the company isn't necessarily looking for a 15 percent increase in sales. They're looking for an increase of sales revenue. That could mean a number of things.

For starters, focusing on higher-dollar sales could be the answer. Selling more to existing customers versus selling to more customers are considerations. Price increases, shallower discounts, and generating more direct-to-consumer sales can all be part of the answer. The point is that you need to be very succinct with your team member about what it is the organization needs. You are, after all, hopefully, aligning what your organization needs most with what your team member does best.

As with every commitment conversation component, you will not only include your team member's input in the formation of the commitment and resulting covenant, but you'll also solicit it. You do not want to create a potential disconnect later on by giving your team member an opportunity to say, "I would have told you about that if you would have asked me." Never stop asking.

"Are their more people that need to be involved or on our progress report distribution list than I've mentioned? If you can't think of any right now, as we move ahead with this assignment, a need to involve someone else might come up. I'll be confronting you about the project status on a regular basis. The door is always open for adjustments. The same goes for revisiting *what* we're doing and discussing if any aspect of that should be added to or changed. If you think we need to adjust *who* is involved, let me know."

When?

Put a time frame on the task, assignment, project, or initiative. A time frame might have been imposed on you by those higher on the organizational food chain. If not, it will be hard to enforce one except through consensus with your team member about *when* this should be done. To not have a clearly defined time frame invites Parkinson's first law, and work will probably expand to fill the time available for its completion.

One aspect of the visionary skill required by leaders is putting time into perspective. If the organizational policymakers want to see new numbers reflected by the end of the quarter, that's a fast track, and you'll need to pull the fire alarm to get the troops moving on that one. More than likely, you'll have until the end of next quarter to show results. Either way, it's up to you to schedule and structure a conversation that will cover the commitment your team members are going to make to getting the organization's needs met.

When you involve your team members in the decision-making process through your conversations, you have a lot of expert opinion available to you regarding how quickly things can get done. You must also consider the trade-off between speed and thoroughness, between getting things done and getting things done right, and between immediate results versus building relationships that will produce results over time. Being the referee in a discussion of timing trade-offs requires leadership vision and judgment.

When hasn't yet come up in your introductory spiel with Francine. It could very well be one of the first questions she asks you when you open the floor for discussion. Whether or not she picks up that ball, you will, right after putting *who* and *what* out on the table. If she brings up *when*, several things could be cooking in her mind. She might feel that the organization, in characteristic style, will demand the possible on an impossible time frame. Executive muckety-mucks are notorious for ignoring important issues until they become crises; then everyone becomes part of the fire drill.

When it comes to scheduling, you're not only trying to align what your people do best with what the organization needs most but you're also negotiating on behalf of the organization *and* your team members. Nobody ever said leadership is easy. If you see a leader coasting through his or her days wearing a grin, he or she either has incredibly well-developed confrontational skills, or leadership responsibilities have been completely abandoned, leaving his or her team members struggling to stay afloat. Leaders are constantly negotiating.

WHERE?

Are there any geographic considerations to make in the execution of this task, assignment, project, or initiative? Will travel be involved? If so, how much? Who will be doing the traveling? Does the amount and expense of traveling required make the project unfeasible? From the brief introduction you've given Francine, it does not initially appear that much travel will be required.

If travel is an issue, such as might be required of the sales professional who calls regularly on retail accounts across five states, then it will obviously become a major part of the conversation. Your team member will need to make a serious commitment to the travel, and it could have a pronounced effect on his or her emotional purpose (assuming it's to settle down and spend more time with the family).

Sometimes travel isn't the issue in terms of spending time away from the family. Sometimes it's a case of moving the entire family to Senegal. That little relocation will need to be part of your conversation, especially if part of your team member's emotional purpose is to reside in the Western Hemisphere. If there is any travel involved, even a small amount, it's best to mention that early on and not assume it will be okay.

WHY?

Because we like you? No. Because you're after Francine's research experience. Francine might be extremely likable, but that's beside the point. There is a reason why the organization needs this task, assignment, project, or initiative executed. There is a reason why the people involved, starting with Francine, are involved. There is a *why* for everything involved, or there *should* be. Nobody should be drawing a paycheck for no reason.

The old "Five Whys" test is always a quick and effective way to determine how worthwhile something is:

- *Why* does the organization want to increase sales revenues by 15 percent? If the answer is credible, such as, "to stay in business," another *why* is in order.
- *Why* should the organization stay in business? "Oh, I dunno," you say, stroking your chin. "So I can have a job, Francine?"
- *Why* should the organization give you a job? "Perhaps because it can then employ a lot of other people, too. Like Francine. It's a place where high school and college graduates come to launch careers."
- *Why* should the organization exist if it's only making work? "Because it's improving the quality of life for everyone we do business with; plus it's owned by shareholders seeking a return on their investment."
- *Why* should return on shareholders' investment matter? "Because it's much more than that," you say. "It's the medical insurance, orthodonture, child care, and college fund for the families of our team members. It's what encourages investment in new and existing organizations to ensure their success. It's an integral part of the economy and tax base of this community, region, state, and this country. Without our corporate tax dollars, there would be no United Nations, no armed forces, nothing to stand between your children and pets and some tinhorn dictator in a third-world theocracy sworn to make citizens of the United States drink goat milk."

Once you sense that you've overplayed you hand on the *Five Whys* test, move on to issues that are more directly vital to the project itself. However, the *Five Whys* can help reveal that the task, assignment, project, or initiative is not, in fact, targeting the real issue the organization needs addressed. The conversation can reveal these things through the discussion of *why*. It might be good to enjoin the dynamic nature of constructive confrontation and make adjustments right out of the starting blocks.

HOW?

The means of execution is another essential topic of conversation. You will have expectations presented to you by those higher on the organizational food chain. You'll interpret the best ways to pull off the task, assignment, project, or initiative. Your team member will have ideas as well. Often, your team member has more hands-on, rubber-meets-the-road experience to draw on and can help you shape an action plan that will make you look brilliant in the execution.

Discussing how something gets done can bring up fears of micromanagement. Talk it out with your team member. If Francine wants you to keep a safe distance while she does her work, she could be negotiating some wiggle room at the front end. The issue isn't looking over her shoulder as she works. The issue is a scheduled and structured reporting plan under which she will provide progress reports.

Saying, "Let me know when you have something" isn't a credible progress report invitation. Telling Francine that you want to receive an e-mail every Tuesday and Thursday during business hours reporting progress on specified points in the assignment gives her clear and concise direction. Scheduling a meeting, even a brief one, every Friday to discuss progress face-to-face puts a demand on performance.

"That's a *when* thing," you protest. Yeah, sorta. But, it's just as importantly a *how* thing in that progress reporting is a major piece of your continuous constructive confrontation. Inasmuch as she can make it good news or bad news, Francine can exert control. She's empowered. She's participating. She's the captain of her own destiny. *How* is not only the *habits, skills, attitudes,* and *activities* used to execute the task, assignment, project, or initiative. It's reporting on how it's coming. Is the plan working as planned? If not, what needs to be altered?

Don't forget to discuss *how much* in your conversation. Is there extra compensation involved? If so, how much? Are there extra hours that need to be worked? If so, how many? Is compensation for this job tied completely to performance as in the case of commissioned sales people? *How much* of Francine's job does this assignment represent? *How much* of her available time should be spent on this task? *How much* does her performance on this project affect her periodic performance review? Any conversation about *how* should also include ample discussion about *how much*.

The conversation left off with you asking Francine, "Based on your research experience, what kind of information can we get our hands on that they can put to use?" You've begun laying out the task using w*ho, what, when, where, why, and how.* Now Francine is about to give you her input, which, based on her experience and expertise, might alter certain aspects of the task. You listen. The need to increase sales revenues by 15 percent is locked. *How* it gets done is open to negotiation. She might answer you like this:

"I think we can start close to home by examining which sales produce the highest margin. If the point is to increase *revenues* by 15 percent, there could be some obvious answers staring right at us."

"Are you talking about cutting manufacturing expenses?"

"No," she replies calmly, so as not to make you look foolish for asking. "There are sales-related expenses that are charged against sales revenues in our cost-of-sales column."

"Like what?" you ask, surprised that Francine knows so much more than you do about internal accounting procedures.

"Like the time you sent Harry to Moscow to write up that $5,000 order. His expense report was over $5,000, even with him eating at McDonalds."

"Lighten up, Francine," you warn. "Everybody deserves one mistake. And there won't be any travel involved in this project. Do you agree?"

"Absolutely," she says, letting you off the hook. "In fact, I think we can get a comprehensive list of recommendations in six weeks without leaving town, if my hunch is correct."

"That's a good time frame, based on what I've been told," you say, relieved that she covered the *when* thing. "So you think you can determine which sales are the most lucrative?"

"Yes," she assures you. "Then we can break them down by type of customer, products, and services — then determine if shifting emphasis and focus from lower margin sales to higher margin sales won't produce the desired 15 percent increase in revenues."

SUMMING UP THE CONVERSATION

Did you begin with the ending in mind? Francine jumped right in, much to your delight, and was loaded with competent recommendations. That's a good start. Here's a sample of how you're loosely scripted conversation might conclude:

"That sounds doable, Francine. I had a feeling your talent for research and inquiry would play well on this assignment." You get another point for flattering Francine by name. "The first thing I want you to do is put together a comprehensive covenant covering what we talked about and any other details that might occur to you. Have it to me by the end of the day on Thursday and I'll look it over and we'll meet again late Monday with my recommended modifications. The whole thing should take no more than two or three pages, max. But be sure to address who, what, when, where, why, and how. In the who portion, think about the distribution from your end, list who should be copied on our distribution on this. I'll combine our lists when I review your draft covenant."

You've recognized the unique talent, skill, and ability Francine brings to the project and made it clear what her next step will be. Looking forward to her draft covenant, you'll need to insert some language of your own describing the understanding of and the agreement to the roles of team leader and team member. You'll look to see if she's put forth a realistic time frame for completing short-, medium-, and long-term components of the task, especially considering time frames imposed on you from above. You both still need to cover the following:

- Agreement and commitment to the processes to be followed
- Agreement and commitment to the necessary resources and priorities

- Acceptance and agreement to everyone's broad and specific expectations
- Agreement to remain flexible and make course corrections as necessary
- Agreement and commitment to the schedule for confrontation and celebration

To cover all of that in an initial conversation would overload your systems. By sending her off to draft a covenant, she'll be organizing the information covered so far. When you convene again on Monday afternoon to revise the covenant, most of what you are committing to will be on paper. From that platform, your second conversation will move much faster because your thoughts will be that much better organized.

Chapter 3 Summary

The commitment conversation provides the substance you and your team member will use to draft the covenant. It's important for you to maintain a guided agenda so that all that needs to be covered will be covered, even new thoughts contributed by your team member. It's easy to see how this open exchange of information can help people remain better informed. Better informed people function more confidently than people afraid they might be missing a piece of critical information. Key points to remember in guiding a commitment conversation include the following:

- Nothing creates a sense of ownership and propriety on the part of your team members more than a voice in determining *who, what, when, where, why,* and *how* related to a job, task, assignment, project, or initiative. Personal and professional commitment to the circle of confrontation is also based upon a sense of purpose. In Francine's case, this was merely a reference to her skill, aptitude, and desire to conduct research. The sense of purpose revealed in the conversation is not couched in terms of material possessions but in how the work resonates with the team member's sense of purpose.

- On a higher level, commitment involves submission to the guiding principles of the organization and its mission. But *surrender* is a term we are socialized to avoid. It implies loss of freedom. In reality, what many consider freedom in professional pursuits can bind them up, mired in the minutiae of running a business. For intrapreneurial people, surrender to a successful process of achievement provides the greatest opportunity for personal and professional self-actualization. There is no question how Francine's work will benefit the organization.
- The commitment is a two-way street between the team leader and team member. Team leaders must make it clear they are as willing to hold up their end of the bargain as their team members, or all bets are off. Without equal commitment from supervisors, managers, and executives and their team members, the motivation for compliance falls back on the leader's institutional authority.
- The commitment must cover all significant aspects of the expectations being set forth, which include the following:
  - Specific and accurate description of the task, initiative, and responsibilities
  - Understanding of and agreement to the roles of team leader and team member
  - Realistic time frame for completing short-, medium-, and long-term tasks
  - Agreement and commitment to the processes to be followed
  - Agreement and commitment to the necessary resources and priorities
  - Acceptance and agreement to everyone's broad and specific expectations
  - Agreement to remain flexible and make course corrections as necessary
  - Agreement and commitment to the schedule for confrontation and celebration

All of these things and more are covered in the context of *who, what, when, where, why,* and *how* as your conversation with Francine becomes a covenant in Chapter 4. The closer a commitment conversation comes to becoming a covenant, the more comprehensive the conversation becomes. As the leader in the circle of constructive confrontation, you remain keenly aware of how your skill at guiding conversation is leading to actionable behavior and the opportunity for tremendous performance and productivity from your team members.

The Covenant

If MBWA is such a good thing, doesn't it make good sense to expand and strengthen the concept to include *Management by Writing it Down?* A contract is an agreement, whether or not it's written down. But unless it's written down and signed by all parties, it's likely to degenerate into a lightning rod for classic "I said/you said" arguments, misunderstandings, disagreements, disconnects, confusion, and conflicts — in other words, confrontations — old-fashioned, old-school, negative, after-the-fact confrontations to be exact. In the circle of constructive confrontation, the covenant is a *written* agreement, which has a spiritual dimension inasmuch as both parties agree to be subject to whatever guiding principles are included. By putting the commitment down on paper, even if it's only an electronic file stored on your respective computers, the covenant formalizes what has been committed to by your individual team member or your team, and *you,* as a representative of the organization that pays everybody.

The covenant is a living document that needs to be revisited every time a scheduled confrontation takes place, if only to guarantee that progress being reported is consistent with the plan. It's a road map for progress and a game plan for whatever game the covenant covers. As crucial as this written agreement is to the circle of constructive confrontation, the covenant does not replace or contradict the team member's customary documents on file in HR. If anything, a copy of the covenant should be forwarded to HR to be stored in the team member's file. But it's a *working* document, used and referred to constantly. It's not a static piece that ends up in a file, never to be seen or used again. File folders with covenants in them get mighty worn around the edges.

DOUBLE USAGE

Everybody's covenant file folder, containing progress reports and meeting notes, becomes well worn pretty quickly because confrontation is not a one-way street. All parties to the covenant are obligated to confront the others to ensure the task, assignment, project, or initiative is executed as agreed. The covenant grants team members written permission to confront their team leaders as necessary to stay the designated course. More importantly, the document obligates team leaders to regularly confront their team members or teams and needs to be constantly close at hand for all parties involved.

The covenant is the merger of principles and practice. The language of the covenant is intentionally active, as opposed to passive. It's not about what ought to or should be done. It's about what *will* be done. The covenant outlines the theoretical guiding principles behind how the commitment will be operationalized. More than merely a commitment on paper, the covenant serves as a reference and the agenda for constructive confrontations to follow. The covenant is the basis for the continuous circle of confrontation, and the team member and team leader will use the document to remain clear on how the policies, practices, and procedures they've committed to need to be realized.

It's the leader's responsibility to guide the identification of, and engineer the connection between, the individual's emotional purpose and the resources, rewards, and realities of the job. The conversation(s) that led up to drafting the covenant set the stage, clarified the terms, determined the rules of engagement, and essentially wrapped your arms and your team member's arms, around the issue. Conversations leading up to drafting a covenant are much more than goal-setting sessions. Conversations are the *courtship* between what your people do best and what your organization needs most. Covenants are the *vows*.

THE CEO WALKS A FINE LINE

The research you're asking Francine to conduct comes out of an irregular request from the CEO's office. This *could* have been a covenant between a sales division executive and a sales division team member. That's what you'd expect, right? XYZ Corp, however, has a progressive CEO, and she thinks that people sometimes operate too close to the forest to see the trees. So she asked the head of Training and Development to see to it that this research was conducted. That's the role you're playing vis-à-vis Francine. The CEO is also savvy enough to know that the sales division folks are unlikely to consider research on sales to be credible if it comes from outside of their territory. That's why she's planning to turn the recommendations over to the sales division executives as the basis for their own research project, which will immediately follow Francine's work.

As a staunch believer in constructive confrontation, the CEO will see to it that the sales division is every bit as effective with their portion of the project as Francine is with hers. It's her way of triangulating information from the sales division itself, what you and Francine come up with, and (perhaps) an internal or external consultant. You discuss this openly with Francine because it's important for her to understand the entire context and scope of the research project. Like anyone else, her role in the project will make more sense when framed in the big picture. It's almost never a good idea to keep people in the dark about anything. The "need-to-know," as in "I know and when I want you to know I'll tell you," stuff is a power play 99 percent of the time. It's also a silly way for you to open the possibility of a disconnect between you and your team members. It's hard enough keeping them connected in the first place.

FRANCINE'S COVENANT

Following the prescribed format for creating a covenant, Francine sends you an e-mail, as requested, on Thursday afternoon. You read it carefully to make sure that it covers all of the points the two of you committed to. You're particularly interested in the clarity of the language, which is always enhanced by its concision. Covenants and the conversations that lead up to them can become anchors in organizational progress. You and Francine must consciously resist the temptation toward paralysis by analysis. Your covenant might wind up looking like this, or you might be more creative. Either way, it needs to be thorough more than it needs to be long.

To: Your Name
From: Francine France (her parents are French)
Date: Day of Week/Month/Day/Year
Subject: Covenant: Conduct Research to Increase XYZ Corp Sales Revenues by 15 Percent

Who:
1. Francine France will conduct research into the fastest and most effective ways that sales revenues at XYZ Corp can be increased by 15 percent.
2. Francine will report directly to (Your Name) as a representative of XYZ Corp for supervision and necessary guidance.
3. Francine will consult with members of the XYZ Corp sales division as needed to gather data to complete her research.
4. Francine will consult with XYZ Corp customers, as specified by XYZ Corp sales management, as needed to enrich the data she is collecting to complete her research.
5. Francine will copy the following people on her progress reports and preliminary suggestions: (Your Name) and (selected members of the sales division).

What:
1. The XYZ Corp is seeking recommendations on how to increase sales revenues by 15 percent.
2. The desired increase must be in *revenues,* whether related to volume of sales or any other factor.
3. Research must be conducted in order to present a list of objective recommendations on how to most effectively increase XYZ Corp sales revenues by 15 percent.
4. The initial research will be conducted by the Training and Development department to provide an objective analysis of the criteria determining sales margin.
5. When completed and submitted, the list of recommendations will be reviewed and acted upon by the sales division, subject to their own research.

When:
1. Francine will begin her research immediately upon signing this covenant.
2. Francine will submit a written progress report of her findings to (Your Name) every Thursday via e-mail attachment.
3. Pending (Your Name)'s approval, Francine will distribute copies of her progress report to the agreed upon distribution list.
4. At the end of six (6) weeks following the signature date of this covenant, Francine will deliver her final list of recommendations to (Your Name).
5. Pending (Your Name)'s approval and any additions/corrections, Francine will distribute her final recommendations to the agreed upon distribution list. No more than two (2) business days will expire between item 4 and item 5 in this section.

Where:
1. Francine will conduct the research, for the most part, on the XYZ Corp headquarters campus by reviewing historical sales data.
2. Francine will expand her research data through discussions with XYZ Corp sales team members, via telephone, e-mail, or in person at the XYZ Corp headquarters campus.
3. If it is determined that regional focus groups will help validate the collected data, Francine will set up off-campus focus group sessions, subject to (Your Name)'s approval.
4. If it is determined that interviewing customers on their sites will help

(continued)

broaden and validate the collected data, those visits will be set up and carried out, subject to (Your Name)'s approval.

5. Meetings to discuss the progress reports and final recommendations will be held on the XYZ Corp headquarters campus.

Why: 1. XYZ Corp stockholders' equity has been steadily decreasing for seven quarters.

2. A review of expenses has been conducted, and the recommendations to reduce have been in effect for two quarters.

3. Despite expense reduction efforts, profits continue to lag behind projections.

4. Alternative opportunities are being sought to strengthen XYZ Corp's bottom line, including, but not limited to, increasing revenues from sales.

5. Because increasing revenues by 15 percent is a more critical issue than arbitrarily increasing sales by 15 percent, research needs to be conducted and recommendations delivered that expose below-the-surface opportunities to increase margin if possible.

How: 1. Francine will develop a short survey to serve as a standard questionnaire for gathering comparable information from all sources.

2. Francine will conduct telephone, e-mail, or face-to-face surveys to collect data, both internal and external to the organization.

3. Francine will examine historical sales data to make comparisons of various sales in an attempt to isolate key elements of the more lucrative sales in terms of margin.

4. Francine will compile this information into progress report form and distribute it to the agreed upon distribution list, subject to (Your Name)'s approval.

5. Francine will ultimately compile her collected data into final recommendations and distribute them to the agreed upon distribution list, subject to (Your Name)'s approval.

RESPONDING TO THE FIRST DRAFT

Francine did a good job of documenting the content of your discussion and finding some additional information to boot. The point of having your team member compile the first daft is to etch these things in his or her mind. The team member is doing the work, and you, as a leader, are providing guidance and support. To write the covenant yourself would mean doing a major part of your team members' work for them and thus robbing them of the many benefits that come from the experience. They might not jump up and down and thank you for the assignment to write up their own covenants, but their level of knowledge, awareness, and participation are significantly increased. If they have any loyalty to the organization at all, they'll appreciate how much more effective you're helping them become. In fact, you're teaching them constructive confrontational skills that will enhance other areas of their lives, especially their home lives.

You're impressed with the detail Francine was able to secure regarding the company's profit-enhancement initiative. She is obviously a self-starter, which is every manager's dream. If you don't go any farther in the constructive confrontation process than this point, you'll be light years ahead of most supervisors, managers, and executives in giving well-thought-out, precise, and substantive direction to your people. That, in itself, would exponentially increase productivity and performance. The meaningful conversation and exchange of information between you and your team members has already reduced ambiguity and confusion, while building a clearer image of what needs to be done. But you won't stop here. You've had a glimpse of the Promised Land, and you can't wait to get there.

Your job now is to review what Francine has prepared and put the finishing touches on it. Since the art of constructive confrontation is new to XYZ Corp, Francine isn't aware that you're making a commitment to her as much as she's making a commitment to you. She's not aware until you tell her and then, more importantly, *show her* through your consistently supportive behavior over time. To make the point about mutual support, you add a few points to the covenant she drafted to make it clearer.

If you discussed the concept of mutual support between team members and team leaders during your initial commitment conversations with Francine, great. Make sure those thoughts are reflected in the covenant. Never assume people will simply remember important issues or what exactly you said about them. Of course, putting language into the covenant about supporting Francine obligates *you* to perform. So you'd better mean it.

It's apparent that certain elements overlap in *who, what, when, where, why,* and *how.* That's normal. The covenant must always be considered in its entirety to be effective. It can't be partially considered any more than you can partially enforce it. If you choose to confront your team members on some elements of their covenants and not others, you disqualify yourself to do any constructive confrontation and plunge you and your team back into the dark ages when confrontation was always negative, generally avoided, and occurred only when things fell in the tank.

ITEM-BY-ITEM

You and Francine now meet face-to-face, as scheduled, in order to have as complete a conversation as possible as you go over her draft of the covenant. You want everything in play, verbal and nonverbal signals, real-time interaction, and so on. As you make additions, deletions, or alterations to your team member's covenant, discuss them thoroughly as a means of honoring his or her original intent while still sharpening it.

You can choose to highlight, underline, or otherwise indicate visually on the covenant the changes you make so that you can be held responsible for them, *and* your team member can take credit for his or her original concepts. Nothing deflates enthusiasm more than a boss stealing the credit for a team member's idea. You'll see in the upcoming example that the changed or altered items in Francine's original draft covenant are underlined.

The first thing you spot in Francine's draft is her suggestion in the *who* section that she interview customers "as needed." You go ahead and suggest that she plan on interviewing customers instead of leaving it "as needed." You recommend that she request a specific sampling from sales management. Your thought is to give some early control to the sales division so as not to get their nose bent too far out of shape because the CEO wanted some objective analysis done outside of their division. It's a simple change to remove the words "as needed" and make a specific number of "10." The bottom line is that you want Francine to make a more specific request and leave it less to interpretation.

"This will give us an early test as to how cooperative our sales people might be to assist you in this initial research," you tell Francine. "I don't anticipate any resistance on their part, but if you encounter any, tell me about it, and I'll see what can be done. Do you think 10 is a good number?"

"Yes," she says, with a little hesitancy. "I'm not sure if we need quite that many. Then again, a few more might not hurt either. I really won't know until I see what other information I have to compare it with."

"This is a dynamic process," you assure her. "You and I are going to meet once per week to confront the progress you're making. If anything needs changing, we'll discuss it and, if needed, change it."

That's good enough for her, but she suggests adding the words, "unless otherwise decided by (Your Name) and (Her Name)." Note that Francine's revision in the revised covenant that follows is not underlined. That's so it's not later confused as *your* addition, even though you both agree to it. Your signatures on the finished covenant will signify your mutual agreement, which includes all changes and additions, no matter who they came from.

You also mention that the CEO should be copied because this is a project she has taken heightened interest in; in fact, the idea originated with her. One reason is because you want the CEO to see what Francine is doing directly and don't want Francine to think you're filtering or plagiarizing her work. If the CEO doesn't want to be copied until the recommendation stage, take her name off of the list.

"Francine, I added the word 'measured' in item two of the *what* section, because it seemed to help clarify the point the CEO is trying emphasize."

"No problem," Francine assures you. "I know she doesn't want any confusion around that."

"I added the word 'objective' in item three in the *what* section for the same reason," you go on.

"Do you think that'll set off the sales division?" Francine asks. "It kind of makes it sound like we're hammering them for not being objective."

"Good point," you agree. "But the CEO specifically used the word 'objective' over and over, so if we need to err one way or the other, I'll argue that we're following her lead . . . just in case anyone questions why *we're* doing this research."

"Don't you think my reference to objectivity in item three in the *what* section is sufficient?" Francine challenges.

"Your language about objectivity in item three in the *what* section stands well on its own. I'm just more comfortable with the added emphasis."

"But I'm the one working with them," she trumps you.

"True," you retreat. "And I *do* want them to see a copy of our covenant and understand there's no hidden agenda."

"So it's out?" she asks.

"I'll take it back out," you promise. "And I'll make sure it doesn't appear in any form in the final draft, so it won't bug 'em. What do you think of adding the words, 'as per the CEO's directive' in item four?"

"That makes a good point," she agrees. "But I think it will be stronger if you add it to item *five* in the *what* section instead of item four. That way they won't think you're telling them what to do."

"Good point. I'll strike it from item four and move it to item five. Are you okay with the addition of 'with the meeting time to be set no later than 24 hours in advance' I added to item two in the *when* section?"

"Yeah," Francine says. "I can see that we need to have a specific meeting time. But we don't need to set it a week out. Your way leaves it somewhat flexible up to the day before."

"I added 'item five in the *who* section' to item three in the *when* section," you go on, "so you only have to include that list once in the covenant."

"Good idea."

"I liked the language in items four and five in the *when* section," you say. "It will be good for us to go over the final recommendations together. But when they're distributed, they should come from you. After all, you will be the one who did the research."

"Darn tootin'," Francine says. "And delivering in six weeks will give the sales division six *more* weeks to meet the CEO's ninety-day target to take action."

"How did you know about the ninety days?" you ask in amazement.

"You said yourself that I was a good researcher."

"Touché," you say. "Actually," you add, "with your weekly progress reports, the sales division can have a lot of their preliminary thinking done long before your recommendations are delivered."

"Do you ever wonder if we're too nice to those guys?" Francine jokes.

"Let's just hope they appreciate it," you confirm. "I think you should go ahead and just plan on doing three off-campus focus groups."

"I see that in the way you edited item three in the *where* section," she replies. "If the sales guys want to participate should I let them or tell 'em to do their own groups?"

"I think, in keeping with the CEO's objectivity thing, you can allow them to observe. But be clear to them about why active participation in your focus groups would compromise objectivity."

"No problem."

"I think you should also go ahead and plan to interview our top ten customers by margin," you say. "That's why I changed the language in item four in the *where* section. It's a good idea. Just go ahead and do it. But you don't need to travel, given our time constraints. Are you okay with e-mail and telephone?"

"Yeah," Francine says. "That's fine. I'll make sure I give sales a heads up before I contact our top ten customers."

"Good idea," you agree. "I'll make it a special point to confirm that the CEO and the sales executives are cool with that, too. Moving on, notice that I also specified that our meetings will be in *your* office, unless we need to make other arrangements for some reason."

"More convenient for me," she appreciates.

"I need the exercise more than you," you compliment her. "The *why* section looks great," you compliment her again. "Is that another example of your comprehensive research?"

Francine touches the end of her nose with her index finger and points at you with the other.

"Before you think I'm trying to micromanage this," you plead. "I added 'and have it approved by (Your Name) before using it for research, individual interviews, and focus groups in section one in the *how* section. That way I can have your back if anyone takes exception to anything. As far as your ability to write research questions, I have complete confidence in you."

Francine's body language indicates she's okay with that. At least she doesn't tense up. But you know that you must make an effort to demonstrate your confidence in her abilities every chance you get. "I added the 'subject to my approval' business in items four and five of the *how* section for the same reasons we already discussed. I want the ideas to have your authorship, but I need everyone to know that we've discussed them and my authority is behind them in case anyone thinks of challenging you."

"It looks to me like we're ready to get started," Francine says, getting a tad impatient. "I'm glad you added the business about flexibility at the end, just in case. And the stuff about providing support . . . I'm glad you put that in writing."

"Like I said," you say, "that's my job. As long as we keep talking, we'll pull this off with flying colors."

To: Your Name
From: Francine France (her parents are still French)
Date: [Revised: Day of Week Weekday/Month/Day/Year/Time]
Changes by: (Your Name) Underlined
Subject: Covenant: Conduct Research to Increase XYZ Corp Sales Revenues by 15 Percent

Who: 1. Francine France will conduct research into the fastest and most effective ways that sales revenues at XYZ Corp can be increased by 15 percent.

---

2. Francine will report directly to (Your Name) as a representative of XYZ Corp for supervision and necessary guidance.
3. Francine will consult with members of the XYZ Corp sales division as needed to gather data to complete her research.
4. Francine will consult with ten XYZ Corp customers, as specified by XYZ Corp sales management ~~as needed~~ to enrich the data she is collecting to complete her research, unless otherwise decided by (Your Name) and (Her Name).
5. Francine will copy the following people on her progress reports and preliminary suggestions: [(Your Name), (selected members of the sales division), and the CEO].

What:
1. The XYZ Corp is seeking recommendations on how to increase sales revenues by 15 percent.
2. The desired increase must be measured in *revenues*, whether related to volume of sales or any other factor.
3. Research must be conducted outside of the sales division in order to present a list of objective recommendations on how to most effectively increase XYZ Corp sales revenues by 15 percent.
4. The initial research will be conducted by the Training and Development department to provide an objective analysis of the criteria determining sales margin. ~~as per the CEO's directive~~.
5. When completed and submitted, the list of recommendations will be reviewed and acted upon by the sales division, as per the CEO's directive, subject to their own research.

When:
1. Francine will begin her research immediately upon signing this covenant.
2. Francine will submit a progress report of her findings to (Your Name) every Thursday, with the meeting time to be set no later than 24 hours in advance.
3. Pending (Your Name)'s approval, Francine will distribute copies of her progress report to the agreed upon distribution list (item five in the *who* section).
4. At the end of six (6) weeks following the signature date of this covenant, Francine will deliver her final list of recommendations to (Your Name).

(continued)

5. Pending (Your Name)'s approval and any additions/corrections, Francine will distribute her final recommendations to the agreed upon distribution list. No more than two (2) business days will expire between item 4 and item 5 in this section.

Where: 1. Francine will conduct the research, for the most part, on the XYZ Corp headquarters campus by reviewing historical sales data.

2. Francine will expand her research data through discussions with XYZ Corp sales team members, via telephone, e-mail, or in person at the XYZ Corp headquarters campus.

3. ~~If it is determined that regional focus groups will help validate the collected data,~~ Francine will set up and facilitate three off-campus focus group sessions~~, subject to (Your Name)'s approval~~.

4. ~~If it is determined that interviewing customers on their sites will help broaden and validate the collected data, those visits will be set up and carried out, subject to (Your Name)'s approval.~~ <u>Francine will interview XYZ Corp's ten largest customers via telephone or at the customer's property if the customer is local</u>.

5. Meetings to discuss the progress reports and final recommendations will be held on the XYZ Corp headquarters campus <u>in Francine's office, unless otherwise arranged in advance</u>.

Why: 1. XYZ Corp stockholders' equity has been steadily decreasing for seven quarters.

2. A review of expenses has been conducted and the recommendations to reduce have been in effect for two quarters.

3. Despite expense reduction efforts, profits continue to lag behind projections.

4. Alternative opportunities are being sought to strengthen XYZ Corp's bottom line, including, but not limited to, increasing revenues from sales.

5. Because increasing revenues by 15 percent is a more critical issue than arbitrarily increasing sales by 15 percent, research needs to be conducted and recommendations delivered that expose below-the-surface opportunities to increase margin if possible.

How: 1. Francine will develop a short survey to serve as a standard questionnaire for gathering comparable information from all sources <u>and have</u>

it approved by (Your Name) before using it for research, individual interviews, and focus groups.

2. Francine will conduct telephone, e-mail, or face-to-face surveys to collect data, both internal and external to the organization.
3. Francine will examine historical sales data to make comparisons of various sales in an attempt to isolate key elements of the more lucrative sales in terms of margin.
4. Francine will compile this information into progress report form and distribute it to the agreed upon distribution list (in the *who* section above), subject to (Your Name)'s approval.
5. Francine will ultimately compile her collected data into final recommendations and distribute them to the agreed upon distribution list, subject to (Your Name)'s approval.

Other Items:

1. This covenant is a dynamic document, detailing a dynamic process. Changes can be made as needed and justified, contingent on the mutual agreement of both signature parties.
2. This covenant is intended to be a guide to the execution of the project titled: Research to "Increase Sales Revenue by 15 Percent." Nothing in the covenant should be construed as to alter Francine France's conditions of employment with XYZ Corp. The covenant, however, establishes this initiative as Francine's top professional priority until completed.
3. It is always expected that everyone involved will continuously use his or her best judgment and bring any issues affecting the successful execution of this initiative to the other party's attention for resolution as soon as the issue becomes known.
4. To the best of [his or her] ability, and to the full extent of [his or her] authority within XYZ Corp, (Your Name) will provide Francine France with the best possible guidance, coaching, and access to XYZ Corp information.
5. To the best of [his or her] ability, and to the full extent of [his or her] authority within XYZ Corp, (Your Name) agrees to the most appropriate and adequate resources to ensure success of this initiative.

Signature: Francine France [Date, Time, and Location]
Signature: (Your Name) [Date, Time, and Location]

The underlying principles that guide your behavior and Francine's behavior in an organizational context are extremely important to discuss and document. If this acknowledgment that a philosophy of doing business exists, the whole covenant and circle of confrontation process can be sunk with a single torpedo. There are certain fairly universal and unspoken understandings about how to conduct business, inside and outside of the organization. Speak them. As long as they remain unspoken, they remain open to liberal interpretation to perhaps justify irrational or irresponsible behavior. Writing things down strengthens understanding and reinforces the beliefs.

CONGRATULATIONS

You've just pulled off an excellent constructive confrontation — and you're only in the covenant stage. You and Francine just confronted the initiative with the covenant at the center of your conversation. Your next confrontation is scheduled for the following Thursday. In less than 15 minutes of face time you've covered more territory and provided more explicit direction to your team member than most managers and executives do in a calendar quarter. You should hear the stories. It's not that managers and executives don't talk to their team members a lot. But the distilled, concentrated information and direction in the constructive confrontation process is like a laser beam compared to scattered and diffused information in a poorly planned ad hoc conversation.

This confrontation conversation was also constructive. Moreover, Francine is completely *accountable* for the important stuff around this initiative. This is practical stuff. Team leaders need to be organized and deliberate about how they set up and guide the activities of those who report to them. Constructive confrontation is just such a structured and deliberate exercise. Not to go through this detail is to leave too much to chance. The formality of the covenant and the distinctly intentional nature of the conversations you have with your team members, commitment, confrontation, and celebratory, will mean you spend less time in their business over time, while still increasing accountability and decreasing conflict.

All the while, the time you *do* spend with them will be much more focused and productive. What can't be measured can't be managed, remember? Constructive confrontation is all about measuring the *habits, skills, attitudes,* and *activities* of your team members. Managing those things is simply the next logical step. If nothing else, regular, meaningful, face-to-face conversations are a radical improvement in leadership performance for most.

If what you've learned about constructive confrontation so far doesn't sound like conflictual confrontation as you've known it, *good.* Negative after-the-fact confrontation exposes that the bases weren't adequately covered to begin with, and opportunities for constructive confrontation were missed. If you do nothing beyond getting a covenant drafted, you've set the stage for increased productivity, performance, and achievement as only a better understanding of the objectives will bring. You'll also enjoy a greater sense of participation and ownership from Francine and anyone like her who experiences constructive confrontation. Of course you're not going to stop here. You're going to complete the cycle. Before that, it will help to expand beyond Francine's experience to see how diverse the constructive confrontation challenge can be.

COMPLEX COVENANTS

Many covenants will be more complex and comprehensive than the one you just arranged with Francine. Like anything else in life and business, the more that's at stake, the more devils there are in the details. Francine's covenant covers *what* is to be accomplished, *when, where, how,* and *by whom.* All covenants should do that. However, in more complex covenants, goals are further broken down into tasks, and tasks are plotted on time lines. Tasks are purposefully broken down into the *habits, skills, attitudes,* and *activities* necessary to complete the cycle of success and bring it back to the starting spot. In other words, a covenant can really *spell it out,* not because your team members are morons, but because the amount of detail tunes you and your team members into the same radio station with the clearest signal possible.

Even on more complex covenants, once the merger of principle and practice is defined and agreed to, it needs to be written down by the team member. As in less complex covenants, having the team member draw up the first-draft document increases the team member's comprehension and understanding of the context and meaning of each component. It's also incredibly empowering, thus increasing the team member's sense of ownership and the resulting buy-in.

It isn't always necessary to underline changes and strike outs to identify where they came from. If time is of the essence and the temperament of your team member is such that a fully executed agreement needs to be drafted as soon as possible, you can rely on your signatures and copious notes to keep it clear you're both operating on the same page. The finished complex covenant is signed off on by the team member and the leader, just as in a simpler covenant. The team leader's signature binds the organization to the covenant, just as a sales contract establishes price and other criteria, and binds the organization to perform for a customer. The team member's signature represents his or her agreement to the terms and conditions of the task, assignment, project, or initiative. A complex covenant is not necessarily that much longer than a simple covenant, but its implications can be farther reaching.

HARRY'S JOB

You're now cast in the role of sales director. "Sorry about that Moscow thing," you tell Harry as soon as his rear end hits the chair across from your desk. "I appreciate that you ate at MacDonald's every day to keep expenses down," you continue as you stand up and move to a chair out where Harry is so as not to have that enormous, intimidating expanse of desktop between the two of you as you talk. Unlike Francine, who does various things as part of her job, Harry is a sales representative. He's paid to sell. He's paid *for* what he sells. As a commissioned sales professional,

100

Harry is part of a rare breed and one of the most misunderstood creatures on the planet.

You've seen how a simple task or assignment, like Francine's research, can be handled in conversation, commitment, and covenant. The recommendations she will come up with will be extremely important to the life and vitality of XYZ Corp. The nature of the covenant and the need for constructive conversation in the organization varies with occupational challenges. While Francine might need to dodge some bullets from the sales division, she can successfully navigate her waters with a diplomacy and quid pro quo here and there. Francine won't be subjected to a disproportional amount of abuse as she fulfills her covenant. As a sales pro, Harry takes a severe beating every day.

The extremes of constructive confrontation between Francine's and Harry's situations pretty well leave everything else somewhere in the middle. Marketing tasks, that is, assignments, projects, or initiatives to make the telephone ring, require intelligence, creativity, resourcefulness, and the like. But Harry is in sales, not marketing. He has to sit face-to-face with customers and ask them for orders. While marketing and operations people, engineers, and software designers are engaging their intelligence, creativity, and resourcefulness on behalf of the organization from the relative safety of corporate headquarters, Harry is running for his life with a pack of hounds biting at his ankles, or avoiding the accusing glares of a surly secretary in the tomb-like silent tension of a waiting room outside some muckety-muck's office, or listening intently as the muckety-muck shows him pictures of his family at Disney World last summer.

Harry's situation calls for an explanation of constructive confrontation right off the bat, lest he feel manipulated. A discussion of emotional purpose quickly follows just to begin focusing him on what's truly important about this often thankless work he does. You know Harry benefits a great deal from frank and open discussion. So you don't beat around the bush.

COMMITMENT CONVERSATION WITH HARRY

"You have one of the toughest jobs in the world, Harry," you say as your rear end hits the chair beside Harry's.

"No argument here," Harry sighs.

"You make the XYZ Corp's cash register ring. There's no more important job here at XYZ or any other corporation."

"Just show me the money, baby," Harry laughs, mostly serious.

"Money you'll get anywhere you work, *babe*," you retort, trying to be clever. "I mean a ten percent commission is a ten percent commission anywhere, right?"

"I suppose."

"The difference at XYZ Corp, besides the superior products and services we offer, is that I'll confront you on a regular basis."

"Gee, thanks," Harry mumbles. "I guess."

"Seriously, I've been trained in this new concept of constructive confrontation, and I think it can increase my ability to help you sell. It's not a new concept, really. It's a composite of proven encouragement techniques that are sophisticated in their sheer simplicity. It's *acting on them* that makes the difference."

"That sounds like a brochure," Harry says.

"I memorized it," you confess. "But this stuff really works. My boss is more involved, in a positive way, in my success than she's ever been before."

Harry's eyes grow wider, surprised to hear anyone talk about their boss in a positive way, especially when she's not around. "What's the big deal?" he asks. "I know the drill. You give me an unreasonable quota to attain, a pep talk to distract me from the abuse I'm going to endure attaining it, and then confront me when I come up short."

"That was the *old* me," you assure him. "I now know that there are *good* reasons to use confrontation in a constructive way. Better yet, there are methods and techniques to make it simple and straightforward to do."

"Like what?"

"Like this conversation, for starters."

"We've been talking for less than two minutes and we're ready to segue into your emotional purpose."

"My what?"

"The reason you're working. What are you doing this all for? Do you want your family to live in a big house in the suburbs? Do you want to send your kids to private school? Or do you want your wife and kids to live in a double-wide trailer and attend public schools while you race one-hundred-thousand-dollar Formula One Indy cars as a hobby? Do the kids need orthodonture?"

Harry nods his head for a moment. "The house."

"Tell me more," you coax.

"The most important thing to me these days is making sure Brenda gets to live in a house she likes and raise the kids in a good school district."

"Have you figured out how much that will cost? How much you'll need to earn?"

"We actually talked about that recently," Harry admits. "For us to live where we want to live and live a good life with vacations, drive decent cars, and that sort of thing, I need to earn about one hundred fifty thousand per year."

"After taxes?"

Harry nods his head.

"So we're talking a gross between two hundred and two hundred twenty thousand," you calculate.

"Something like that."

"That means selling two-point-two million."

Harry nods his head.

"That's great," you gush. "XYZ Corp would love nothing *better* than for you to sell two-point-two million."

"But that's more than I've ever sold before," Harry says, shaking his head back and forth.

"This is the first day of the rest of your life, Harry," you preach. "The biggest difference between then and now is the structured approach we'll take to support you."

"More pep talks?"

"Constructive confrontation."

Harry leans forward, suddenly all ears. Now that you touched, even briefly, on the emotional purpose of Harry's work and the desired fruits of his labor, the methods and techniques of collecting that fruit are much more interesting. Are most people more cynical than Harry? Yes. They'll *act* enthused and excited on the front end. But, it will take *consistent* constructive confrontation over time to make them believers. At first, they might only go with the program to get out of your office. But once they know you mean it, they'll be dragging you along like an overzealous sled dog. During their cynical stage, constructive confrontation will increase their performance and productivity by virtue of the enhanced contact and vigilance on your part. That alone makes it worthwhile. How many professionals have you heard say, "I would have succeeded if my boss *hadn't* provided me with so doggone much support, encouragement, training, and resources?" Never heard that said? Didn't think so.

THE CONVERSATION TURNS TO COMMITMENT

You deserve points for following your notes in these conversations. The legal pad on your lap has *who, what, when, where, why,* and *how* written on it. It also has *emotional purpose* written on it. You made mental notes and actual check marks beside topics you've discussed. As with Francine, you want the conversation to be affable and pleasant, but you also want it to cover the important points. With your rarely idle pen, you also made a note to cover *habits, skills, attitudes,* and *activities.* You've made some notes beside emotional purpose, like home, neighborhood, schools, kids, Brenda, income breakdown, and two hundred twenty million dollars in sales.

"Let's take our target of two-point-two million and back out of it what you'll need to do to get it," you say. "*And* what the organization needs to do to help you get it."

"Back out of it . . . ?" Harry says curiously. "Do you mean *break it down?*"

"That's a good way to start," you say positively, realizing Harry is on top of your lexicon. "What's your current closing percentage?"

"Ten percent."

You note that. "Your average sale?"

"Last year it was seventy thousand dollars."

You calculate as you scribble notes. "It looks like you need to close about thirty-two sales to make your goal."

"That sounds about right," Harry agrees.

"What are the most you've ever closed in a twelve-month period?" you inquire. You have all this data on Harry already. But having him regurgitate it in front of you gives the appearance of crunching the numbers on the spot, being spontaneous, and brainstorming. Most importantly, you now know that *he knows* the right numbers and has a realistic assessment of the situation. You're modeling strategic thinking for Harry, especially how information feeds the planning process. Many managers or executives, and almost all supervisors, beat their people up with information. "I know what your numbers are and they're crap!" shouts the power-crazed manager. Good motivational maneuver there. It also offers nothing in the way of solutions, remedies, or incentives.

We all know by now that motivation is all about people acting independently. Well-motivated people will do what they know needs to be done, whether or not someone is there to hound them about it. Your conversation with Harry is building a foundation that includes his participation from the ground up. You're not going to hand him his quotas, like the old days, order him to go out and attack the market, and remind him on his way out the door that there will be consequences for failure. As long as you're covering your constructive confrontation bases on the front end, you're in the game, and so is Harry.

"The most I've closed is twenty-three," he admits, knowing *you know*, or could find out pretty darn quickly.

"Two million is the minimum according to the XYZ Corp manifesto," you remind him. Rather than drag him back through his ignominious sales history, you move ahead. "This target of two-point-two million will get you into that envelope. Yep," you say, rechecking your figures. "It looks to me like two-point-two million, at seventy thousand per sale, breaks down to approximately thirty-two sales closed."

"Sounds like that to me," Harry agrees, glad that you're not hammering him for lagging behind the company minimum. "That breaks down into three hundred twenty presentations," he offers, doing his own math.

"You're going to be a busy boy," you empathize. "Assuming Brenda won't want you working on weekends, vacation, or holidays, that means you'll work about two hundred thirty-five days in the next twelve months. It also means you need to average one-point-four appointments per working day for new business or renewals. Does that sound doable to you, Harry?" (It's about time you snuck his name in there.)

Harry nods. "I don't have any trouble setting up appointments."

"Then let's also break that down in our covenant," you suggest.

"Say what?" Harry asks.

"The document that will chronicle our commitment," you explain. "I don't know what all the words mean either, but I get the concept."

"Which is . . .?" Harry presses on.

"We agree on *what* we want to do, *who* needs to be involved, a *time line* for knocking off the tasks and reaching your goal, *where* all of the activities need to take place, *why* we're doing this, and *how* we're going to pull it off. Plus, we make any other notes we need so that I'm on paper agreeing to support your efforts in any way necessary, and you agree on paper to get it done."

"Sounds cool," Harry offers.

"We'll also stay on top of your *habits, skills, attitude,* and *activities,*" you assure him. "It will all be there."

"What's that all about," he asks. "The *habits* and *skills* thing . . .?"

"If you're making your target number of appointments and presentations but having difficulty closing, we'll look at your selling *skill set* and see how we can tune up your script. If your closing rate improves but your ability to set appointments drops off, we'll examine your *habits* and see if you're engaging in the right *activities* day in and day out. If you make no appointments and, of course, close no sales, we're going to talk about what's troubling you. Something will probably be disturbing or deflating your *attitude.* But with this circle of confrontation going, you're involved in the process from day one, and there should be no surprises. You're already halfway to writing this thing up."

"I'm writing this thing up?" Harry asks in an astonished tone.

"Don't worry," you reassure him. "I'll give you these notes on what we're covering. I'll even give you a copy of a sample covenant. You should keep it simple, direct, and to the point. If you're rewriting *War and Peace,* you're going too far. Between your own thoughts and the things I know need to be included we'll have a covenant hammered out within the week, and you'll be on your way to making Brenda a happy woman. This covenant is your top priority until we get it done. Can you e-mail me a draft by Thursday? Seriously, I'm only talking two or three pages. Brief, but thorough. Numbered points, that sort of thing."

HARRY'S COVENANT

After additional clarification on some of the finer points, Harry departs for his new assignment, to prepare the covenant. He's not the writer Francine is, and you know he's unsure about this new approach. It's new to you, too. But you must resist the temptation to take on Harry's responsibility for writing at least the first draft of his covenant. If he doesn't do it, he won't receive the benefit of the exercise. Neither should you give in to the fact that neither Harry nor you especially care for writing and would be happy to just let the covenant part of this thing slide. Doing so will deprive Harry, you, and your boss a tremendous tool for promoting efficiency, performance, and productivity:

- Harry won't focus on the all-important issues he desperately needs to learn about.
- You won't focus on the all-important issues you and Harry both desperately need to learn about.
- Your boss won't have an organized and comprehensive way to confront you on how effectively you're coaching and confronting your people.
- None of you will have a well-documented history of what you set out to do, how you managed the progress of the job, task, assignment, project, or initiative, and how you measured results.

You're encouraged because you've already seen it all start working with Harry, even as he takes off to draft the covenant. For example, Harry has never been as concerned with "the finer points" before. His attention level has already gone up. After another covenant-composing session and several clarification phones calls and e-mails, Harry's game plan for the next 12 months is set:

To: Your Name
From: Harry Harris
Date: Day of Week/Month/Day/Year
Subject: Covenant: To Close $2.2M in Gross Sales Before (Specific Date)

Who:
1. Harry Harris, working under the guidance of (Your Name) will increase his gross sales to $2.2M for XYZ Corp on or before (Specific Date) following the detailed plan worked out with (Your Name) and referred to herein.
2. (Your Name), as a representative of XYZ Corp, will provide Harry with all necessary information, resources, and direction as mutually agreed between the two of them to reach the $2.2M goal.
3. Harry and (Your Name) will conduct themselves within the highest professional standards and will do everything in their power to keep their communications and regular confrontations constructive. If communications or other aspects of their professional relationship become problematic for either party, Harry and (Your Name) will submit to joint and individual counseling and coaching as stipulated by the Human Resources department with the intention of ensuring that Harry's best interests and the interests or the organization are both protected and preserved.

What:
1. Harry Harris will average 1.4 sales presentations per day (for a minimum of 320 presentations on or before (Specific Date). At no point will he fall more than one week behind in his appointment schedule (seven per week), after vacations, holidays, and personal days have been considered.
2. Harry Harris will average not less than $70,000 per sale for the twelve months and close no less than 10 percent of his sales pitches. Only gross sales at or above the $2.2M for the twelve month period

---

will justify adjustment of the minimum per sale average and/or closing ratio.

3. (Your Name) will provide or make available to Harry all necessary
training, coaching, and XYZ Corp resources necessary to maximize
Harry's potential as an XYZ Corp sales representative, including, but
not limited to, weekly constructive confrontation, more frequently if
necessary.

When: 1. Harry will have no less than six (6) new sales presentations scheduled
by 9:00 A.M. each Thursday and no less than seven (7) by the end of
the day Friday.

2. Harry will submit his written progress reports covering *who, what,
when, where, why,* and *how* via e-mail covering all of his sales activities by 4:00 P.M. each and every Wednesday.

3. Harry and (Your Name) will meet face-to-face each Thursday at 9:00
A.M. to confront the progress on Harry's covenant, evaluating the degree of compliance with documented tasks and milestones, and discussing the best ways to remedy any variations in the established plan.

4. Harry will contact (Your Name) and/or (Your Name) will contact
Harry *whenever* additional confrontation is necessary, based on new
or urgent information. Information can be shared between Harry and
(Your Name) at any time.

Where: 1. The scheduled Thursday meetings will be in Harry's workspace, unless
otherwise agreed to in advance.

2. Harry's sales presentations will be conducted within a 50-mile radius
of XYZ Corp headquarters, unless a more extensive trip is mutually
agreed upon by Harry and (Your Name).

3. Harry will make himself reasonably available at XYZ Corp headquarters to XYZ staff members and researchers seeking ways to improve
sales performance and margin.

Why: 1. XYZ Corp requires that all full-time sales professionals generate two
million dollars in gross sales revenues annually.

2. Harry desires to provide a lifestyle for his family that will require him to
generate no less than two-point-two million dollars annually in gross
sales revenue.

(continued)

3. Using constructive confrontation, (Your Name) is committed by covenant to the growth and development of Harry's career and the health and well-being of Harry's family by whatever means are within his [or her] authority within XYZ Corp.

How: 1. Harry will research and qualify as many leads each week as necessary to achieve the face-to-face presentation quotas stipulated above. Exceeding the appointment-setting goal in any given week does not adjust downward the preset goals for any subsequent week.

2. Harry will present (Your Name) with a written report each week, conforming to a mutually agreed upon format and delivery mechanism, detailing each performance element of the covenant. Harry will make himself available for whatever coaching and training is necessary to accentuate and accelerate the successful execution of his covenant and exceeding the specified goals whenever possible.

3. (Your Name) will make reasonably available all XYZ Corp tools and resources to assist Harry in setting up presentations, making presentations, and closing sales. This includes (Your Name) and Harry constructively confronting one another regularly to ensure that neither (Your Name) nor Harry will settle into the prescribed performance envelope and back off forward pressure toward generating new and renewal sales revenue.

Other Items: 1. This covenant is intended to be a guide to the execution of the project titled: "To Close $2.2M in Gross Sales Before (Specific Date)." Nothing in the covenant should be construed as to alter Harry Harris' conditions of employment with XYZ Corp. The covenant, however establishes this initiative as Harry's top professional priority.

2. This covenant is the core commitment and agreement between (Your Name) and Harry in their official XYZ Corp capacities; it is not expected to address each and every aspect of Harry's employment. This covenant is subject to the rules, regulations, and standard operating procedures for XYZ Corp, unless otherwise specified and duly authorized.

3. To the best of [his or her] ability, and to the full extent of [his or her] authority within XYZ Corp, (Your Name) will provide Harry with the best possible guidance, coaching, and access to XYZ Corp information.

---

4. This covenant is a dynamic document in a dynamic working environment and can be altered or modified as needed and agreed to by both parties in order to better achieve the stated outcomes.
5. It is expected that everyone involved will continuously use his or her best judgment and bring any issues affecting the successful execution of this initiative to the other party's attention for resolution as soon as the issue becomes known.

Signature: Harry Harris [Date, Time, and Location]
Signature: (Your Name) [Date, Time, and Location]

Who, what, where, when, and *how* are great overall guides to covering the territory necessary to create a commitment to be chronicled in a covenant. Your covenants might look like Harry's, or they might look completely different. It is most important to understand and apply the principles and practices *behind* the concept of constructive confrontation conversations, commitments, and covenants. Then you can craft your covenant in a manner that suits you best. The elements necessary to cover what you and your team members need to have covered are all that are required — no more, no less.

The covenant shouldn't get bogged down with superfluous and unnecessary language. Such things increase the possibility of confusion, internal contradiction, and diminish the document's effectiveness. The ultimate goal is to chronicle a plan that best aligns the emotional purpose of your team member, your best ability to guide his or her progress through constructive confrontation, *and* what the organization needs most.

Obligations and Opportunities for Everyone

As you can see in Harry's example, this covenant pins down expectations for both you and Harry in specific, realistic, and achievable ways. The covenant obligates you to ongoing and regular involvement with Harry's progress through scheduled constructive confrontation. You might still argue that you "don't need no stinking covenant" to manage Harry's progress, and you'll be involved with Harry as much as you see fit and don't need a written agreement to prompt you. This argument invites several potential disconnects.

First, you might not be as involved in the structured encouragement of your team members as you'd like to *think* you are. At least you might not be giving the perception of involvement to your team members or people above you on the organizational food chain; either one of which are final arbiters, each in their own way. The conversations that lead to a commitment, which forms a basis for the covenant, clear up any ambiguity or miscalculation about how much involvement is enough.

Covenants help prevent disconnects by demonstrating your commitment to the growth and development of your team members. If your team members harbor any doubt or misgivings about your commitment to them, the covenant, along with how faithfully you follow it, should erase those doubts. The covenant is likewise your road map to focusing your energies on the growth and development of your people, especially if you haven't polished those skills lately, if ever.

Perhaps most of all, a covenant binds the organization's commitment to you. Although you don't need to have those above you on the organizational food chain sign off on the specific covenants you negotiate with your team members, it's always highly advisable to keep them copied, alerted, and in the loop. Copy HR on the covenants to ensure a lot of eyes see them. Involving HR in approving each tiny detail in the covenant might lead to permanent paralysis. Make everyone copied on the covenant acknowledge that they received it (through an electronic acknowledgment), so you'll have a paperless paper trail.

This creates a tacit obligation on the part of the organization to back you up. If they feel any need to modify anything you're doing, it's their responsibility to let you know. If you keep your covenants, policies, and procedures secret from those with influence beyond the range and scope of your own, there's no guarantee they'll have your back if and when you need it. In the best of all possible worlds, you'll have a covenant negotiated with your boss.

Actively engaging in the circle of constructive confrontation focuses the needs of the organization, through you, to your team members and their efforts on behalf of the organization. The more skilled you become at the circle of constructive confrontation, the more that flow of energy begins to resemble a laser beam, capable of cutting through the thickest organizational blockages and inertia. The more skilled you become at constructive confrontation, the more impressive you'll be to those above you on the organizational food chain. Your effectiveness, if visible to the muckety-mucks you report to, is your ticket to success when the opportunities arise.

You need to convey that same message to your team members. Opportunities for promotion don't come by every day. But when they do, anyone's best chances are exponentially improved by a documented track record of proven performance. That means being visible and on the record for the *right things*. For you, that means encouraging the growth and development of your people as it translates into actual performance improvement that helps achieve clearly articulated departmental, divisional, and organizational goals.

For your team members, promotability is tied to the successful history of accountability you've helped them achieve. It also means a record of dependable achievement through documented performance improvement. That's why you shine a spotlight on the good things your team members do. It helps them, and it doesn't make you look bad either. After all, having a low-performing team isn't going to propel you toward fulfilling *your* emotional purpose.

CHAPTER 4 SUMMARY

Chapter 4 outlines how the covenant is used to translate principles into practice. It forces thinking to become focused and deliberate. Clearly defined goals and objectives are only as good as the plan to achieve them. Crafting and drafting constructive confrontation covenants removes ambiguity and establishes a working process. Some of the key points to remember as constructive confrontation increases accountability and reduces conflict between you and your team members include the following:

- It's the leader's responsibility to guide the identification and engineer the connection between the team member's emotional purpose and the resources, rewards, and realities of the job, with the understanding that a contract is being forged.
- This is much more than a goal-setting session. The covenant is the enforceable document for the circle of confrontation to follow. The team member and team leader must be clear on how the policies, practices, and procedures they are committing to will be documented and used on an ongoing basis.
- Once the merger of principles and practice is defined and agreed to, it needs to be written down in a covenant by the team member and revised by the team leader. In the end, it's a collaborative document. By having the team member draw up the document, he or she is sure to understand the context and meaning of each component. The core elements to be included are designated by the team leader, with additions made by the team member.
- The covenant covers *what* is to be accomplished, and *when*. It also defines *who* is involved, *where* things will take place, and *how* the activities will go down. The reasons for the initiative are covered in the *why* section. Goals are broken down into tasks, and tasks are plotted on a time line. Purposeful goals are broken down into the *habits*, *skills*, *attitudes*, and *activities* necessary to complete the cycle of success and bring it to the starting spot once more.
- The finished document is signed off on by the team member and the leader. The team leader's signature binds the organization to the covenant, just as a sales contract establishes price and other criteria, and binds the organization to perform for a customer. The team member's signature represents his or her agreement to the terms and conditions of the task, initiative, or job.
- The covenant is a living document that needs to be revisited every time confrontation is scheduled. The covenant grants the team

member written permission to confront the team leader as necessary to stay the designated course. More importantly, the document obligates the team leader to regularly confront the team member and needs to be close at hand for the team leader and the team employee.

The value of comprehensive conversations, meaningful commitments, and well-crafted covenants will become increasingly evident as the confrontations themselves are described in Part II. Staying positive, making course corrections, facing new challenges, and cementing the team leader/team member bond are all about to be addressed. None of these valuable leadership activities would be possible without prior conversations, commitments, and covenants.

PART II
Confrontation

CHAPTER 5

Confrontation

If you've been holding your breath in anticipation of the actual confrontation itself, relax. Blue is not your color. Besides, you've been confronting for a long time now. It hasn't killed you yet, has it? Every time you've addressed an issue head on, looked it square in the face, and dealt with matters in a realistic manner, you've confronted. The constructive confrontation difference is the use of confrontation in the systematic, purposeful pursuit of well-defined goals and objectives. Constructive confrontation replaces scattered, haphazard, negative, after-the-fact confrontations with the well-organized, premeditated use of confrontation as a preemptive, anticipatory intervention. Rifle versus shotgun. Laser beam versus incandescent bulb. Mascara brush versus hair styling brush.

Constructive confrontation is, in large part, about regularly tracing results back to what's producing them or keeping them from happening, so you're never far from the problem or the solution. The covenant is the document you operate from; that's why it's important to have your ducks in a row when you write the commitments down. The commitment conversation and covenant have made it clear that constructive confrontation is an obligation that the team leader and team member have to one another, not a burden to be endured. "How are things going?" is not a competent confrontational question. Confrontations must be item-specific: "Have the phone center calls been increased by five percent this week, the way we planned?"

TRUTH EQUALS EFFICIENCY

The *who, what, when, where, why,* and *how* components of constructive confrontation must be framed in truth and honesty. Truth and honesty can live together or apart, so it's important to consciously consider both. Truth is what is. We might make truth fuzzy with how we interpret it, and that will always happen, but facts are facts. What is truth to one is not falsehood to another. Although interpretations of facts can vary, the facts remain the same. The photocopier is broken: truth. Is it true that Fred broke the photocopier? Maybe, maybe not.

Is it important to know who was present when the photocopier went south? Does it really matter? Before hunting Fred down to string him up by his thumbs, ask yourself, "What's the best use of my time, determining who broke the photocopier or getting the thing fixed as soon as possible?" Fred might be a good candidate to head up that effort, but that's up to you and your personal sense of irony.

Honesty is knowing the truth and telling it. Withholding, deceiving, manipulating, downright lying, and any number of other unethical behaviors are committed by people who know the facts but spin an intentionally skewed interpretation, usually as an end to a means or a means to an end. People can also withhold truth because they're afraid of the consequences of telling it. Messengers are still routinely sacrificed in organizational life for no other reason than telling the truth (see whistle-blowers). The truth, in these unfortunate scenarios, exposes the mess for what it really is and implies that other approaches that could and should have been taken would have produced better results.

When the truth is in short supply, effort is wasted. When various individuals are maliciously or innocently withholding valuable or potentially valuable pieces of information, business is being conducted in at least partial, if not complete, darkness. There is no way to maximize efficiency, performance, and productivity when you're flying blind. The best you can hope for is luck. If that's how little the stockholders' investments are being valued, if that's how little your team members' efforts are being valued, and if that's how little value you place on your own career success, you might as well take the operating budget to Las Vegas and park yourself at the craps table. You'll probably have as much success turning a profit there as you will when you operate without internal or external honesty.

You can't build trust without honesty. There's no way you can build and sustain the type of effective internal and external working relationships you want for your organization in an atmosphere of suspicion and distrust. Trust can only be earned through the consistent demonstration of honesty over time. Saying to someone, "You'll have to trust me on this," is not going to make them sleep well at night. The more often you or your organization ask to be trusted, the more opportunities you and your organization have to prove you're trustworthy.

Building trust takes time. Trust can be lost in an instant. If your team members nod their heads but roll their eyes, you probably have a trust problem. They're not buying that the organization, or you as a representative of the organization, are trustworthy. Don't expect them to pour heart and soul into anything you ask them to do, no matter what formalities (like conversation, commitment, covenant, confrontation, and celebration) you put them through.

To say, "I don't know," when you *do* know is dishonest. It's better to say, "I'm not at liberty to share that information right now." If that's the truth, you're being honest. Being honest, even when not sharing all the information your team members ask for, will build trust. This doesn't mean you should spill all kinds of classified information where it doesn't belong. If there are things your team members want to know that you're obligated to keep secret, say so. Claiming that you're not at liberty to share certain information when you *are* is dishonest and will come back

121

to bite you. Worse yet, sharing privileged information with your favorite folks and not with others will undermine working relationships in the worst way. Few things will turn team members more cynical than favoritism, especially when parceling out information.

Ninety-nine percent is not enough when it comes to truth. One percent of falsehood will corrupt the rest. Being authentic and honest is the only way to create an environment in which your team members will truly give it up for you. Dealing off the bottom of the deck or being disingenuous, even just a teeny-tiny bit, will impeach everything else you're trying to do. People will distrust on a lot less evidence than it takes to earn trust. To earn trust faster, make small promises that you can consistently keep. Large promises, even if you keep *most of them*, will still erode trust. Keeping your focus "in the moment" as much as possible will also keep you from wandering off into blue-sky predictions or promises.

WHO TO CONFRONT

You will confront those with whom you have outstanding covenants. If you don't have a covenant with someone, you don't have the right to confront them. If, by invoking your institutional authority, you feel you have the right to confront anyone, anywhere, at any time, you could be causing yourself innumerable problems and making yourself extremely unpopular. Even if covenants are not written down, as in the case of spouses, children, coworkers, the kid behind the counter at Starbucks, or postal workers, there are certain commonly accepted social and familial expectations. A healthy (i.e., constructive) confrontation might be in order if those commonly accepted social and familial expectations are blatantly violated. However, any confrontation based on unwritten understandings will always be mitigated by the other party's interpretation of the agreement.

If you want constructive confrontation to build and sustain positive relationships of any kind or provide a clear and unambiguous road map for workplace productivity and accomplishment, it must contain a written covenant. As you've seen, part of that covenant describes and designates *who* is involved, ergo *who* is expected to confront *whom*. Consider marriage, for example. People usually enter the relationship large on promise, small on detail. The covenant, if there ever is one, is drafted at the time of the divorce. Most, if not all, of the confrontation during the course of the relationship is based on contradictory interpretations of the verbal agreement.

Marital disputes fuel a hostile and adversarial relationship more than they build a sense of warmth and intimacy. The same is true in professional relationships. If you take an honest inventory of the expectations and positive outcomes of best-laid plans within your organization, how would the percentages compare to the 50 to 60 percent of marriages that fail in the United States each year? If you're heavily invested in the performance and productivity of another person, constructive confrontation, with all of its critical components, is called for. Just relying on people to keep their word (as you understand it) and then getting upset when they don't is amateur city.

If you report to someone on the organizational food chain who cares enough to engage you through constructive confrontation, count yourself among the lucky ones. If your boss deals with goals, objectives, expectations, and such only at your annual performance review, you have nothing but wiggle room the rest of the year. For most, that might sound appealing: a carefree working environment with no hoops to jump through or reports to write. It also means you're back at that Las Vegas craps table when it comes to vertical mobility. If no one has made it clear what exactly is expected of you, how can you count on being recognized when you achieve it?

The same thing applies to the people who report directly to you. Engage each and every one of them in constructive confrontation. You're not being paid to lead some of them and not others. If you truly lead the way you like to be led, the type of recognition and encouragement that stokes your boilers will do the same for your team members. "Exactly who do I confront," you ask? Everyone whose performance and productivity you're responsible for, which means engaging the complete circle of constructive confrontation: conversation, commitment, covenant, confrontation, and celebration.

WHAT TO CONFRONT

Confront everything in the covenant. Make confrontation notes with the same headings as contained in the covenant. If it will help, print out the template with the name of the covenant and all the other elements: *who, what, when, where, why,* and *how.* Some people make confrontation notes on the covenant itself to verify that the confrontation took place when and where designated and, if not, why. Note the date and time of the confrontation. Are you meeting the schedule that you and your team member agreed to? Are you slipping and letting other things throw you off schedule? Are things going so smoothly that you feel like relaxing on the regular conversations that you originally planned on? Words to the wise: stick to the plan, *especially* when things are going well.

Confronting progress on the covenant doesn't need to be a time-consuming activity. But it should be thorough if you expect it to be effective. Pilots go through a check list before each and every take off. The check list is always the same. If they blow it off because most things they check never malfunction, how safe would you feel flying on that aircraft? If you discover there is too much detail on the covenant, you and your team member can agree to adjust it. Constructive confrontation is a dynamic process. But just because something is working as planned most of the time, you still want to know when it ceases to work as planned, and you want to know as soon as possible. It's not the strong and dependable links that typically fail in the process chain, but they can.

Constructive confrontation is a diagnostic tool to determine where and why breakdowns and disconnects occur. Are the initial commitment or covenant flawed? Have internal or external conditions changed significantly? The circle of confrontation ensures that the organization keeps learning, and the lessons are fresh.

The entire circle of confrontation is a documentation process that creates a case history and reference library for future performance expectations. As such, everything needs to be at least touched on at every confrontation session. Confrontation notes are made by both the team leader and the team member. Performance tracking applies to team members and team leaders alike. This documentation is a positive opportunity for everyone involved to have their efforts acknowledged. Both the team leader and the team member have a vested interest in shared success. If and when a link in the chain fails, everyone loses. Confront everything.

Confrontation is an opportunity to propel things forward and build enthusiasm. That won't happen if you only confront progress inconsistently, selectively, or haphazardly. Since the days of the Western Electric Hawthorne studies in the 1920s, management attention paid to work efforts has been known to improve performance, if for no other reason than the fact that they paid attention. The team leader's regular assessments of the team member's performance are opportunities for continuous recognition and reinforcement of positive behaviors.

WHEN TO CONFRONT

Depending on the scope and complexity of the job, task, assignment, project, or initiative, constructive confrontations should be held weekly, if not more often. If your team member is working on something that doesn't require a weekly confrontation, he or she is not doing very important work. You can request more comprehensive and formal presentations, perhaps to the department staff, on a monthly or quarterly basis. But the check-ins between the parties to the covenant need to take place regularly and should not allow too much time to pass between them.

Violate the schedule if circumstances dictate. If you observe or it comes to your attention that the covenant or the way your team member is carrying it out needs immediate attention, pay your team member a visit. Explain why you're confronting progress on the job, task, assignment, project, or initiative ahead of your regularly scheduled confrontation. If it's a false alarm, so be it. If a course correction is needed, better to make it sooner than later. Don't be jumpy, though. Every little bump in the road doesn't call for a redrafting of the covenant or a visit from you. Discretion is the better part of valor.

You need to demonstrate as much trust in your team member's abilities as possible. Jumping in and prematurely snatching responsibility out of his or her hands is not a trust builder. It demonstrates not only a lack of trust in your team member but also in your judgment. If you and your team member do your jobs thoughtfully and thoroughly on the front end, you won't need to doubt your judgment on the back end. Any good plan anticipates some amount of adversity and adjustment.

The key to timing is to keep it realistic. The frequency of the confrontation conversations in any given job, task, assignment, project, or initiative depends upon the execution time line you and your team member establish. If the two of you allow for too much wiggle room so as to not pressure yourselves too much, you're compromising performance and productivity. That's up to you and how dedicated you are to the health and well-being of the organization you're working for. If you're a believer in fair-but-firm expectations, you'll schedule the work and the confrontations to check progress in a reasonable, yet prudent, manner.

WHERE TO CONFRONT

Conduct your regularly scheduled constructive confrontations as close to where the actual work is being done as often as possible and practical. It's best to do your regularly scheduled confronting in a place that least disrupts your team member's activities. It's a common practice in large organizations to fly operatives into headquarters to hold court with their bosses. If you've set up your constructive confrontation properly, your team members are actively engaged in important work, producing results. If it makes more dollar-for-dollar sense to take them away from what they're doing than to inconvenience yourself, go ahead.

If your team member's activities are less important and vital to your organization's success than your time to confront them, you might want to reconsider what you have your people doing. In most organizations, executive time is not used in such an efficient way as to warrant postponing real rubber-meets-the-road activities. Your job is to lead and guide the activities of your team members. They're more likely to be up to their necks in it than you are. In other words, you're more mobile. Get off your backside and do more MBWA.

CONFRONT IN THE OPEN

As important as regular confrontations are, they need to be made with consideration for the needs and productivity of your team members. You and your team member need to make a decision about how important it is to disrupt real-time work. We live in a virtual world. Although face-to-face meetings are always the best for collecting data and observing complete communication (verbal, nonverbal, etc.), contact via telephone, e-mail, and carrier pigeon is still contact. Where constructive confrontation takes place should be decided so as to minimize slippage of responsibility. A phone call or e-mail now and then is not going to promote accountability as much as staring into someone's eyes. If you're a supervisor, manager, or executive who prefers not to deal with people directly, in-person, and stare into their eyes, leadership of people is not the best career choice for you.

Constructive confrontation doesn't necessarily call for convening secret summits. Regular confrontation, if it's constructive and objective, is not usually as personal as the commitment conversation about emotional purpose. In fact, the highlights of all circles of confrontation should be public knowledge in order to engage team support for everyone's efforts. That will be tough to do if everybody's agenda is top secret. By making announcements in staff meetings and posting progress reports in newsletters, intra- and internet web sites, and other media, you're helping your entire team swim in a vast pool of potentially helpful data.

Assessing and confronting mainstream issues related to the circle of confrontation can take place in the open, at staff meetings, over meals, even at the water cooler. Don't allow the assessment and confrontation conversations appear to be overly glib or inconsequential. This is important stuff, and you, the leader, need to keep written progress notes on the written covenant, complete with dates and times of conversations.

The more public you make the workplace agendas, the more you invite peer feedback that might expose things you and individual team members have overlooked. Announcements of a celebratory nature should be as public as possible, without getting gushy and gooey about it. Such an open atmosphere around *habits, skills, attitudes,* and *activities* helps people help each other. Openness can build synergy as the team effort eclipses isolated individual efforts.

PERSONALIZE IN PRIVATE

If the confrontation conversation takes on "come to Jesus" implications, it's better in private so as not to humiliate anyone. As tempting as humiliating people sounds to die-hard intimidation-style supervisors, managers, and executives, it's a no-no. Confrontation conversations about poor performance or productivity need to be focused like a laser beam on diagnosing and correcting the problem. Extra tension that public scrutiny adds will only hinder the process.

If, after all the geographical considerations mentioned, the regularly scheduled confrontation winds up in your office anyway, resist the temptation to jump behind your desk. When your team members are struggling and need your help, it's more important than ever to be physically and emotionally available to them. In the vulnerability of their failures the last thing they need is judgment or condemnation. They need serious medicine, for sure. It's your job to create the best possible opportunity for your team members to receive their medicine — along with the safest and most encouraging environment in which to take it.

HOW TO CONFRONT

As mentioned, confrontations are made in person, via telephone, via e-mail, or in any way the team leader and team member agree to in the covenant.

The means of the confrontation needs to be appropriate for the questions and conversation required. Just as broad, closed-ended questions fail to produce quality information, vague contact diminishes the effect. Confrontation is not a casual encounter.

Confrontation conversations are not a time to gloss things over. Instead of hammering on the negative in your private session, accentuate the mutual commitment you've made to help your team member succeed. The most important message after "the objectives are not being met," is "we started this together, and we'll straighten it out together." The more potentially troubling the news about the covenant, the more specific you need to be.

Remember inviting Fred to confront the Bigsby account? When he shows up in your office or you show up in his, get down to business in a timely yet prudent manner. This shows respect for Fred's time, your time, and respect for the constructive confrontation process. After you've made small talk with Fred, don't say, "How's the Bigsby account coming?" and leave it at that. That's not constructive confrontation. It's not even credible confrontation. If you have set a marker in your covenant that the Bigsby account should be at $100,000 by May 15, and it's May 15, the specific and appropriate question is, "It's May 15; is the Bigsby account at $100,000?" Ambiguous questions leave lots of wiggle room. Wiggling never got a sale closed, a customer's problem solved, or a project completed.

FRANCINE'S SCRIPT

A week has gone by since you finalized your covenant with Francine. She's been working independently since then. Every indication in her mood and attitude is positive. When it comes time for her progress report to show up in your e-mail in-box, there it is. As you stroll toward Francine's office at the appointed hour on Thursday, take a moment to review her covenant. You've also armed yourself with a legal pad to take notes on *who*, *what*, *when*, *where*, *why*, and *how*. Your pending confrontation conversation with Francine has been loosely scripted.

To: Your Name

From: Francine France (her parents are still French)

Date: [Revised: Day of Week Weekday/Month/Day/Year/Time]
Changes by (Your Name) Underlined

Subject: Covenant: Conduct Research to Increase XYZ Corp Sales Revenues by 15 Percent

Who: 1. Francine France will conduct research into the fastest and most effective ways that sales revenues at XYZ Corp can be increased by 15 percent.

2. Francine will report directly to (Your Name) as a representative of XYZ Corp for supervision and necessary guidance.

3. Francine will consult with members of the XYZ Corp sales division as needed to gather data to complete her research.

4. Francine will consult with ten XYZ Corp customers, as specified by XYZ Corp sales management, ~~as needed~~ to enrich the data she is collecting to complete her research, unless otherwise decided by (Your Name) and (Her Name).

5. Francine will copy the following people on her progress reports and preliminary suggestions: [(Your Name), (selected members of the sales division), and the CEO].

What: 1. The XYZ Corp is seeking recommendations on how to increase sales revenues by 15 percent.

2. The desired increase must be measured in *revenues*, whether related to volume of sales or any other factor.

3. Research must be conducted outside of the sales division in order to present a list of ~~objective~~ recommendations on how to most effectively increase XYZ Corp sales revenues by 15 percent.

4. The initial research will be conducted by the Training and Development department to provide an objective analysis of the criteria determining sales margin. ~~as per the CEO's directive~~.

5. When completed and submitted, the list of recommendations will be reviewed and acted upon by the sales division, as per the CEO's directive, subject to their own research.

When: 1. Francine will begin her research immediately upon signing this covenant.

2. Francine will submit a progress report of her findings to (Your Name) every Thursday, <u>with the meeting time to be set no later than 24 hours in advance</u>.

3. Pending (Your Name)'s approval, Francine will distribute copies of her progress report to the agreed upon distribution list (<u>item five in the</u> *who* section).

4. At the end of six (6) weeks following the signature date of this covenant, Francine will deliver her final list of recommendations to (Your Name).

5. Pending (Your Name)'s approval and any additions/corrections, Francine will distribute her final recommendations to the agreed upon distribution list. No more than two (2) business days will expire between item 4 and item 5 in this section.

Where:

1. Francine will conduct the research, for the most part, on the XYZ Corp headquarters campus by reviewing historical sales data.

2. Francine will expand her research data through discussions with XYZ Corp sales team members, via telephone, e-mail, or in person at the XYZ Corp headquarters campus.

3. ~~If it is determined that regional focus groups will help validate the collected data,~~ Francine will set up and facilitate three off-campus focus group sessions~~, subject to (Your Name)'s approval~~.

4. ~~If it is determined that interviewing customers on their sites will help broaden and validate the collected data, those visits will be set up and carried out, subject to (Your Name)'s approval.~~ <u>Francine will interview XYZ Corp's ten largest customers via telephone or at the customer's property if the customer is local</u>.

5. Meetings to discuss the progress reports and final recommendations will be held on the XYZ Corp headquarters campus <u>in Francine's office, unless otherwise arranged in advance.</u>

Why:

1. XYZ Corp stockholders' equity has been steadily decreasing for seven quarters.

2. A review of expenses has been conducted and the recommendations to reduce have been in effect for two quarters.

3. Despite expense reduction efforts, profits continue to lag behind projections.

(continued)

4. Alternative opportunities are being sought to strengthen XYZ Corp's bottom line, including, but not limited to, increasing revenues from sales.

5. Because increasing revenues by 15 percent is a more critical issue than arbitrarily increasing sales by 15 percent, research needs to be conducted and recommendations delivered that expose below-the-surface opportunities to increase margin if possible.

How:

1. Francine will develop a short survey to serve as a standard questionnaire for gathering comparable information from all sources, <u>and have it approved by (Your Name) before using it for research, individual interviews, and focus groups</u>.

2. Francine will conduct telephone, e-mail, or face-to-face surveys to collect data, both internal and external to the organization.

3. Francine will examine historical sales data to make comparisons of various sales in an attempt to isolate key elements of the more lucrative sales in terms of margin.

4. Francine will compile this information into progress report form and distribute it to the agreed upon distribution list (<u>in the</u> *who* section above), subject to (Your Name)'s approval.

5. Francine will ultimately compile her collected data into final recommendations and distribute them to the agreed upon distribution list, subject to (Your Name)'s approval.

Other Items:

1. <u>This covenant is a dynamic document, detailing a dynamic process. Changes can be made as needed and justified, contingent on the mutual agreement of both signature parties.</u>

2. <u>This covenant is intended to be a guide to the execution of the project titled: Research to "Increase Sales Revenue by 15 Percent." Nothing in the covenant should be construed as to alter Francine France's conditions of employment with XYZ Corp. The covenant, however, establishes this initiative as Francine's top professional priority until completed.</u>

3. <u>It is always expected that everyone involved will continuously use his or her best judgment to bring any issues affecting the successful execution of this initiative to the other party's attention for resolution as soon as the issue becomes known.</u>

4. <u>To the best of [his or her] ability, and to the full extent of [his or her]</u>

authority within XYZ Corp, (Your Name) will provide Francine France with the best possible guidance, coaching, and access to XYZ Corp information.

5. To the best of [his or her] ability, and to the full extent of [his or her] authority within XYZ Corp, (Your Name) agrees to the most appropriate and adequate resources to ensure success of this initiative.

Signature: Francine France [Date, Time, and Location]
Signature: (Your Name) [Date, Time, and Location]

"Thanks for getting your initial report in to me on time, Francine," you say as you cross the threshold of her office for your first weekly confrontation. "I heard from two people on your distribution already who weren't aware we are doing this research. They're all for it."

"I wish I could say the same for everybody in sales," Francine sighs.

"Problems?" you ask.

"*Potential* problems," she qualifies. "As you predicted, not everybody is happy with outside involvement."

"Anybody refusing to cooperate?" you inquire.

Francine shakes her head, "No."

"Should I get hold of the sales VP and have another chat?" you offer.

"Let's hold off on that," Francine concedes. "Give me another week to see if I can get them to warm up."

"It's your call," you assure her. "Just let me know if I can assist."

"I will," she says.

"I noticed that you've contacted all ten of the customers sales gave you as interview candidates."

"Yes," she reports. "I've already heard back from five of them and everything looks good for the focus group."

"Excellent."

"So-o-o," she continues, "I shouldn't give the impression that *nobody* in sales is cooperating."

"Duly noted," you nod. "I see that you also have about fifteen people set up for the focus groups."

"Right. But I'm thinking that to get at least five in a group, we'll need to conduct one group per week for three weeks."

"How does that affect getting your recommendations finished on time?" you ask.

"If I hold the first focus group next week," she explains, "I think everything will still be on time."

"Good," you say, sounding relieved that things are going smoothly. You look down at your legal pad and make a check beside *when*. "Is there anybody else, other than who we already have noted, to report on or to involve?"

"Nobody beyond who's on the covenant," she says.

"Okay," you say, making a check mark beside the *who* on your checklist. "Any other pieces of the process to report on?"

"Nothing that's not in my report," she replies.

You glance down at her report. "Your survey looks great, by the way."

"Thanks."

"Everybody seems to be clear about *what* we're doing, *why* we're doing this research, and *who* asked for it?" you ask, reading from the covenant.

"Check."

"Everybody's clear that the desired outcome of the recommendations is a fifteen percent increase in sales *revenues?*"

"Check."

"Any need to alter *where? Places? Locations?*"

"Nope."

"Where do you think we'll be by this time next week?"

"Same as the report states," she confirms. "I plan on having half of the interviews completed, one focus group completed, and a raw data pack for you to review."

"Great," you say, noting her comment on the report she sent. "You're moving this along nicely."

"It's a pretty good plan," she says.

"I think we've covered the *who, what, when, where, why,* and *how* of it," you conclude. "Any questions for me right now?"

"Nope."

"If there's anything you want me to deal with before next Thursday," you offer again, "let me know."

"Will do," she says.

"Have a good weekend if I don't talk to you before," you say as you turn to leave.

"Thanks, (Your Name)," Francine offers, cordially. "You, too."

In that short amount of time, you've confronted all of the predictable issues around the "Increase sales revenues by 15 percent" initiative. All of the issues covered in your covenant with Francine, that is. But there's nothing so far to indicate that you've allowed anything to slip through the cracks.

You just seized the multiple opportunities to congratulate and compliment Francine on the work she's doing and the way she's going about it. Words can scarcely capture how important this form of recognition is. Francine is obviously self-motivated, and you're cheering her along. She is not likely to feel you're blowing smoke or complimenting her gratuitously because everything you're referring to is actual performance, something she's actually doing or has already done. Never miss the opportunity to deliver a sincere compliment. Constructive confrontations, like the one you just had with Francine, are replete with such opportunities.

HABITS, SKILLS, ATTITUDES, AND ACTIVITIES

What actually takes place as a result of constructive confrontation that makes a genuine impact on personal and organizational performance? All of the constructive confrontation components work together to heighten awareness for everyone as to what needs to be done and the best ways to go about doing it. To operationalize that awareness, the performance issues addressed by constructive confrontation can be separated into four categories: *habits*, *skills*, *attitudes*, and *activities*.

It's important to have a solid, practical answer when problems need to be addressed. Times of crisis or urgency are not times for theorizing. *Habits*, *skills*, *attitudes*, and *activities* are the handles that allow both team leaders and team members to get a grip on solutions. These four categories encompass the human behaviors required to get things done. Habits represent the discipline to act. Skills refer to trained and refined natural abilities to act effectively. Attitude refers to the desire to do the job well. Activities are the actual tasks that comprise the overall effort. Constructive confrontation conversations use *habits, skills, attitudes,* and *activities* to frame solutions that arise through confrontation. Take a moment to refresh yourself with Harry's covenant.

To: Your Name
From: Harry Harris
Date: Day of Week/Month/Day/Year
Subject: Covenant: To Close $2.2M in Gross Sales Before (Specific Date)

Who: 1. Harry Harris, working under the guidance of (Your Name) will increase his gross sales to $2.2M for XYZ Corp on or before (Specific Date) following the detailed plan worked out with (Your Name) and referred to herein.

2. (Your Name), as a representative of XYZ Corp, will provide Harry with all necessary information, resources, and direction as mutually agreed between the two of them to reach the $2.2M goal.

3. Harry and (Your Name) will conduct themselves within the highest professional standards and will do everything in their power to keep their communications and regular confrontations constructive. If communications or other aspects of their professional relationship become problematic for either party, Harry and (Your Name) will submit to joint and individual counseling and coaching as stipulated by the Human Resources department with the intention of ensuring that Harry's best interests and the interests or the organization are both protected and preserved.

What: 1. Harry Harris will average 1.4 sales presentations per day (for a minimum of 320 presentations on or before (Specific Date). At no point will he fall more than one week behind in his appointment schedule (seven per week), after vacations, holidays, and personal days have been considered.

2. Harry Harris will average not less than $70,000 per sale for the twelve months and close no less than 10 percent of his sales pitches.

Only gross sales at or above the $2.2M for the twelve month period will justify adjustment of the minimum per sale average and/or closing ratio.

3. (Your Name) will provide or make available to Harry with all necessary training, coaching, and XYZ Corp resources necessary to maximize Harry's potential as an XYZ Corp sales representative, including, but not limited to, weekly constructive confrontation, more frequently if necessary.

When:
1. Harry will have no less than six (6) new sales presentations scheduled by 9:00 A.M. each Thursday and no less than seven (7) by the end of the day Friday.
2. Harry will submit his written progress reports covering *who, what, when, where, why,* and *how* via e-mail covering all of his sales activities by 4:00 P.M. each and every Wednesday.
3. Harry and (Your Name) will meet face-to-face each Thursday at 9:00 A.M. to confront the progress on Harry's covenant, evaluating the degree of compliance with documented tasks and milestones, and discussing the best ways to remedy any variations in the established plan.
4. Harry will contact (Your Name) and/or (Your Name) will contact Harry whenever a confrontation is necessary, based on new or urgent information. Information can be shared between Harry and (Your Name) at any time.

Where:
1. The scheduled Thursday meetings will be in Harry's workspace, unless otherwise agreed to in advance.
2. Harry's sales presentations will be conducted within a 50-mile radius of XYZ Corp headquarters, unless a more extensive trip is mutually agreed upon by Harry and (Your Name).
3. Harry will make himself reasonably available at XYZ Corp headquarters to XYZ staff members and researchers seeking ways to improve sales performance and margin.

Why:
1. XYZ Corp requires that all full-time sales professionals generate two million dollars in gross sales revenues annually.
2. Harry desires to provide a lifestyle for his family that will require him to generate no less than two-point-two million dollars annually in gross sales revenue. *(continued)*

3. Using constructive confrontation, (Your Name) is committed by covenant to the growth and development of Harry's career and the health and well-being of Harry's family by whatever means are within his [or her] authority within XYZ Corp.

How:

1. Harry will research and qualify as many leads each week as necessary to achieve the face-to-face presentation quotas stipulated above. Exceeding the appointment-setting goal in any given week does not adjust downward the preset goals for any subsequent week.

2. Harry will present (Your Name) with a written report each week, conforming to a mutually agreed upon format and delivery mechanism, detailing each performance element of the covenant. Harry will make himself available for whatever coaching and training is necessary to accentuate and accelerate the successful execution of his covenant and exceeding the specified goals whenever possible.

3. (Your Name) will make reasonably available all XYZ Corp tools and resources to assist Harry in setting up presentations, making presentations, and closing sales. This includes (Your Name) and Harry constructively confronting one another regularly to ensure that neither (Your Name) nor Harry will settle into the prescribed performance envelope and back off forward pressure toward generating new ad renewal sales revenue.

Other Items:

1. This covenant is intended to be a guide to the execution of the project titled: "To Close $2.2M in Gross Sales Before (Specific Date)." Nothing in the covenant should be construed as to alter Harry Harris' conditions of employment with XYZ Corp. The covenant, however, establishes this initiative as Harry's top professional priority.

2. This covenant is the core commitment and agreement between (Your Name) and Harry in their official XYZ Corp capacities; it is not expected to address each and every aspect of Harry's employment. This covenant is subject to the rules, regulations, and standard operating procedures for XYZ Corp, unless otherwise specified and duly authorized.

3. To the best of [his or her] ability, and to the full extent of [his or her] authority within XYZ Corp, (Your Name) will provide Harry with the best possible guidance, coaching, and access to XYZ Corp information.

4. This covenant is a dynamic document in a dynamic working environ-

---

ment and can be altered or modified as needed and agreed to by both parties in order to better achieve the stated outcomes.

5. It is expected that everyone involved will continuously use his or her best judgment and to bring any issues affecting the successful execution of this initiative to the other party's attention for resolution as soon as the issue becomes known.

Signature: Harry Harris [Date, Time, and Location]
Signature: (Your Name) [Date, Time, and Location]

You arrive at Harry's desk promptly at 9:00 A.M. on Thursday, as scheduled, with your legal pad, a copy of the covenant, and the progress report Harry e-mailed to you at 3:40 P.M. Wednesday afternoon. In your other hand is a coffee mug. There's some slippage already in Harry's performance, which means Harry will be defensive when you arrive. That's a secret of constructive confrontation. You're anticipating what attitudes *might* exist based on experience. When someone knows they've fallen short of the boss's expectations, even when they agreed to the expectations, their energy tends to be focused on defensive behavior rather than on problem solving. You don't know this is the case with Harry before you arrive, but you're aware of the possibility. Therefore, you're cautious not to throw gasoline on a potential fire by challenging Harry right off the bat. Your opening remarks are scripted.

"Morning, Harry."

"Hi, (Your Name)," Harry returns the greeting. "Did you get my progress report?"

He's more preemptive than you expected. You would have predicted a "Dog ate my report" sort of thing. But you recover quickly thanks to your anticipation and loose scripting. "Have it right here," you acknowledge. "But, I wanted to ask if you and Brenda had a chance to discuss the two-point-two million target we decided upon for you." Back on script.

"Yeah, we talked about it."

"What did she think?"

139

"She's all for it," Harry relays. "She thinks we can live nicely on one-hundred-fifty thousand after taxes."

"It must feel good to have her solidly behind you."

"She's all about 'Show me the money'," Harry jokes.

You decide to forget he ever said that in case Brenda ever asks. "She's probably also about the safe and secure family," you add.

"True," Harry agrees, slightly disappointed that you didn't romp down that "let's exchange clichés about women" road with him. As a matter of protocol, decorum, and the fact that you'd never say anything about Brenda outside of her presence that you wouldn't say *in* her presence, you put the "C" in *constructive* confrontation.

Notice that you've immediately and intentionally introduced Harry's emotional purpose into the conversation to vector him away from excuses and defensiveness and set the context of the confrontation. In practically the same breath, you've tied his financial goals to his emotional purpose. You referenced his wife, Brenda, by name because you've already established that intimacy during commitment conversations and the process of crafting the covenant.

"Shall we take it from the top?" you offer, sitting in a chair across the desk from Harry.

"I set up another presentation since I sent you that progress report," Harry blurts.

"Great," you assure him. "Do you think you'll have three more by the end of the day tomorrow?"

Harry's covenant calls for him to have six presentations set up by 9:00 A.M. Thursday. As of his progress report at 4:00 P.M. Wednesday, he only had three. He's now reporting four, so you affirm his progress and ask if he can make up the deficit to be back on plan by end of the day Friday. As you expected, he begins tap dancing around the deficiency.

"Brenda had to take our oldest boy to the dentist on her way to work on Tuesday," Harry explains. "So I had to drop the others off at school, which is out of the way to get in here."

"I understand," you empathize. "I have kids, too. Getting organized and out the door in the morning can be a zoo."

140

"You can say that again," Harry agrees.

"Can you get your other three appointments set before the end of the day tomorrow," you ask, bringing him back on task.

"Yes," he says. "I'll just get more organized."

"Organization helps," you agree. "Let me ask you, Harry, do you and Brenda extend your business planning into your home?"

"I'm not sure I follow," Harry says with a confused look on his face.

You've decided to have a coaching moment with Harry because he's introduced the "family zoo gets in the way of work" excuse. He's probably right about the conflict between family responsibilities and work. But you recognize this as a habits and activities issue. The sooner you start teaching on those points, the better it will be for Harry, you, and XYZ Corp.

"Hearing you describe the kind of morning you had on Tuesday," you begin, "reminds me of the *habits, skills, attitudes,* and *activities* we talked about."

"How so?" Harry is still in the dark.

You're patient, as all good teachers are, praying that Harry's memory isn't *that* short. "The trip to the dentist and dropping kids off at a school that's not on the way to the office are habits and activities issues," you explain. "You just said that it will take better organization here at work to get more productivity."

"Yeah . . ." Harry agrees, sort of.

"Remember how we talked about your emotional purpose for work, tied that into a target income, and broke it down into weekly activities?"

"Sure."

"It's important to build habits based on that breakdown," you go on. "Do you and Brenda talk about the activities for the week ahead?"

"When we hit the pillow Sunday night," Harry chuckles, "we complain about how wasted we are and how much we have to do starting Monday. One of us usually says, 'We need a vacation.'"

"So Monday morning hits you like a linebacker running loose in the backfield."

"You've got that right," Harry agrees.

You draw in a deep breath, pleased with the precision of your diagnosis, right down to the linebacker analogy. "Have you tried setting aside a half hour *before* you go to bed Sunday night and planning the week?"

"With everything we have to do," Harry complains, "that would take two hours. We just catch as catch can."

"So there's no habit in place to plan how home activities affect work activities?"

Harry gives you a suspicious look. "If this is about my coming in late now and then," he confesses, "I'll stay a few minutes longer at the end of the day."

"Nobody's counting the minutes you're at work, Harry," you assure him. "That's not what's most important here. I know people with families live on a roller coaster. Do you remember how we broke down the work activities required for you and Brenda to get the income you want?" you ask, pointing to the covenant in your lap. "Do you still think these figures in our covenant are still accurate and realistic?" (They're only a week old, for heaven's sake, but you're making a point.)

Harry shrugs his shoulders. "Sure."

"Do you think you could attach the organizing you do at the office to accommodate these activities to the organizing you do at home, so everything will run more smoothly at both ends?"

"Now, (Your Name), my private life is my private life . . ." Harry begins, defensively.

"Absolutely," you agree. "*And* when you bring it up as a factor in work performance, my instincts tell me that one might be getting in the way of the other." [Note the use of "and" instead of "but" so as not to cue a defensive response.] The only legitimate concern I have for how things are going at home is how they affect you here. We already know how your *success* here affects your lifestyle at home."

"What do you suggest," Harry challenges.

"Like I said," you begin, shifting forward in your chair and laying your hand on the covenant in your lap for emphasis. "Do you have your copy of our covenant there?"

Harry pulls his copy of the covenant in front of him.

"You know how many appointments you agreed to set up by Wednesday afternoon at 4:00 P.M. and by the end of the day Friday," you continue.

"Right," Harry says, examining the document.

You can tell that you're on thin ice here. Harry is feeling defensive, which is how he's been taught his whole life to feel when underperforming in the presence of "the boss." He even feels victimized by his own kids. Now he's transferring the feelings of victimization to *you.* You know you're about an inch away from becoming the oppressor. A lesser person than you would cave into the urge to start beating Harry over the head with his own covenant *or* changing the subject to avoid an unpleasant confrontation. But you use the document wisely, choosing to remain the teacher and coach.

"You also know about the dentist appointments, what time school begins, soccer practice, and that sort of thing."

Harry looks up at you. There is a faint light flickering behind his eyeballs. You coax it out.

"It's all part of the same master plan," you say. "Setting up sales appointments, getting the kids to school, earning one-fifty after taxes so Brenda and the kids can spend it . . ."

Harry nods, the light getting brighter in his eyes.

"I don't care as much about when or how you go about getting all the activities worked in," you assure him. "As long as they all get worked in."

"I suppose it wouldn't hurt to have a weekly family planning meeting on Sunday evening," Harry agrees. You can tell he's wondering if he can pull such a thing off at home. "At least we can alert each other to the big stuff."

"Some people do it during a special meal," you offer. "Pizza, whatever. They even have a calendar on the side of the fridge."

"It wouldn't hurt for the kids to get more organized," Harry confesses.

"Good habits are good habits," you encourage. "Especially, if they bring in one-fifty per year after taxes."

Harry raises his eyebrows in agreement on that one. You have now confronted the fact that Harry is behind on his activities (setting up sales appointments) and framed the problem in the context of *habits* and *activities*. You won't know if you've made the point strongly enough until end of the day Friday. Moreover, his performance over the next week and the week after that will tell you if he's making any behavioral changes at home to support his efforts at work. The bottom line is that he told you where his disconnect was (family issues), and you seized the opportunity to teach. That's the type of opportunity constructive confrontation creates. In the same way you had the opportunity to compliment and encourage Francine, you could have just as well had the opportunity to teach.

"Let me know Friday afternoon if you managed to line up your three additional appointments for the week," you say, offering Harry a chance to redeem himself and a deadline to do it. "I know it will be a scramble, but I'm sure you can do it if I get out of your hair."

By letting Harry know that you're on top of his performance and still expect compliance by the end of the day Friday, as designated in the covenant, you've placed a performance demand on him. You intentionally used the number "three" because "seven" is more intimidating. Harry is only *three* short. His magic number is *three*. So avoid going big picture and saying, "Seven, Harry. You promised seven."

He hasn't reported any closings on his progress report, and you've already noted that his first appointment isn't until next week anyway. So you take the high road on that one, too. "Good luck on the appointments you have lined up for next week. If I can help with anything, let me know."

"Thanks," Harry replies.

"I'm serious," you say, looking him dead in the eye. "If there's anything about your emotional purpose, the *activities* outlined in our covenant, the time schedules, whatever, let's talk about it. I want you to hit these targets. You're certainly capable. The last thing I want is for lack of communication or misunderstanding between the two of us to block you from getting what you want or the organization to get what it needs from you."

"I know," Harry nods.

You can tell that he's close to "tilt," so you slide forward in your chair, prepared to stand. You refer to the covenant in your hand.

"There are no changes in *who* is involved, except that the kids need to be *more* involved in planning the week," you say lightheartedly.

Harry half nods, half wags his head in agreement.

"We're still looking at 1.4 sales presentations per day average and seven new appointments per week," you go on. "So, you'll have a hot week or two in your future." That's the *what*.

Harry nods again, knowing that these things come in cycles. When it rains it pours, yadda, yadda, yadda.

"Our reporting schedule stays the same, except that you'll let me know about those last three appointment schedules for this week late Friday afternoon, or whenever you set them up." That's the immediate *when*.

"Right," Harry acknowledges.

"If there's anything you need," you go on, "or anything I need to tell you, we'll get in touch with each other right away."

"Right," Harry acknowledges, again.

"Nothing's changed about *why* we're doing this," you note. "Methodology remains the same . . . *who*, *what*, *when*, *where*, *why*, and *how* are still good to go it looks like."

You glance at Harry to read his body language and to see if he's agreeing with you. He's nodding, so you stand and head for the door. "I promised I'd get out of your hair," you repeat, "so I'm out of here, as promised. Let me know if you need anything."

"I will," Harry agrees in parting.

You return to your office and put a copy of Harry's progress report *with your notes from the confrontation on it*, along with the covenant, into Harry's project file. You also make a quick note on your calendar for Friday afternoon at 5:00 P.M., "Heard from Harry on last three appointments scheduled?" From the time you left your office with a fresh cup of coffee on your way to Harry's office, you spent all of 15 minutes confronting Harry. Yet you learned a great deal and you seized the opportunities to address a deficiency in *habits* and *activities*.

Everybody seems to lag a little out of the starting blocks on new covenants, so you didn't freak out to find he wasn't exactly on plan. That doesn't mean you don't rejoice when someone hits the ground running, like Francine, and congratulate them accordingly. Never, never, never skimp on encouragement.

In keeping your expectations realistic about Harry's progress, you positioned yourself to keep things in perspective and in context. He might have attitude issues to deal with later on. You'll know more about his skill level as he reports on his closing ratio. No need to set him up for disappointment early on. Give him all the air and space he needs by keeping things constructive. Keeping things constructive sometimes means *not confronting* issues not relevant to the immediate situation. There will be plenty of time to confront skills and attitude issues as they come up. By jumping the gun you can contribute to an attitude problem.

Constructive confrontation, as you just experienced with Harry, is like tickling the dragon's tail. You need to get his attention. But you don't want to agitate him to the point where he bites your head off. Advocates of old-school confrontation would have you believe that you should rile him up and then invoke your institutional authority to bite *his* head off. Wrong. You want the conversation between Brenda and Harry to be about how they can organize their home activities to best support his work activities. You don't want Brenda and Harry to spend their time talking about what an unreasonable boss you are.

CHAPTER 5 SUMMARY

Chapter 5 is a blueprint for regularly tracing results back to what's producing them or keeping them from happening. Those things that need addressing as a result of the constructive confrontation should be classified as *habits, skills, attitudes,* or *activities.* The constructive confrontation conversation is an excellent opportunity to teach and coach. Other important constructive confrontation concepts include the following:

- The commitment conversation and covenant have made it clear that constructive confrontation is an obligation the team leader and team member have to one another, not a burden to be endured. "How are things going?" is not a competent confrontational question. Confrontations must be item-specific. "Have the phone center calls been increased by five percent this week, the way we planned?"
- Confrontations are made in person, via telephone, via e-mail, or in any way the team leader and team member agree in the covenant. The means of the confrontation needs to be appropriate for the questions and conversation required. Just as broad, closed-ended questions fail to produce quality information, vague contact diminishes the effect. Confrontation is not a casual encounter at the water cooler. When you met Harry in his office, there was a lot of nonverbal body language you would not have wanted to miss.
- Confrontation notes are recorded directly on the progress report itself to verify that the confrontation took place when and where designated and, if not, why. Answers to specific confrontation questions should be written down as well. *The entire circle of confrontation is a documentation process* that creates a case history and reference library for future performance expectations.
- Confrontation notes are made by both the team leader and the team member, even if the only documentation on the team member's part is his or her progress reports. Encourage extra note taking so the details of your confrontations don't evaporate after the session is over. *Performance tracking applies to team members and team leaders alike.* This documentation is a positive opportunity for everyone involved to have their efforts acknowledged. Both the team leader and the team member have a vested interest in shared success.
- *Confrontation is an opportunity to propel things forward and build enthusiasm.* Since the days of the Western Electric Hawthorne study in the 1920s, management attention paid to work efforts has been known to improve performance. The team leader's daily, weekly, monthly, and quarterly assessments of the team member's performance are

opportunities for continuous acknowledgment and growth for both *leader* and team member.

- Constructive confrontation is a diagnostic tool to determine where and why breakdowns and disconnects occur. Is the initial commitment or covenant flawed? Have internal or external conditions changed significantly? *The circle of confrontation ensures that the organizations keep learning, and the lessons are fresh.*

You can now stop holding your breath in anticipation of confrontations. They're fantastic opportunities to get a great deal done in a relatively brief time. They're structured, well-planned, yet flexible in the way they're loosely scripted. All of this should be assuring to you and build your confidence. You're not learning how to confront anymore as much as you're now learning how to make confrontations work *for* you instead of against you.

You're still alive and feeling better and better about your effectiveness as a leader. Every time you address an issue head on, look it square in the face, and deal with matters in a realistic manner, your confrontation skills improve and increase. The systematic, purposeful pursuit of well-defined goals and objectives that you now know as constructive confrontation replaces the scattered, haphazard, negative, after-the-fact confrontations of the past.

CHAPTER 6

Staying Positive

Negative energy will multiply in your workplace like rabbits from hell if you don't consciously and consistently exert positive influences. Research indicates that it takes 50 positive affirmations to balance out one negative comment. Unfortunately, there seems to be a natural human default setting that runs to negativity and cynicism. Many department heads, supervisors, managers, team leaders, and executives think that staying holed up in their offices and allowing the inmates to run the institution will produce the least conflict. Apparently these leaders are oblivious to all the demonic bunnies hopping around everywhere, from under desks, out of filing cabinets and photocopiers, to riding in the mail room guy's delivery basket.

On the other side of the coin are the micromanagers who think that sharing their employees' clothing is the way to engender positive relationships. "If everybody thinks and behaves the way I do," these leaders think, "we'll all get along great." Because leaders who think this way usually only have one fan in the office, that being him- or herself, it makes perfect sense — to them. That would explain the rabbit with the glowing red eyes riding on his or her shoulder.

Constructive confrontation is not micromanaging. Micromanaging is butting into work processes and a team member's schedule uninvited. Every micromanaging intervention carries with it the implication that you, as the leader, are more capable of doing a person's job than he or she is. That's deflating and leaves a sour aftertaste. The type of contact and time schedule for the circle of confrontation are agreed to in the commitment and covenant stages. Issues with micromanaging, if any, need to be ironed out at that point to avoid negative reactions down the line. You must make it clear to your team member that the *high contact* involved with constructive confrontation is about keeping everybody and everything focused on the project and objective, not merely looking over someone's shoulder.

We can put a man on the moon, but it's still tough to control our emotions. Negative energy and behavior in the workplace usually result from frustration. Frustration usually results from confusion and unrealistic expectations. Expectations are often unrealistic, not because they're unachievable, but because they're not based on clearly defined objectives in the first place. Positive vibes and energy will emerge from constructive confrontation when specific *habits, skills, attitudes,* and *activities* help team members reach their objectives and fulfill their part in the covenant.

Staying positive and maintaining emotional control, at least as far as work is concerned, are largely functions of consistent confrontation of the progress being made in executing the covenant. If the circle of confrontation turns out to be very different than the team member expected, adjustments are called for, perhaps as far back as step one. Consistency is critical to the successful circle of confrontation. Of course, consistent *failure* to support your team members in the execution of their covenants will cause them to withdraw their support for *you* and anything you want them to do. Even when your intentions are honorable, inconsistency will derail even a well-organized and systematic approach to accomplishment.

Establishing a positive atmosphere in the workplace requires a conscious, deliberate, premeditated program of making positive statements, spreading around positive affirmations, and providing positive support and encouragement *to everyone.* Saying the positive stuff only to your fa-

vorite folks will just breed more demon rabbits. If the research on negativity is valid, and most management and executive experience will validate it, 1 negative, cynical antagonist in an office can stink up the joint
for 50 positive people. That's why it's so important that leaders bring all
of the institutional and popular authority they can muster to bear on the
positive side of the ledger. If the one negative party poop is the department head, the department is sunk.

FOCUS ON PROGRESS

The primary confrontation conversation, as you've already seen, focuses
on the progress being made, or not being made, on the execution of the
covenant. This focus on the project, not the person, keeps the *constructive*
in constructive confrontation. The commitment conversation, covenant,
and subsequent constructive confrontations all need to keep the emotional purpose of the work in the forefront of the team member and team
leader's consciousness. The emotional purpose is positive. It focuses on
the wants and needs of the team member and the team member's family.

In no case should the tone of the confrontation conversation become
accusatory. Even when you're dealing with deviations from the covenant,
unmet goals, or failure to perform agreed-upon activities, you must speak
in solutions and practice the language of *habits, skills, attitudes,* and *activities* until it becomes second nature to you and your team members. Framing anything or anyone in failure guarantees demotivation and deflation
of ego. If you have a team member who actually *is* motivated or inspired
to do good work by criticism or negativity, send that person to Johns
Hopkins University Hospital for neurological research or lease him to
Ripley's Believe It or Not. You have an uncommon perplexity on your hands.

You've heard it a million times (twice now in this book) attack the *problem,* not the *person.* Believe it. Attacking the person won't put a dent in the
problem. Focus all available energy and resources on getting the covenant executed. Energy and resources spent on any form of complaining
or criticizing are *wasted* energy and resources. Beyond the waste is a trail
of destruction, where singed remains of your team member's ego can be

151

found. Despite the rah-rah that takes place around a pep rally or a motivational seminar, pumping people up for more than 24 hours isn't easy. Keeping them pumped up is even harder. This is made even harder when you don't know what you're up against.

ENCOURAGEMENT IS THE LANGUAGE OF LEADERSHIP

Encouragement is a never-ending task for leaders because you have no way of truly knowing what is discouraging your team members. You certainly don't want it to be *you* or your attitude. But it could be something far beyond the workplace and beyond your control. Constant, almost relentless, reinforcement of the efforts your people are putting forth are the best hedge against negativity they might import into the organization from outside. Whether there are family problems, addiction problems, money problems, romance problems, or all of the preceding, you're limited in your ability to address problems beyond your sphere of influence. Being positive and establishing and supporting an encouraging agenda is the best you can do to ward off negativity from the outside. You might succeed in making the workplace the safest and friendliest port in your team member's emotional storm.

Encouragement is also an important weapon in your battle against negativity in the work place because negative people tend to find and feed off of one another. Positive people seem to be fine working in isolation or in groups because other people's attitudes might or might not affect them. Negative people, although they often *appear* to be working in isolation, are aware of each other's existence. Somehow they have extrasensory perception — a sort of radar — that alerts them to one another's presence. Their unspoken allegiance and unholy alliance always seems to keep them on the same page, ready to attack the weakest link in your organization at the worst time. Maybe the demonic rabbits carry messages back and forth between them.

Indeed, battling negativity can be difficult because you can never be sure where it's coming from. What you *can* do is make sure you're not stirring up any new negativity on the job. In fact, the best and most productive use of your time and resources is to create a positive, supportive, and encouraging working environment for your team members. That includes focusing on the progress of the covenant. Progress is positive. Lack of progress is repairable and need not be negative. In fact, it's more repairable if it's not approached negatively. Being off track is fixable. Your focus should continually be on reinvigorating progress and getting your team members back on track, *not* on beating them up for being off the pace or off track. Unfortunately, many who learned to lead by imitation will do a lot of beating because they've never seen a more positive and proactive approach. With constructive confrontation the positive approach is built in.

DON'T BE A BLOWFISH

When the commitment and covenant are clearly defined and free of ambiguity, the team member has something concrete to hold the team *leader* accountable for and vice versa. This can be empowering. When the time comes to deal with adherence, there's no reason for either party *not* to couch the confrontation in positive terms of getting back on track to fulfill the emotional and organizational purpose agreed to in the beginning. Nobody's trying to pull a fast one. The more specific the question, suggestion, complaint, or grievance, the less likely it will be catastrophized and made into something larger. Avoid the blowfish syndrome. A misunderstanding between team member and team leader can be a fish, easily swallowed. Or it can be an easily swallowable fish blown up into something the size of a sperm whale, way out of proportion to the problem. Part of your job as a leader is to keep things in perspective.

Another of the unfortunate default settings human beings seem to have is catastrophizing. Sometimes people catastrophize their problems because they think people with the biggest problems are the most important people. How often have you heard, "If you think *you've* got problems, listen to this." Some people really think that anything negative or contrary that happens to them is a life and death situation. As a leader, you need to help them regain perspective. Sometimes they catastrophize just to be a squeaky wheel in search of some grease. Constructive confrontation will keep things in proportion through the consistent conversation that moves from commitment, to covenant, to confrontation, into celebration.

One of the most frequent activities for skilled leaders is to listen to a catastrophized account of a situation and then demonstrate how only a slight real-world adjustment is required to correct the variance. Over time, this reduces your team members' anxiety and renders them less likely to blow things out of proportion. The more frequently you check your course, the less drastic any single course correction needs to be. When your team members are sensitive enough to interpret course correction as criticism, and some will be that sensitive, the smaller the correction the better. Letting things go too long, thus requiring drastic course correction, will feed that sense of disaster, not to mention undermining your team's confidence in you.

NEVER DISCUSS A PROBLEM
WITHOUT OFFERING A SOLUTION

Focusing on solutions forces positive thinking. When someone is burning leaves down the block and one of your team members runs into your office to report that the entire Sequoia National Forest is ablaze, outplace that person to the Cable News Network (CNN). News bureaus want to hear about train wrecks more than they care about trains that arrive on schedule. Someone who constantly sees the sky falling is not good for morale. He or she is not helping maintain perspective in the office. Ask someone who reports a forest fire (when it's really Harry sneaking a cigarette in the men's room) how she or he intends to *solve* the problem.

Going to solution instead of lingering on the problem drives people's thinking into their left brains. All the theatrics and histrionics of the catastrophe are playing in the IMAX theatre otherwise known as the right brain. The left brain contains a bunch of Cal Tech rocket scientists in white lab coats waiting with arms folded and massive gray matter ready to engage in possibility thinking. As a leader, you are often called upon to usher the panicked team member out of the IMAX and into that cerebral situation room and introduce him or her to the team. "Ladies and Gentlemen, this is Fred. Fred seems to think the Sequoia National Forest is on fire."

The linear-thinking scientists will immediately engage Fred in research and inquiry. "Did you see this fire with your own eyes?" one scientist asks, pencil poised over her clipboard to chronicle the answer.

"Well," Fred hesitates, looking to you as if to seek your support, of which you offer none except to motion him to answer the question, "No. I smelled smoke, though."

"Were you anywhere in the *vicinity* of the Sequoia National Forest at the time you smelled the smoke," asks another scientist.

Fred looks your direction for relief again. You merely nod toward the questioner. "N-no," Fred admits sheepishly.

"Did someone in or near the Sequoia National Forest call or contact you to report an incendiary incident?" a third scientist asks.

"No," Fred confesses. "Look, maybe I exaggerated a little."

The scientists all stand frozen, looking at Fred for a moment, and then return to busily scribbling on their clipboards. Real scientists are good that way, totally professional. They're never negative in an emotional sense. They won't tell Fred he's an idiot. They're all *thinking* he's an idiot, of course. But they won't say that out loud until they're slamming back a few brewskies after work at the Afterburner Lounge and Karaoke Palace down the street.

As a leader, constructive confrontation is one of your best tools for teaching Fred that whenever he brings a problem to your attention, he's getting marched straight into that room full of white smocks and clipboards. Crying wolf is not allowed. Even if the Sequoia National Forest *has* turned into a gargantuan inferno, who do you want to help you put out the fire, Wolf Blitzer and a CNN news crew or Red Adair? Red will brush aside the cameras and get to work.

Operating out of the linear left brain is a good way to stay positive.

Psychologically, you're distancing yourself from emotion entirely as you move out of the right brain. Working on solutions, which is a critical thinking activity, will be more or less devoid of emotion based simply on which hemisphere of the brain is engaged. As a result, there are two primary approaches to developing and sustaining positive thinking: (1) intentional injection of positive and progressive thoughts and ideas, as in the pep rally, motivational seminar, or the personal compliment, and (2) forcing the discussion into the linear left hemisphere of the brain, which will lock emotion outside the door. Absence of emotion means no negative *or* positive affect, which is just fine now and then, considering the alternative.

Research indicates that locking out emotion works better for males, who typically have more difficulty switching between hemispheres of the brain than do females. Neuropsychologists report that accelerated interhemisphere data transfer in females is one explanation for their remarkable intuitive abilities. Describing interhemisphere data transfer in females as "accelerated" sounds much better than describing interhemisphere data transfer in males as "retarded." You can form your own conclusions on that.

DISPLACEMENT THEORY

Remaining positive is always a matter of choice. It's not only the team leader's responsibility to *model* a positive attitude, you must decide to *take the steps* necessary to develop and sustain a positive atmosphere. The circle of confrontation removes most of the snares and entanglements that result from poor planning and team leader and team member misunderstandings. This makes it easier for both the team leader and the team member to choose a more positive attitude and stick to it.

In contrast to those whose default settings go to the negative, the person whose default setting goes to the positive is refreshing, but not the norm. Positive versus negative displacement theory refers to the belief that a positive thought and a negative thought can't occupy the same space in the universe at the same moment. Therefore, if anyone, including leaders, observes discussions deteriorating into debates or conversations becoming criticisms, the best way to stop the movement toward the negative is to displace it.

Once a discussion becomes negative it tends to become *increasingly* negative until it no longer holds any redemptive potential. Spiraling into the negative is common in the workplace, especially when egos and pride are involved. Accusations and counteraccusations are ego defenders. The fact that few, if any, people ever advanced their career by proving their boss wrong doesn't seem to stop many from trying. The fact that few negative confrontations ever resolved the issue that the confrontation was ostensibly addressing doesn't seem to reduce the occurrence of negative confrontations, either.

Because negativity tends to feed on and fuel itself, it doesn't take much thoughtful effort to escalate a dispute. To deescalate a negative, adversarial, or hostile situation requires thoughtful, intentional, premeditated, and strategic insertion of positive thoughts into the conflict. You must remain vigilant to stay aware of the good progress being made on the covenant. Mentioning something that needs improvement, no matter how delicately, might send your team member into a self-critical spiral. He or she might go off on you, because he or she is cynical enough to "just be waiting" for you to go negative. Have some positive ammunition to fire back. A compliment will displace the negativity, hopefully long enough to make the confrontation constructive again.

Even if your team member tries to drag you down a critical path (i.e., baits you to criticize), don't go there. Stay on point and continue displacing his or her negative comments with compliments. Compliments can include the amount of effort you see being invested, including the effort to expand his or her horizons to come up with new solutions. His or her tolerance and patience in putting up with the incredible bureaucracy in your organization can be a good pat on the back that reflects understanding and empathy on your part. People will forgive you for a multitude of sins as long as you feel their pain.

Don't block legitimate concerns from your team members. They'll feel ignored, unheard, and disenfranchised. If you pick up on a negative theme and your team member doesn't seem inclined to spin it more positively, offer some help. "I think I'm following you, Harry. Can you reframe that thought in terms of executing the covenant?" If Harry isn't speaking in terms of executing the covenant, what's he talking about, anyway? Put the weight of being the positive-thinking police on your own shoulders. That's why you get paid the big bucks. Say, "I want to make sure I understand." Or say, "Let me see if I understand," and then restate what your team member just said in your own words. As long as you're legitimately attempting to achieve understanding, you're displacing your team member's ability to hide behind confusion.

Clarity, concision, and specificity are your friends. Invite your team member to restate what you're saying by asking, "I want to make sure I'm not missing anything. How would *you* sum up where we are?" The more you can steer the entire confrontation conversation into constructive waters, the farther you're steering it away from negativity, which could be called large-scale displacement. If you don't like what's being said or the attitude with which it's being said it's up to you to invoke displacement theory and put something positive in its place.

No "Buts . . ."

You've heard it before and you'll hear it at least one more time: avoid using the word "but." You can pour on the positive affirmation, load up your team members with compliments, and praise them until their cups runneth over, but . . . See how that works? As soon as you utter the word "but," your team members roll their eyes, literally or figuratively, and say, "That's the sound of the other shoe dropping."

Using the word "but" impeaches everything you said before it. The only way to convince your people that you're a sincere and authentic person is to say what you mean and mean what you say, in a way that doesn't reek of disingenuousness to them. You may think brutal honesty is virtuous. But if your honesty impugns their intelligence or is just plain critical, they tune out and your effectiveness as a leader has been seriously compromised.

Don't disqualify your good and wise counsel by attempting a back-handed criticism or trying to sneak in a scolding dressed in sheep's clothing. People have such finely tuned radar that an Academy Award winner would have a tough time convincing them that a criticism is a compliment. If you manage to make someone think you're complimenting them when you need to draw their attention to an area that needs improvement, what have you accomplished?

Give your compliments honestly. Then use the "and" to connect thoughts. "You've put a lot of effort into this, Harry. I think you're going to see your closing percentage start to increase any day now. And, with a temporary increase in the number of prospecting calls, the odds are going to shift in your favor." No "buts," see? Using "and" forces you to keep the comment positive and encouraging.

"You've put up with some attitude from the sales division, Francine. With a slightly altered approach and a break to cool off, I think you'll be able to up their cooperation level, and they might even enjoy themselves in the process. Let's try giving a dozen golf balls to the one who gives up his top clients first or a lunch certificate at the Afterburner Lounge and Karaoke Palace if he or she is not a golfer."

"Buts" cause disconnects. It's always a worthwhile investment for you to become known as a builder of relationships and a seeker of the high ground. You want to be known for being a solution hound. What you have to say is either important or it's not. Hopefully, you don't feel that what you have to say is so marginal that you don't mind disqualifying yourself with a cheap "but." You might as well imitate Austin Powers and say, "Having said that . . ."

POSITIVE EXPERIENCE BUILDS CONFIDENCE

Positive experiences make staying positive easier. Confidence is the belief that what you expect to happen *will* happen. This involves being realistic in the first place. Every stage of the constructive confrontation process contains sufficient flexibility to recalibrate the commitment and covenant in case you and your team member have overreached. One of your principle responsibilities as a leader is to make sure your team members don't set themselves up to fail. Even if you manage not to overburden them, they might, in their exuberance, overburden themselves.

Overburdening themselves is not just *their* problem; it's your problem, too. Every time a team member fails or falls short, his or her confidence is compromised. They'll begin the next day farther back in the pack. Productivity and performance will suffer. It doesn't need to be that way. You can do a lot to help avoid it by keeping goals and objectives reasonable.

Make sure your team members don't have too much wiggle room, either. If their goals and objectives are far below their capabilities, they won't experience a sense of accomplishment, even when they hit their goals. Some leaders conspire with their team members to set low expectations, so they won't have to confront their team members' progress — more specifically — their *lack* of meaningful progress. When this happens, the team leader and team members are stealing money from the organization that pays them. If that's allowed to continue for long, leadership up the organizational food chain is obviously disengaged or simply disinterested.

Create the optimal balance between what your team members are capable of accomplishing and the opportunities available to succeed. If it's a fairly new relationship, allow your people to play it soft until you begin to get a sense of what they're capable of. You'll know that by gauging the amount of effort required to hit the targets you agree upon.

Your leadership radar sweep will also be searching constantly for imbalances in *habits, skills, attitudes,* and *activities* among your team members. Very few folks are good at everything. The diversity of strengths and weaknesses among your people will surface soon enough. All of your observations will sharpen your skill set in aligning what your people do best with what your organization needs most.

BEING POSITIVE STARTS WITH YOU

You can't instill confidence in your team members when you're awash in self-doubt yourself. That's not going to produce a positive scenario, no matter how you cut it. You might be able to fake it temporarily, but your fool's paradise will implode sooner or later. Building leadership confidence is the same process as building team confidence, with repeated successful experiences. This means you need to set expectations for your own performance expectations within reasonable parameters.

The more consistently you guide your team members to successful outcomes, the more confidence you'll have a right to claim. This puts the obligation and responsibility of proper planning squarely on your shoulders. If you dial in coordinates for targets beyond your range to hit them, how can you expect to set your people up for success? You can't teach what you don't know. You might learn the lesson 24 hours before passing it on to your team, but who's going to be the wiser? The important thing is that you arrive at the knowledge and awareness first.

Winning builds confidence. The circle of confrontation, with its commitment conversations, covenant, confrontation, and celebration components, gives you a chance to tighten up the reins a little or let them out whenever necessary to give yourself and your team members the best chance to win. Confident people tend to be positive people and vice versa. When you're able to establish and sustain a positive atmosphere in your department or organization over time, positive thinking and behavior will actually begin to feed on, and perpetuate, itself. You can never stop stoking the furnaces, though.

POSITIVE CONVERSATIONS

You've been around long enough to realize that a conversation, unguided and left to drift aimlessly, can turn negative fast. Backbiting, gossip, kvetching, and complaining can mix together in a bubbling cauldron of stinking sludge that people are all too eager to stir but unwilling to eat. You don't want the putrid odor wafting through the hallways of your organization. The best way to clean the air is to stop the negativity. This begins with how you conduct your conversations with team members.

You already know that a conversation with team members is an opportunity to learn where their heads are as well as to get them involved in planning the execution of the organizational agenda. Therefore, don't just bark orders at them or spend the entire conversation voicing your agenda as it was handed to you from above. Put the issues in front of your team members and listen for their responses, paying particular attention to their *attitudes*.

When you notice attitudes going south or comments becoming caustic, you actively engage in redirecting the conversation back to the agenda using the language of encouragement and solutions. This doesn't mean disagreeing or getting argumentative with your team members. That will only generate or escalate negativity. Nod your head and acknowledge whatever it is they're feeling, avoid using the word "but," and steer the conversation back on course.

Francine might start to complain early on that the sales division is notorious for not sharing information. Don't let that negativity derail what needs to be done. You can even position the situation as part of a long-range improvement. "I understand why you might feel that way, Francine," you assure her. "The CEO is highly concerned with increasing sales revenues, though. That's where *this* effort needs to remain focused. Perhaps executing this initiative will be a first step in improving information flow between the divisions. If nothing else, it will give us a proven model to build on."

POSITIVE COMMITMENTS

You acknowledged what Francine was feeling, just as you established the importance of staying on task. Your job as a leader conducting commitment conversations is to listen, learn, and refocus; listen, learn, and refocus; listen, learn, and refocus. It's a never-ending cycle. The result is a much more positive commitment. You must exert the conscious effort to ensure that everything your team members are committing to is framed in positive progress for them, the organization, and for all the internal and external stakeholders.

It wouldn't be hard for you to conspire with Francine to compile an enemies list. Most people around the workplace already have one in their heads. The easiest thing for leaders to do is appeal to their team member's sense of victimization and abuse. If the leader is part of the conspiracy to abuse the team members, that cheerleading role gets a little dicey. Nevertheless, team members with those naturally negative default settings will expend untold amounts of energy planning and executing an all-out assault on an uncooperative division or department.

To steer them away from battlefield tactics and toward cooperative, collaborative commitments, you must appeal to what's in it for them. If they have an insatiable urge to kill, maim, and pillage, remind them of how the successful execution of their job, task, assignment, project, or initiative will crush the competition. If your team members can't imagine someone winning without someone else losing — if life is a zero-sum game to them — make sure they perceive your side as the winner and your marketplace adversaries as the losers.

POSITIVE COVENANTS

At the end of the day, the commitment needs to be fully framed in positive and productive descriptions of *who, what, when, where, why*, and *how*. It's a complete waste of time to form a covenant based on what someone else, or another organization, might or might not do right or wrong. The behavior of others is beyond your control. The covenant needs to be constructed of positive components. Each element or building block of the covenant needs to describe the *right things* you and your team members can do to achieve the desired outcomes. That's what's meant by *activities*.

The covenant is the written road map that describes *who* is involved, based on positive reasons for involvement. You don't include everyone *not involved* because of the negativity they would bring or the fact they having nothing to do with the initiative. *What* is being done is described in positive terms to keep the focus intentional rather than avoidant. The timing issues of *when* things are to be accomplished can become negative if they're not realistic. An achievable time line adds to the positive effect of the covenant by accumulating an ongoing sense of accomplishment.

The geographical references to *where* things will take place serves a similar purpose of creating clarity and diminishing confusion by leaving less to chance, misunderstanding, or misinterpretation. *Why* something is being done, as well as the methods of doing it (*how*), are very obviously couched in positive terms of encouragement and accomplishment, both for the team member's emotional purpose and the organization's best interests.

POSITIVE CONFRONTATIONS

Because scheduled and ad hoc confrontations are continuations of the commitment conversations, they need to remain positive for all of the same reasons. Frustrations from lack of progress can contaminate the continuing conversations if you don't anticipate such emotions and aren't prepared to deal with them. This is where a leader's empathic capacity will be sorely tested. Supervisors, managers, and executives with A-type impatient personalities have a tough time with this. But leadership is not about *you* being comfortable. It's about getting the best possible performance out of your team.

If you can successfully work through your own instincts to go negative as the execution of a covenant unfolds, you can help your team members do the same. In fact, assuming you can grow and develop as a leader to the point where you can stay positive and constructive no matter what, what good would it do if you were the only one to remain positive in the circle of constructive confrontation? Without dismissing the fact that your team members will get frustrated and will have a tendency to go negative from time to time, you must keep the focus on solutions, keep the language positive, and keep the confrontations consistent and constructive.

You don't need to play shrink to your people during confrontations. In fact, it's better if you don't. If frustrations abound, remind them that you can't help them with how they feel about something, but you can guide them through *what to do* in order to produce positive results. Remember that confidence, which is always a good feeling, comes from multiple successes. You can rely on the fact that winning feels good and exert all of the influence you have at your disposal to ensure that you and your team engage in winning activities. Strategically steer them away from regrets of the past and fantasies about a glorious future. For you, that means protecting the positive by bringing your team members back into the moment and focusing them on doing the next right thing.

POSITIVE CELEBRATIONS

Okay, go ahead and pontificate and prophesy a little on the glorious future, but only during celebrations. Although the specifics of celebrations will be covered in Chapter 9, it's important to note that every component of constructive confrontation must be intentionally and premeditatedly kept positive. If the celebration of accomplishment is dropped or devalued, your team members will wonder just how much your heart was in this thing to begin with. Even the most minor celebrations, like bringing in doughnuts, carrot sticks, or candy, are physical evidence that you're aware that good things are being done.

In terms of reinforcement, positive rewards build attraction. Punishment increases avoidant behavior. Celebrating the positive results of the constructive confrontation process encourage more willing, enthusiastic involvement in the future. To not celebrate or acknowledge positive progress and results will increase cynicism and muffle enthusiasm. Celebrating in ways that have no meaning to your team members will demonstrate that you haven't been paying attention to what they're all about.

Celebration is acknowledgment. It's up to you as the leader to make sure the timing and methods used to acknowledge progress and accomplishment reinforce the most positive aspects of your constructive confrontation efforts. Your team members might tell you (in fact, they *should* tell you) what constitutes a meaningful and rewarding celebration to them. Your responsibility is to make sure the celebration is (1) warranted and appropriate for the scope of the accomplishment, and (2) will happen in a way that will charge your team members' batteries for the next step.

CHAPTER 6 SUMMARY

Chapter 6 provided an agenda for keeping the focus on the wants and needs, not the failures and deviations. In doing so, it is a proactive program to keep things positive. Among the following are the highlights worth repeating:

- Constructive confrontation is not micromanaging. Micromanaging is butting into work processes and a team member's schedule uninvited. The type of contact and time schedule for the circle of confrontation are agreed to in the commitment and covenant stages. Issues with micromanaging, if any, need to be ironed out as soon as possible to avoid negative reactions down the line. Skilled leaders can impress the need for constructive confrontation on their team members so as to create a distinction between meddling and a good team leader and team member tandem.

- We can put a man on the moon, but it's still tough to control our emotions. Negative energy and behavior in the workplace usually result from frustration. Frustration usually results from confusion and unrealistic expectations. Staying positive and keeping emotional control are largely functions of proper commitment and contracting. If the circle of confrontation turns out to be very different from the team member's expectation, adjustments are called for, perhaps as far back as step one.

- Expectations are often unrealistic, not because they're unachievable, but because they're not based on clearly defined objectives in the first place. Positive vibes and energy will emerge from constructive confrontation when specific habits, skills, and attitudes help team members reach their objectives and fulfill their part in the covenant.

- When the commitment and covenant are clearly defined and free of ambiguity, the team member has something concrete to hold the team leader accountable for. This is empowering. When the time comes to deal with adherence, there's no reason for either party *not*

166

to couch the confrontation in the positive terms of getting back on track to fulfill the emotional and organizational purpose agreed to in the beginning.

- Remaining positive is often simply a matter of choice. It's the team leader's responsibility to model a positive attitude. The circle of confrontation removes most of the snares and entanglements that result from poor planning and team leader and team member misunderstandings. This makes it easier for both team leader and team member to choose a more positive attitude about anticipated behavior.
- Displacement theory means intentionally taking a positive idea and using it to displace a negative idea. A compliment displaces a criticism. Talking in terms of the solution displaces dwelling on the problem. Keeping the continuing conversations positive and encouraging will displace the opportunity for them to become critical and cynical. It can take as many as 50 positive affirmations to displace a single disparaging remark. It's never too soon to start with the positive affirmations.
- Positive experiences make staying positive easier. Confidence is the belief that what you expect to happen *will happen.* As a leader, it's important for you to set up situations in which you and your team members have the best opportunities to succeed. Once a pattern of success at one level is established, ratchet up the bar and elevate the performance of an already confident team. Allowing people within your sphere of influence to elevate at their own pace is fine, as long as their levels of performance don't become so dispersed and fragmented that they cease to work with any type of synergy.

Staying positive under uneventful circumstances is one thing. Staying positive in the face of challenging circumstances is something altogether different. You will deal with changes and challenges. It's not a matter of "if" as much as it's a matter of "when." That's part of the game. But the cycle of constructive confrontation can prepare you to deal effectively with changes and challenges, whether they are generated internally or externally.

CHAPTER 7

Changes and Challenges

No plan is perfect. Constructive confrontation is a dynamic and fluid process. The fluidity and flexibility should be used in response to changes in the internal and external marketplaces, not to provide wiggle room for underperformance. If commitments and covenants are constantly changed and modified, they will be devalued. However, dealing with unforeseen change and meeting new challenges are important to keeping the circle of confrontation valid.

Honoring the covenant doesn't mean arbitrarily adhering to rules for rules' sake. Your best judgment is called for when dealing with change and rethinking the commitment without discrediting, revoking, or rescinding the covenant. It's important not to allow changes or new challenges to render the circle of confrontation irrelevant. Dealing with long- and short-term challenges by the seat of the pants is more common than uncommon in management circles. But cold turkey confrontation (that's often adversarial) seems to come out of nowhere also and usually accomplishes nothing more than generating hostility and resentment.

As a case in point, Francine's research work has taken a turn for the better. Upper management in the sales division, once opposed to the intrusion of a researcher from Training and Development, has now taken to the idea. In a recent sales management meeting, someone said, "What good is researching why people buy? We really need to know why people *don't buy*, so we can fix it." That thought flashed with everyone present and the executive vice president of sales went to the CEO, who agreed that such additional research might prove equally valuable.

You were consulted and asked how you could go about expanding the research and still work with the sales division to get some recommendations implemented within the original 90-day deadline. Being the enthusiastic positive thinker you are, you promised to consult with Francine immediately. Francine has become an increasingly important player since this research project kicked off two weeks ago. She has reported on schedule with timely progress for both of those weeks and managed to establish workable relationships with the sales division folks, with only minimal nudging from you. You're aware, however, that this expansion of her responsibilities will add to her burden, so she definitely needs to be consulted as soon as possible.

"If all I have to do is modify the survey questionnaire," Francine says, with a concerned look on her face, "that would be one thing. But we're talking about interviewing a separate population of people if you want me to contact people who *didn't buy* from us."

"I know," you sympathize. "That's why I told the CEO and executive vice president of sales that I needed to run this by you."

"When do they want this done?" Francine inquires.

"I'm glad you're sitting down," you say, only half joking.

"Same deadline?" she asks.

You nod your head. "Sort of . . ."

Francine rolls her eyes.

"I don't think we're married to the original six weeks you had," you report. "Now that sales has taken a more active interest in this, they don't need their own six weeks following yours. They'll act on your recommendations straight up. So you could say we just doubled your time to ninety days."

"If that's the case, then I can research the potential customers who didn't buy from us with a new survey questionnaire as I wrap up the interviews and focus groups I'm doing now."

"So, as far as *who* is concerned," you summarize, consulting the covenant in the "Conduct Research to Increase Sales Revenue by 15 Percent" file you brought with you to Francine's office, "everyone remains the same except for the addition of the group of potential customers who didn't buy from us."

"That group is going to be a bigger challenge since we don't have a relationship with them," Francine points out.

"Any thoughts on how to approach them?" you ask.

"They'll need some extra incentive," Francine ponders. "Perhaps we can give them dinner certificates in exchange for filling out our questionnaire. To *good* restaurants," she adds. "None of this Afterburner Lounge stuff."

"Any other changes in *who?*"

"I could use an extra pair of hands to analyze the data now that I'm moving straight from one population to another."

"Does anyone come to mind?"

"Marvin."

"Marvin?"

"Marvin Michaels who does button-up work for the sales division," Francine explains.

You raise your eyebrows slightly. You hadn't thought of an interdisciplinary team. But now that she mentioned it, the possibility for synergy between departments makes sense.

"He can help with lining up the nonbuying customers as well as crunch data for me as I gather it," she continues. "That will leave me free to keep contacting these people."

The scope and dimensions of the project are changing right before your eyes. But Francine is all over it in this guided conversation. You and Francine resolve to use your best discretion in a project that could easily get outside of its lines and overreach its practical usefulness. You continue to take notes with your perpetual-motion pen as the two of you discuss changes to the *what, when, where, why,* and *how.*

The two of you meet with the executives from the sales division and get their okay with the expanded plan, securing a commitment for Marvin's participation. Given how the parameters of the new initiative dovetail into the existing one, you and Francine decide to modify the existing covenant rather than adding a second one. Anywhere an item has been added or amended, you insert [New]:

To: Your Name
From: Francine France
Date: [New] Day of Week Weekday/Month/Day/Year/Time
Subject: Covenant: Conduct Research to Increase Sales Revenue by 15 Percent

Who:
1. Francine France will conduct research into the fastest and most effective ways that sales revenues at XYZ Corp can be increased by 15 percent.
2. Francine will report directly to (Your Name) as a representative of XYZ Corp for supervision and necessary guidance.
3. Francine will consult with members of the XYZ Corp sales division as needed to gather data to complete her research.
4. Francine will consult with ten XYZ Corp customers, as specified by XYZ Corp sales management to enrich the data she is collecting to complete her research, unless otherwise decided by (Your Name) and (Her Name).
5. [New] At the request of the sales division and CEO, Francine will also include ten potential customers called on by XYZ Corp in the past twelve months, yet did not purchase.
6. [New] With the ongoing cooperation of the sales division, Francine will receive the assistance of Marvin Michaels to help gather and assess research data. Marvin will also assist Francine directly with identification and contact with identified, non-purchasing potential XYZ Corp customers.
7. [New] Marvin's ongoing contributions will be duly noted on Francine's progress reports.
8. Francine will copy the following people on her progress reports and preliminary suggestions: [(Your Name), (selected members of the Sales Division), <u>and the CEO</u>].

What: 1. The XYZ Corp is seeking recommendations on how to increase sales revenues by 15 percent.

             2. The desired increase must be measured in *revenues,* whether related to volume of sales or any other factor.

             3. [New] Research must be conducted *in collaboration with* the sales division in order to present a list of recommendations on how to most effectively increase XYZ Corp sales revenues by 15 percent.

             4. [New] The initial research will provide an objective analysis of the criteria determining sales margin *and* gather data as to why potential customers decided not to purchase from XYZ Corp.

             5. [New] When completed and submitted, the list of recommendations will be reviewed and acted upon by the sales division, as per the CEO's directive, as the recommendations are received.

When: 1. [New] Francine will continue the research she has begun, adhere to the existing schedule, and conduct the additional research in the subsequent six weeks.

             2. [New] Francine, in collaboration with Marvin Michaels and sales division executives, will integrate whatever tasks they deem necessary to conduct the existing and additional research in a timely and effective manner.

             3. Francine will submit a progress report of her findings to (Your Name) every Thursday, with the meeting time to be set no later than 24 hours in advance.

             4. Pending (Your Name)'s approval, Francine will distribute copies of her progress report to the agreed upon distribution list (<u>item five in the *who* section</u>).

             5. [New] At the end of twelve (12) weeks following the signature date of this covenant, Francine will deliver her final list of recommendations to (Your Name).

             6. Pending (Your Name)'s approval and any additions/corrections, Francine will distribute her final recommendations to the agreed upon distribution list. No more than two (2) business days will expire between item 4 and item 5 in this section.

Where: 1. Francine will conduct the research, for the most part, on the XYZ Corp headquarters campus by reviewing historical sales data.

(continued)

2. Francine will expand her research data through discussions with XYZ Corp sales team members via telephone, e-mail, or in person at the XYZ Corp headquarters campus.

3. Francine will set up and facilitate three off-campus focus group sessions.

4. Francine will interview XYZ Corp's ten largest customers via telephone or at the customer's property if the customer is local.

5. Meetings to discuss the progress reports and final recommendations will be held on the XYZ Corp headquarters campus in Francine's office, unless otherwise arranged in advance.

Why: 1. XYZ Corp stockholders' equity has been steadily decreasing for seven quarters.

2. A review of expenses has been conducted and the recommendations to reduce have been in effect for two quarters.

3. Despite expense reduction efforts, profits continue to lag behind projections.

4. Alternative opportunities are being sought to strengthen XYZ Corp's bottom line, including, but not limited to, increasing revenues from sales.

5. Because increasing revenues by 15 percent is a more critical issue than arbitrarily increasing sales by 15 percent, research needs to be conducted and recommendations delivered that expose below-the-surface opportunities to increase margin if possible.

How: 1. Francine will develop a short survey to serve as a standard questionnaire for gathering comparable information from all sources and have it approved by (Your Name) before using it for research, individual interviews, and focus groups.

2. [New] Francine will develop a second survey to serve as a standard questionnaire for gathering information from nonpurchasing XYZ Corp potential customers and have it approved by (Your Name) before using it for individual interviews. This questionnaire will specifically target reasons why these potential customers *did not purchase*.

3. [New] Because of the nature of the relationship between nonpurchasing customers and XYZ Corp, the research conducted among nonpurchasing customers will be limited to individual interviews.

4. [New] XYZ Corp will provide incentives as agreed upon between (Your Name) and the sales division in exchange for the participation of the nonpurchasing potential customers.

5. Francine will conduct telephone, e-mail, or face-to-face surveys to collect data, both internal and external to the organization.

6. Francine will examine historical sales data to make comparisons of various sales in an attempt to isolate key elements of the more lucrative sales in terms of margin.

7. Francine will compile this information into progress report form and distribute it to the agreed upon distribution list (in the *who* section above), subject to (Your Name)'s approval.

8. Francine will ultimately compile her collected data into final recommendations and distribute them to the agreed upon distribution list, subject to (Your Name)'s approval.

Other Items:

1. This covenant is a dynamic document, detailing a dynamic process. Changes can be made as needed and justified, contingent on the mutual agreement of both signature parties.

2. [New] This version of the covenant was revised and agreed to on [Day of Week Weekday/Month/Day/Year/Time]

3. This covenant is intended to be a guide to the execution of the project titled: Research to "Increase Sales Revenue by 15 Percent." Nothing in the covenant should be construed as to alter Francine France's conditions of employment with XYZ Corp. The covenant, however, establishes this initiative as Francine's top professional priority until completed.

4. It is always expected that everyone involved will continuously use his or her best judgment and bring any issues affecting the successful execution of this initiative to the other party's attention for resolution as soon as the issue becomes known.

5. To the best of [his or her] ability, and to the full extent of [his or her] authority within XYZ Corp, (Your Name) will provide Francine France with the best possible guidance, coaching, and access to XYZ Corp information.

6. [New] To the best of [his or her] ability, and to the full extent of [his or her] authority within XYZ Corp, (Your Name) agrees to the most appropriate and adequate resources to ensure success of this initiative, including coordination with the sales division (as necessary) and contact with the CEO.

Signature: Francine France [Date, Time, and Location]
Signature: (Your Name) [Date, Time, and Location]

TIME WELL SPENT

Your revised covenant with Francine chronicles the changes in the *who, what, when, where, why,* and *how* of the initiative. Your original hope was to increase cooperation with the sales division regarding the CEO's desire for research and recommendations. You got more than you bargained for when the sales division folks got with the program. But you responded nicely, making the best of the situation for all concerned. Most importantly, you kept Francine right in the middle of the action and aware of the political implications of what she's doing.

All told, it took a couple additional hours of your time and Francine's time to revamp the covenant, including all the meetings on the topic. Time is precious. But you're keenly aware of the excessive amounts of time that could be wasted down the road if you don't get things clear *now*. Because there is an end time associated with the project, you are especially anxious to get it right the first time. The revised covenant represents the new expectations for the project and details important elements that must be considered if the changes are to be sustained. Here are some items on which you received high marks:

- You kept the transition copasetic by involving Francine in proposed changes right away. Whenever possible, someone executing an initiative, like Francine, should be involved in the highest level meetings from day one. That way you don't have to play messenger. Francine's example in this book assumes you're working in a moderate bureaucracy, ergo you're in the loop perhaps more than you might need to be in a more progressive organization.
- You helped keep Francine engaged by allowing her to express her feelings about the changes without judgment. Nor did you allow your conversation to disintegrate into a gripe session.
- You kept the process constructive by immediately guiding your conversation with Francine into solution thinking with your line of questions.
- You helped keep Francine enthusiastic by *giving her the choice* of

176

personnel. Obviously, you couldn't give her an entire department. But she made a reasonable request for help, and it turned out to be someone in sales, thus fostering an even stronger working relationship between your departments.

- Marvin Michaels isn't a party to your covenant because he doesn't report to you. As it stands he is an interdepartmental collaborating partner with Francine, and his activities are well documented in the covenant and in Francine's progress reports. That makes the quality and quantity of his contributions easily traceable. Marvin's work won't get lost in the translation thanks to your constructive confrontation process.

- You helped Francine expand her influence as a result of her efforts to work with the sales division. When they decided to expand the study, Francine was perfectly positioned. True to the nature of constructive confrontation, you gave her every opportunity (and the guidance and resources) to succeed.

- The changes should hold because you were able to work out a consensus about *who, what, when, where, why,* and *how.* Buy-in by all is always best scenario whenever and wherever possible.

- The transition from covenant version A to covenant version B should be relatively seamless because you adhered to the established customs and practices of constructive confrontation.

The real you reading this book (not Francine's boss) might find different considerations necessary in your organization, depending upon your circumstances. The changes you face might or might not be similar to those at XYZ Corp. Even though you will probably construct a different covenant to cover the varied circumstances you and your team members face, it should be clear by now how the circle of constructive confrontation is fluid and dynamic. Despite its flexibility, constructive confrontation provides a solid foundation for *continuous accountability.* When executed properly, constructive confrontation will *decrease* workplace *conflict* by minimizing or eliminating confusion and ambiguity.

FLEXIBILITY AND YOU

Sometimes the team member's quantified performance, as defined in the covenant, doesn't turn out to be the most productive and efficient plan of attack after all. Whatever course corrections are called for, it should be noted whether or not the problem is related to the team member's *habits, skills, attitude,* or *activities.* Being cast in the wrong role is most likely not the team member's fault. However, proper casting is a matter of concern for the team leader *and* team member.

Harry, for example, was cast correctly according to his emotional purpose and the type of work he signed on to do. Some realignment of the individual's emotional purpose to the wants and needs of the organization might be necessary if real-world conditions change for the organization or the team member. Course corrections, based on the realities of the internal or external marketplace, aren't the same as renegotiating the terms of the covenant because someone changed his or her mind.

Bear in mind that the dynamic and fluid nature of the constructive confrontation process shouldn't be interpreted as wiggle room for either party. New or unforeseen challenges, moves by competitors, or other changes might call for recalibration of the guidance system the covenant represents. The tendency to overcommit should be dealt with during the initial commitment conversation to avoid a tug-of-war later on.

Sticking with the circle of confrontation has its benefits. Tossing aside a formalized approach to confrontation in favor of doing whatever feels "right" in the moment sooner or later pits the team leader's "right" against the team member's "right." The team leader, by virtue of institutional authority, can, and usually does, impose what feels "right" to him or her, leaving the hapless team member to be "wrong." Invoking institutional authority usually comes at the expense of team members' enthusiasm and best efforts.

HARRY'S CHALLENGE BECOMES A SCRIPT

Despite your best efforts through the commitment conversation, covenant, and initial confrontation stages, Harry is struggling. Everything in the circle of confrontation seems to be intact. You've been vigilant about guiding the conversations and allowing yourself or Harry to set unreasonable expectations or overcommit. Harry's performance targets are well within the standard range for other XYZ Corp sales executives. In fact, almost everyone else is outselling him. It's time to study the Harry challenge in terms of *habits, skills, attitudes,* and *activities.* Your conversation with Harry is loosely scripted before you get to his office. You already know he's scrambling to close sales, so you're mentally prepared in case he's defensive.

"Hello, Harry," you say spryly as you enter his office at the appointed time for your weekly confrontation.

"Oh, hi," he replies, his voice cloaked in nervous anticipation.

"I thought your progress report yesterday was very thorough," you say as you sit down.

"I know there's a problem," he says preemptively.

"The way you present your information is clear and thorough, Harry," you insist. "It's important for me to point that out because I think that'll help us get to the blockage quicker and remove it."

"How do you know that *I'm* not the blockage?"

You intentionally take a long sip from your coffee mug and rest your Harry Harris file on your lap. This is a moment of truth for a leader. Harry's bringing his personal frustration and self-defeating attitude to your doorstep and dumping it there. You swallow your coffee and take a deep breath. "People are rarely the problem, Harry," you assure him. "Relax."

"So if I'm not making these numbers," he says, half sarcastically, "is it the weather?"

"I can't stop you from being hard on yourself when you're not at work, Harry," you chuckle. "But around here we look at *habits, skills, attitudes,* and *activities.*"

Harry sits back in his chair. "Oh, yeah," he says, recalling your earlier conversations. "So which is it?"

Just that quickly your confrontation conversation is back on track. "I'm not sure which it is," you say as you shift forward in your seat. "Do *you* have any sense of what's breaking down?"

"I just don't think I can pull it off anymore."

"I can't help the way you feel, Harry," you confess. "I *can* help you do the things that will bring you success. Are you interested?"

"I feel like I've tried everything," Harry bemoans.

"If you keep deferring to your feelings, we're likely to miss the real reason your numbers are down."

"Okay," he finally agrees. "Where do we start?"

"Let's start with *habits*."

"You mean when I get to work, how long I take for lunch, and that kind of thing?"

"That's right," you confirm.

"I come in at eight, take an hour for lunch at twelve-thirty, and go home between five and five-thirty. When I have a presentation to make in the morning, I'll go straight there from home if it's between my house and the office. If it's not, or if it's later in the day," he goes on, "I'll come through here and make some calls first."

"During the time you're here," you say, "your progress report indicates you're able to get all your calls in."

"Yeah," Harry agrees. "The calls are no problem." He points at the progress report in your hand. "I make the right number of appointments, seven or more per week."

"We can cross *habits* and *activities* off the list," you say. "That leaves *skills* and *attitude*."

"I guess my attitude has been pretty crappy lately," Harry admits.

"Do you think that's the chicken or the egg?"

"Say again."

"Do you think your attitude is costing you closings or have the reduced closings dampened your attitude?"

Harry thinks for a minute. "I'm not sure," he says. "How can I tell?"

"I'm no shrink," you qualify. "But I wonder if there are days when you feel better than others?"

"Sure there are," Harry confesses. "Doesn't everybody go through that?"

"Good point," you agree. "Is there a difference between your closing rates on days you feel good versus days when you don't?"

"I've never paid any attention to that."

"Maybe you should record that on your progress report over the next week or two," you suggest. "Just make a note of the mood you're in at every presentation, and we'll see if there's any correlation to your closing ratio."

"I can do that," Harry says.

"As a hedge," you say, "let's go over your script."

You spend a half-hour with Harry going over his scripted pitch and close (*skill*). He seems to have them down pretty well, but you detect a certain flatness in his delivery. You point out several spots in the script where Harry could punch up the dynamics in his tone, spots that call for active listening to read the customer's reactions, and some revisions that Harry can try based on his interpersonal interaction style. The sales scripts are continuously revisited and revised at XYZ Corp to keep the sales staff as well prepared as possible, so nothing gets stale.

Harry's issue might well be related to fluctuations in daily mood. You suspect it's a combination of how Harry presents his script *and* the mood he brings into the presentations. Thanks to constructive confrontation you're on top of Harry's situation, and you have a structured approach to remedy whatever is ailing his performance. Moreover, you have the wherewithal to address Harry's situation in an organized and objective manner. No "buts." Even when Harry is reluctant to take an objective and positive approach to his performance problem, you have the covenant to work from as well as a record of his specific performance since he made the formal commitment.

The flexibility to change and meet new challenges never comes easily in an organizational environment. But having a cohesive structure from which to operate (vis-à-vis constructive confrontation) will keep your ducks in a row and enable you to provide the consistency necessary to build the kind of trust required to sustain change and elevate your team members' performance to meet new challenges.

CHAPTER 7 SUMMARY

Constructive confrontation establishes parameters and provides an agenda for dealing with change and new challenges without discrediting, revoking, or rescinding the covenant. Even when the covenant is adapted or modified to accommodate change or new challenges, the principles of constructive confrontation will preserve the spirit of the original commitment. The following are some of the Chapter 7 high points to remember:

- No plan is perfect. Constructive confrontation is a dynamic and fluid process. But the fluidity and flexibility should be used in response to changes in the internal and external marketplaces. If commitments and covenants are constantly changed and modified, they will be devalued. Dealing with intentional and unforeseen change and meeting new challenges are important to keeping the circle of confrontation valid, *not* to compensate for poor workmanship on the front end.
- The team member's quantified performance, as defined in the covenant, might not turn out to be the most productive and efficient plan of attack after all. Whatever course corrections are called for, the problem identified in terms of the team member's *habits, skills, attitude,* or *activities.* Being cast in the wrong role is most likely not the team member's fault. However, proper casting is a matter of concern for both the team leader and the team member alike.
- Realignment of the emotional purpose of the individual to the wants and needs of the organization might be necessary if real-world conditions change for the organization or the team member. Course

corrections, based on the realities of the internal or external marketplace, aren't the same as renegotiating the terms of the covenant because someone changed his or her mind.

- The dynamic and fluid nature of the constructive confrontation process shouldn't be interpreted as wiggle room for either party. New or unforeseen challenges, moves by competitors, or other changes might call for recalibration of the guidance system the covenant represents. The tendency to overcommit should be dealt with during the initial commitment conversation to avoid zigging and zagging later on.

- It's important not to allow changes or new challenges to render the circle of confrontation unimportant or irrelevant. Dealing with long- and short-term challenges by the seat of the pants is all too common in contemporary management circles. But so is cold turkey confrontation that's often adversarial, seems to come out of nowhere, and usually accomplishes nothing more than generating hostility and resentment. Sticking with the circle of confrontation has its benefits.

- Tossing aside a formalized approach to confrontation in favor of doing whatever feels "right" in the moment sooner or later pits the team leader's "right" against the team member's "right." The team leader, by virtue of institutional authority, can impose what feels "right" to him or her. Invoking institutional authority usually comes at the expense of team members' enthusiasm and best efforts.

All leaders face changes and challenges. Depending on the volatility of your industry and marketplace, you might face changes and challenges constantly. Depending on the volatility and temperament of your team members, you might face even more challenges. Winging it is appealing when there is little at stake. But taking risks with the organization's resources and your team members' careers is serious business.

With constructive confrontation you have a system that equalizes your management applications across your direct reports and provides consistency. When you're trying to sustain change or encourage your team members to rise to meet growing challenges, their trust in you will be determined in large measure by the consistency of your leadership. The next step is to ensure that the bonding material in your workplace relationships is strong and resilient.

CHAPTER 8

Cementing the Bond

Trust was alluded to in Chapter 7. It must reach critical mass when it comes to cementing a bond between a team leader and his or her team members. There is a natural cynicism when it comes to relationships between anyone on the payroll and the next-highest person on the organizational food chain. Ideally, organizations would take on a molecular organizational structure, with working cells expanding, contracting, or going away altogether depending on the workload.

Unfortunately, most organizations still use a Napoleonic, militaristic, bureaucratic, hierarchical model of organization. Privates report to corporals. Corporals report to sergeants. Sergeants report to lieutenants. Lieutenants report to captains. And so on, and so on, and so on. Majors make more than captains, and generals make more than anybody else. Organizational power (institutional authority) is concentrated at the top and diminishes as you move down the power chart (i.e., organizational chart).

If you want to explore the possibilities of doing more with less or getting greater productivity from fewer people than molecular organizational structures make possible, try reading *Unleashing Leadership: Align-*

ing What People Do Best with What Organizations Need Most (Franklin Lakes, NJ: Career Press, 2005). If your organization will be operating in the hierarchical model for the foreseeable future, you'd best learn how to bond up with your folks in spite of the structural disconnects hierarchical organizational models impose.

In a militaristic model, you need more than ever to create a strong, trusting bond with your people to overcome the system-imposed disincentives. When policies and standard operating procedures are drafted in large or hierarchical organizations, they run to the lowest common denominator, which results in restrictive, constraining policies for the best minds and attitudes in your organizational population. It really can't be helped unless you make the leap to a more progressive model.

Without vectoring off into a treatise on organizational design, let it be noted that constructive confrontation is the closest thing to the high accountability and low conflict you can achieve without a dynamic organizational model and truly progressive, servant-leadership scenario. You can't blend a partially punitive motivational model with an incentive and attraction-based approach. The two are like oil and water. They won't mix. The very possibility of punitive sanctions impeaches all possibility of trust.

This trust and bonding thing is a lot more than providing cookies and tea or pizza and soda in the break room every afternoon. Food is a treat, mind you. It can be used to great effect in rewarding good efforts. But you need to concern yourself more with what feeds a person's soul. That's why "money talk" is only a starting place on the way to defining a true emotional purpose for working.

TRUST

It's as important for the team leader to be consistent as it is for the leader to stay positive. The bond between team members and the team leader is cemented by trust, and constructive confrontation is a trust-building exercise. Its *primary* purpose is to increase accountability, performance, and productivity, while decreasing conflict in workplace relationships. But when the principles underpinning constructive confrontation are practiced, trust is a natural consequence.

Trust, like respect, must be earned. Leaders who deliver on their promises over time earn trust in the same way you come to trust team members who do the same. A major element of the initial commitment conversations, crafting of the covenant, or the constructive confrontations is the promise made by the leader, on behalf of the organization, to each team member. Placing a high priority on following through on that promise is imperative to build and sustain trust.

Think of trust as water stored in a reservoir. A crack in the leader's commitment can cause a dam break on the part of the team member, and rightly so. The leader, as a representative of the organization, is in a position to know exactly what he or she is committing to, as well as the strategic and psychological importance of consistently honoring all commitments and fulfilling all covenants. Inconsistent application of constructive confrontation will discredit both the team leader and the concept. Trust, if there ever was any, will disappear. If a team member sees him- or herself as an exception to the rule, there might as well be no rule. If a team member sees another team member being excepted from a rule, there might as well be no rule.

Consistency in the application of constructive confrontation across the organization is another key element in trust building. Constructive confrontation is self-calibrating to every team member's performance abilities. Some team members have difficulty keeping up with the rest of the department, due to poorly developed *habits*, lower *skill* levels, questionable *attitudes*, or lack of adequate *activities*. If only difficult team members are singled out for constructive confrontation, the entire circle of confrontation process will appear to be punitive and remedial. The process brings out the best in everyone and should never be selectively applied. Such inconsistency will erode and destroy trust — guaranteed.

Organizational rah-rah programs intended to change "the way we do business" are great, if taken for what they are. Marching bands, clowns on stilts, popcorn, and cotton candy . . . who hasn't been involved at one time or another as a participant or producer of such pageantry? But everybody knows deep down that ballyhoo and fanfare, no matter how expensive, don't change anything. Nothing can substitute for consistent behavior over time when building and sustaining trust. Intentional change can only take place when reinforced by consistent, daily, hour-by-hour legitimate behavior, because people won't embrace change until they trust it. If you're the champion of change, even continuous improvement, in your organization, your people won't buy-in unless they can trust *you*.

HONESTY

More than anything else, people want a team leader who tells them the truth. You won't cement any bonds without it. Team leaders who spin and contort information to manipulate team members and situations leave a bitter aftertaste, not to mention team members who are loathe to cooperating and investing themselves emotionally in their work. People are not as afraid of bad news as they're afraid of *no news*. Being left in the dark carries with it the implication that you're not important enough to know. Of course the worst way to treat team members is to lie to them. Being intentionally misleading is a guaranteed relationship killer.

Be honest. If your organization is hierarchical, don't pretend it's not. Freely acknowledge to your people how the organization is structured and how the reward system operates. Remind them that you're swimming in the same water as they are. "We all know why we're here and what we're here to do," you tell your people. "If not, I owe you an apology and an explanation." Some organizational environments have become so cynical that people feel a leader who gets actively engaged in the team members' business is meddling.

Forget about it. It's not up to individual team members to decide arbitrarily why they're there and what their jobs are. Your team member's input in defining the emotional purpose in his or her work — and how his or her work resonates with that emotional purpose and vice versa — is essential to constructive confrontation, but only in collaboration with *you*. Think about how ridiculous the alternative would sound. "None of us

188

knows exactly why we're here or what we're here to do," you confess. "The more confused you are, the easier it is for me to manipulate you." Don't expect to win any votes with that speech, despite its brutal honesty.

There are organizations out there that could honestly make such claims, at least the first part. But it's not typically a result of intentional disinformation as much as it's a lack of interest. Burnout above leads to burnout below. Apathy in the executive suite will quickly infect and contaminate the whole organization. Cynicism breeds cynicism — and nothing breeds cynicism, apathy, and burnout faster than mendacity. Not being honest might appear to be the course of least resistance, the easy way out, the best way to avoid making waves, but the penalty you pay in distrust far outweighs an emotional savings on the front end.

THE TRUTH MADE EASY

The primary reason leaders aren't more truthful with their team members is because they don't want to deal with the emotional push back and backlash to bad news. Who can blame them? But ugly moments are better than ugly careers. Besides, bad news doesn't need to be ugly. Any news needs to be delivered in a constructive way. If you've built up a track record for being truthful, your team members won't take it out of your hide when you need to bring up problems or force them to face things they'd rather look away from. They'll know you have their best interests at heart.

Constructive confrontation is a road map for long-term behavior. Even if a constructive confrontation cycle is short term, as in Francine's situation, the operating principles will "change your way of doing business." Her next job, task, assignment, project, or initiative will be systematically managed through constructive confrontation. Harry's career success over the long haul depends on the expert application of constructive confrontation. Without it, he's stuck. Without it, *you're* stuck in a goal-setting/failure-to-meet-goals/react-and-confront-after-the-fact cycle that will make you yearn for early retirement.

If you look at honesty and telling the truth to your team members as an integral part of the circle of confrontation, it becomes less ominous. Bad news is often taken as criticism by team members, because bad news is often *used as criticism* by team leaders. Shaming folks is a poor choice of motivators. Use Teddy Roosevelt's idea to put situations in perspective: Start where you are, use what you have, and do what you can. Your team members will appreciate your honesty when you use it as a growth and development tool, not as a criticism.

Running a close second to avoiding emotional push back and backlash is the fact that telling the truth requires that you, as the leader, know and accept it. There are many heads buried in organizational sand out there. Why do you think the beach is such a popular corporate retreat location? The use of cyclical and consistent evaluation and feedback, which is the essential nature of constructive feedback, will diminish this ostrich effect. Go back to the notion that you and your team members are all swimming in the same water. If you lose, they lose.

Many managers and executives build fire walls to protect themselves from the failings of their team members. The team members in these situations know they've been left to twist in the wind. Nothing the leader says can overcome the distrust this causes. No pep talk, no marching band, and no pizza party will inspire team members to throw themselves into their work if they suspect they're throwing themselves off a cliff.

In a militaristic, bureaucratic, hierarchical organization it's difficult to smudge the distinction between positions on the organizational food chain. This just gives you more to accept about life in the big city and how you need to relate to your people. Discuss it with them. Tell them how promotion works in your organization. Be honest about what you have the power to do and what you don't have the power to do. They might think you're much more influential than you really are and wonder why you're not exerting more authority on their behalf.

If you and your team members can keep your heads out of the sand and have constructive conversations about the realities of your organization and the solar system in which your organization orbits, the bond between you will strengthen. Don't go to their level to bitch and complain about what a crappy organization it is. Remember that you're part of it. Before you can convince your team members, in an honest and realistic manner, that their roles in the system are important, you must believe yours is, too. Negativity won't make your case compelling.

Whether team members recognize it, the support they receive from team leaders through the circle of confrontation will accelerate successful goal attainment, both personally and professionally. As you're already aware, continued success over time builds confidence. Confidence produces positive feelings about the people and processes the team member is associated with. Confidence won't come without honest disclosure on your part. You're expecting no less from them through every phase in the circle of confrontation. As with every aspect of authentic leadership, you go first.

This is not a lot of rah-rah hyperbole. The issues of honesty and disclosure are critical components of constructive confrontation. If you allow dishonesty and withholding of information in your organization, if only within your sphere of influence, any train you set on the tracks will soon be derailed. If you think honesty is a vague or irrelevant concept, try operating without it. The productivity and performance of your team over time will tank. You can fool some of the people for a short time. But long-term performance requires that you say what you mean and stand by what you say.

Listening

One way that cynical and negative people in the workplace came to be that way is because they were promised one thing and delivered another. If you are promised support, then turn when you need it to find yourself alone in the middle of the Utah salt flats, how likely will you be to believe the next promise? If you're told that specific performance on your part will produce specific rewards from the organization and then deliver on your end of the bargain only to discover that everyone above you on the organizational food chain has amnesia, how eager will you be to play the sucker again?

Another way that people in the workplace come to be cynical and negative is by being ignored. People eager to participate have ideas and sug-gestions. At the very least they want to discuss their roles and be clear about them. When they find no audience for their ideas, suggestions, and role-defining conversations, they head to the water cooler. Who's waiting there to engage a sympathetic ear in conversation? Why, it's the cynical and negative team members who shouted their enthusiasm into deaf ears in the past and got nothing for their efforts. The club just acquired a new member.

Cynical and negative team members don't feel heard. If they're not heard, they're not appreciated. If you don't appreciate them, the best you're going to get out of them are the motions. Even if you don't have a way to quantify it, that attitude and the paltry level of performance neg-ativity brings with it are costing you and your organization plenty in lost productivity. That loud sucking sound is real dollars being sucked out of the bottom line.

People become invisible when they're not listened to. When people go into a disappearing act, it's your job as a leader to make the invisible visible. It's also your job to make sure they don't slip off the radar screen again. That means listening to them. "But if I sit and listen to my team members bitch and whine all day, I'll never get any work done," you whine. "And neither will they."

You're right. Lending an ear to every ad hoc complaint and grievance that pops into your team members' heads will bring your whole depart-ment to a standstill. That's why your listening must be *active*. Here are many ways to define and describe active listening. The important thing to remember is that listening won't become a problem until it's passive. Listening becomes passive when you're not involved.

Don't be like the proverbial husband hiding behind his newspaper while his wife tries to tell him about her day. That type of behavior on your part will send your team member straight back to the water cooler. Make sure that your scheduled commitment and confrontation conver-sations are open-ended enough that if your team member has any addi-tional business, you can accommodate it. The conversations you engage during the constructive confrontation cycle guarantee visibility. In fact, they shine a spotlight on your people.

It's hard to feel invisible when your team leader is regularly seeking you out to talk progress, problems, solutions, opportunities, and the like. Constructive confrontation listening is active. You're recording what's being said because your follow-up will depend on it. How do you know if you're moving in the direction you want if you didn't mark your last spot? You're actively listening for vocal inflection and body posture cues that will tip you off to changes in mood and *attitude*.

You're also actively looking for clues on the status of your team member's current *habits, skills,* and *activities*. This means you're attentive, responsive, you make mucho eye contact, and you're taking notes. Nobody across from you is going to feel ignored or invisible under those circumstances. That problem is solved simply by adhering to the operating principles of constructive conversation.

Of course you can't be listening if you're talking. Because constructive confrontation is a collaborative effort between you and your team members, lecturing is not allowed. What you say must be informed by what your team member tells you as well as the agenda you've loosely scripted in advance. Let it be known that the entire conversation is framed in the needs of the organization and how your team member's emotional purpose, *habits, skills, attitudes,* and *activities* resonate with those needs. This isn't the counseling center, after all.

Part of being an active listener is setting the agenda for the conversation and being prepared with a loosely scripted presentation. Your team member will shift and adjust that agenda, which is okay, if it stays constructive. Skilled conversation management on your part will provide you with good information. Your honest disclosure of information to your team member is critical to his or her ability to return accurate and relevant data back to you. You set the tone, guide the agenda, and remain flexible to accommodate any pressing concerns on the part of your team member.

By doing all of this, you're modeling the organized and productive way you expect your team member to present information to you. You might need to say, "Point taken. Now, back to the original issue . . ." Or, "Those are important issues. Let's schedule a separate conversation to make sure they're covered. Right now I need you to focus on . . ." Your offer to hold a separate conversation will rarely be accepted because, oftentimes, the digression to other issues was probably just that, a digression, a red herring, a smoke screen to distract you from the performance demands being discussed. If your team member does have something extra to discuss, have the conversation. You want to know what's on his or her mind, because it's undoubtedly affecting, or is potentially affecting, his or her performance or attitude. Forewarned is forearmed.

When team members receive consistent attention from their team leaders, it doesn't necessarily need to be frequent or long-winded. With scripted points to cover, a little conversation goes a long way. When team members feel listened to, they will take more risks and work harder to fulfill their end of the covenants they've signed onto. Support and recognition from team leaders is seen by team members as affirmation that their efforts and contributions are truly appreciated. Appreciation builds strong bonds. Unscripted and passive listening equals inertia. Active listening shortens the exercise.

SCRIPTS

Through constructive confrontation you're constantly gaining new information. Constantly retracing the *who, what, when, where, why,* and *how* of everything your team members are doing gives you information about other people. Remember that the information you gather needs to be triangulated. As you triangulate the information gathered from observation, peer feedback, and direct conversations, the reliability of your assessments and analysis will increase. The quantity and quality of the information depends on your skill as an information gatherer and analyst. The better you are at information gathering and processing, the greater the asset you are to your people.

In the same way, the skilled use of information will increase your team member's confidence in you. Reminding them that you're always on the prowl for information is also important. Do you recall the seven-second encounter with Fred in which you interrupted a hallway conversation to make a public demonstration of respect for your team member's time and also to set a meeting? "Excuse me, folks," you said politely but squarely. "Fred," you continued, making eye contact with him, "I need five minutes to check in on the Bigsby matter today. Let me know when is best for you."

Scripting always prepares you to make the most out of confrontation conversations, even minor ones, and guides the conversations. Scripting also makes you appear more confident and knowledgeable, upping your credibility with everyone. By telling Fred you're on top of the Bigsby account, you're telling everyone else to be prepared to discuss *their* work. It's preemptive inquiry, and it keeps people alert. Not frighteningly alert, like indiscriminately setting off firecrackers in unsuspecting people's wastebaskets. But making them aware that it's your job to set the speedometer around the place.

After all you've now learned about constructive confrontation, it should be hard to believe that so many people in positions of responsibility still work up the courage to confront their team members only when things have gone incredible sour and they have no choice. Or they confront people with too little too late only at performance review time. Yet for most supervisors, managers, and executives, that's all they know to do. The conversation should never stop. By making a conscious commitment to keep the conversation current, you make it easier on yourself and your team members to communicate timely and relevant information and keep things from going sour at all.

How many times, though, have you emerged from a "conversation," "performance review," or "character assassination" with the person above you on the corporate food chain muttering to yourself, "That was a waste of time?" Time is too valuable to you and your team members to waste in unscripted conversations. Cementing the bond with your team members means respecting their time and making your contact with them meaningful and productive. Scripting and prethinking conversations and working from a deliberate agenda with premeditated language will increase your chances of making good impressions.

GETTING TO KNOW TEAM MEMBERS IN CONVERSATION

Scripting constructive confrontation conversations is a matter of you, the leader, thinking through what you want the outcome of your conversations to be and preparing to make sure you get the important things said, not wishing later that you had said more important and relevant things. The time you have and the importance of your interaction with your team members are too important to leave to chance. Prepare, practice, and practice some more.

Cementing your bond with team members through loosely scripted conversations doesn't mean caving in to every gripe they have. Anticipating and planning for the responses you're sure to hear is a complex challenge. But you should be prepared nonetheless. Team members are most likely to deal with underperformance in the following ways :

- Blaming conditions at home
- Blaming conditions in the marketplace
- Blaming conditions inside the company
- Blaming the fact that somebody set off a firecracker in their wastebasket

Whatever or wherever your team member places the blame for underperforming, don't disagree. A spitting match between you and a team member accomplishes nothing positive and stains the carpet in the office. You're not getting paid to prove people wrong, even when they are. You're getting paid to help them perform at the most productive level possible. "Fred, I have no doubt that the economic conditions on the street are presenting a bigger challenge than ever before, and the Bigsby account is likely to feel the pinch. We took that into account when we were discussing the conditions of our covenant."

Hopefully you did. If not, Fred's got you over the barrel. Notice the word "but" is conspicuously absent. By now you're keenly aware that injecting the word "but" into a sentence or thought dismisses what came before it. You might as well say, "Fred, I have no doubt that the economic conditions on the street are presenting a bigger challenge than ever before, but I don't care what you have to deal with. Don't come to me with your wimpy excuses. Do what you promised you'd do or the next firecracker goes down your pants."

Try instead, "Fred, I have no doubt that the economic conditions on the street are presenting a bigger challenge than ever before. What do you think has changed since we crafted our covenant? How can we compensate for that without compromising the agenda we committed to?" Scripting your response to their excuses so as not to fracture your relationship is a matter of keeping your eyes on the prize:

- Acknowledge your team members' concerns; don't give them an excuse to disconnect because you *don't give a rip* about them or don't believe them. Respect them enough to hear them out. Then guide the conversation toward solutions.
- Use their expressed concern as an invitation to revisit the basic components of your covenant to see how the problem might already have been accounted for, if not solved. After all, they brought it up.
- Take advantage of the dynamic nature of constructive confrontation and make a change or alter the plan if that's the appropriate thing to do. You'll know it's the appropriate thing to do if it creates a more direct route to the goals you and your team member initially agreed to.
- If your team member is loading unnecessary weight on his or her own shoulders, use your institutional power to remove it. Some team members will take on too much, even if you initially cautioned against it. Help them eliminate some of the load.
- Learn from your team members' resistance, excuses, or push back. These behaviors speak volumes about them. Triangulate that information and use it to be a better communicator and improve your confrontation skills.

Accountability matters. Accountability and authority go hand in hand. Talk about them openly and intentionally. But don't beat people up with their "obligations." If folks feel they've been saddled with a heavy load of responsibility and very little authority to work with, they'll become resentful and cynical. Every person has a maximum accountability setting. Don't exceed yours or your team member's.

SCRIPTS: EXPRESSING CONCERN

When expressing concern for a troubled team member, don't merely say, "How are you feeling, Fred?" You get that ever-popular point for using Fred's name, because you've learned to always include people's names as much as possible in your scripts. But what is it you really want to know and why? If you want to merely let Fred know you care about him, which is a good thing to communicate, there are better ways to do it. "Was your ski vacation all you expected it to be?" shows that you care enough to remember that he went skiing on vacation. "Did your son's little league team win on Saturday?" shows that you care enough to find out that (1) Fred has a son, (2) Fred's son plays little league baseball, (3) there was a little league game on Saturday, and (4) you remembered to follow up on it. It's good to note these little things so you *will* remember to follow up. It goes a long way.

If Fred's attitude is in the dumpster, that's something else. Extend a scripted invitation to chat with him privately. Be specific: "Fred, I want to spend a few minutes with you this afternoon on several things; when can you come by my office?" (or "When can I stop by your office?") Then engage in a premeditated, honest disclosure of your concerns. "Fred, I've noticed that you seem a little [fill in the blank with the appropriate term: down, frazzled, anxious, distant, whatever]. Everything we have planned in our covenant is on schedule, so I don't want to get in your business, except to say that if you need something, I hope you'll let me know."

No threats, no demands, no pressure, just concern — specifically and unambiguously expressed. People tend to be extremely private and with-holding about what's bothering them, especially if it's you. If you suspect it's about your relationship, without getting paranoid about it, leave that door open. "If this is about how I'm handling things or leading you and the team, I want you to know I welcome all comments and suggestions. We rise and fall together. I don't want to hold any of you back or vice versa — especially if telling me about it can fix it."

If Fred's crappy attitude is running parallel to poor performance, as in unmet goals, unfinished tasks, and so on, use another script that specifi-cally addresses both issues. "Fred, I've noticed that you seem a little [fill in the blank with the appropriate term: down, frazzled, anxious, distant, whatever]. Your success and my success are intertwined, as we've dis-cussed many times. So if you need something, as we've *also* discussed many times, it's your job to let me know. I also don't know if how you're feeling has anything to do with [fill in the blank with the appropriate term: making plan, hitting your agreed-upon numbers, getting your cus-tomer service calls up by five percent, delivering your reports on time, whatever], but we're [fill in the blank with: off target, off course, gener-ally off schedule, or whatever]. How do you think we should proceed?"

Remain specific and stick with your scripted priorities. Fall back on the qualifier, "Fred, I can't fix how you feel. Only *you* can do that. But I can help you get back to making the decisions we discussed making in our initial conversations about this project, doing what you need to do to complete this project, and taking the steps you need to take in order to succeed. If we need to revisit the conversation where we defined success, let's do it."

Not being able to take away another person's pain or ending their un-happiness is a basic rule of life, unless you're the one causing it. Talking to Fred this way lets him know you won't take responsibility for how he has chosen to feel. "But I can help fix what's ailing your performance vis-à-vis our covenant. Let's get back to a point when you were [fill in the blank with the appropriate term: making plan, hitting your agreed-upon numbers, getting your customer service calls up by five percent, delivering your reports on time, whatever] and see what's changed, what we need to change now, if anything, or if we need to address your *habits, skills, attitudes,* and *activities.*"

This script demonstrates that you are concerned with your team member's feelings, but not at the expense of the performance both of you owe to the organization that pays you. It also demonstrates that you're flexible, although not to the point of forgetting what you initially agreed to. You will make adjustments if justified, but it's more likely that you'll work with Fred to make necessary course corrections on how the covenant is being executed. Perhaps the most important message is (and you should come right out and say it), "If I'm the problem here, I want to fix it. If you're unintentionally or unconsciously injecting problems into this process, I want to help you identify them and correct the situation. I won't ask you to do anything I won't do." When you're alone again in your office, you can sit back, reflect on your handiwork, and think to yourself, "How about them apples?"

CHAPTER 8 SUMMARY

Leaders who deliver on their promises earn the respect and trust of their team members, thus cementing the bond between them. The systematic and interactive nature of constructive confrontation, if executed properly and consistently, will result in strong bonds between team members and team leaders. The constructive confrontation agenda will squeeze out nonproductive squabbling, gossiping, and irrelevant discussion. The following are the major issues involved in cementing the bond:

- It's as important for the team leader to be consistent as it is for the leader to stay positive. The bond between team members and the team leader is cemented by trust. Nothing builds and sustains trust more than consistent behavior over time. A major element of the initial conversation, commitment, and covenant is the promise made by the leader, on behalf of the organization, to each team member.

Placing a high priority on following through on that promise is imperative to build and sustain trust.

- A crack in the leader's commitment can cause a dam break on the part of the team member. The leader, as a representative of the organization, is in a position to know exactly what he or she is committing to, as well as the strategic and psychological importance of honoring all commitments and fulfilling all covenants.

- Inconsistent application of constructive confrontation will discredit both the team leader and the concept. If a team member sees him- or herself as an exception to the rule, there might as well be no rule. If a team member sees another team member being excepted from a rule, there might as well be no rule.

- Some team members have difficulty keeping up with the rest of the department, due to lower skill levels, lower motivation, or other factors. If only difficult team members are singled out for constructive confrontation, the entire circle of confrontation process will appear to be punitive and remedial. Properly executed, the circle of confrontation brings out the best in everyone.

- When team members receive consistent support from their team leaders, they will take more risks and work harder to fulfill their end of the covenants they've signed onto. Support and recognition from team leaders is seen by team members as affirmation that their efforts and contributions are truly appreciated. Appreciation builds strong bonds.

- Whether team members recognize it, the support they receive from team leaders through the circle of confrontation will accelerate successful goal attainment, both personally and professionally. Continued success over time builds confidence. Confidence produces positive feelings about the people and processes the team member is associated with.

To paraphrase Norman Vincent Peale, nobody cares how much you know until they know how much you care about them. It's one thing to claim you care about the growth and development of your team members. It's much more powerful to demonstrate your genuine concern through honest and consistent interaction. Earning respect and trust take time. There are no shortcuts. You can't be on again/off again. Your words and actions must be authentic and reliable. The payoff to your diligent and vigilant effort is the chance to celebrate achievement. Celebration, as you're about to learn, is an art in itself.

Part III
Celebration

Celebrating
the Right Things

Rewarded behavior is repeated behavior. This popular workplace slogan points to a common leadership mistake: taking small accomplishments for granted. Small stuff is significant stuff. If you want it to keep getting done, recognize it. Unfortunately, most organizational executives have become accustomed to celebrating only extraordinary achievements, assuming that the small stuff will take care of itself. This assumption overlooks and fails to reward the incremental efforts that make the big achievements possible.

It's not the daily home runs that add up to overall success. It's the singles, the doubles, and the bases on balls that lead to more runs. Organizations are not revered on the basis of style unless the style is accompanied by profitability over time.

The circle of confrontation involves celebrating the devotion to daily effort as defined in the covenant through all types of recognition and reward. Covenants begin with the big picture and the ultimate goal. But they immediately break down the grand prize into the *habits, skills, attitudes,* and *activities* necessary to pull it off. If those weekly, daily, even hourly incremental tasks don't get done, you can forget about the grand prize. Celebrating the small stuff sets up the big party later. Split the difference on the old axiomatic "eyes on the prize" bit and keep at least one eye on the details that get you there.

If *habits, skills, attitudes,* and *activities* are important enough to be defined in the covenant and consistently coached, they're important enough to encourage. When loyalty and adherence to the process, as revealed in the smallest efforts, are *sufficiently* encouraged, major results will happen. If the deliberate, daily activities required to achieve larger results are not encouraged and dwindle as a result, the larger outcomes will be jeopardized and probably not be realized, except by coincidence. Do you want to stake your career on such a coincidence?

When targets are not hit and goals are not reached, the team leader, the team member, and the rest of the organization all suffer, although not necessarily in that order. Constructive confrontation is a well-engineered process that breaks down what needs to be done, how it needs to be done, and how often it needs to be done in order to produce higher-profile results. Effort calls for recognition. Results demand it.

Just as success over time builds confidence, appropriate recognition for every level of effort builds goodwill and the desire to meet and exceed expectations the next time around. Anticipation that good effort will be recognized, even on a small scale, is strong motivation. Anticipating that good effort will go unnoticed and unrecognized breeds cynicism. Make sure your deliberate style of recognition and rewards resonates with your team doing the right things.

WHAT ARE THE RIGHT THINGS?

Zig Ziglar built his legendary motivational speaking career in large part by being positive. The incredible vacuum created by the scarcity of intentionally positive reinforcement in the business world gave him a wide open field upon which to play. Minor recognition, even for seemingly innocuous little things will help keep your team members' behavior between the navigational beacons of your organizational agenda. More importantly, consistent recognition is an ongoing acknowledgment that you're on their side, with their best interests at heart, just like Ken Blanchard's Shamu example.

The right things are simply the planned *habits, skills, attitudes,* and *activities* you talk to your team members about day in and day out. If you're not talking to your team members regularly about the small efforts that, taken together, comprise the megaeffort, you're derelict in your leadership responsibilities. Never assume they know. Even if they *do* know, deliberate and intentional encouragement and reinforcement from you makes results exponentially better. But you won't find good behaviors to encourage and reinforce unless you're deliberately and intentionally looking for them.

Pay Attention

Never think you can sign off on a covenant and walk away. More than that, how often have you attempted to manage the productivity and profitability of others with no covenant at all? Most supervisors, managers, and executives walk away from the regular and meaningful contact they should be having with their people without so much as a full understanding of *who, what, when, where, why,* and *how.* To find someone doing well under those circumstances depends almost entirely on free association interpretation of what exactly you mean by "good."

Right things also include the exercise of sound judgment outside of the planned *habits, skills, attitudes,* and *activities* you talk to your team members about. When you've sufficiently converted your team members into believing the guiding principles behind the proper *habits, skills, attitudes,* and *activities,* they'll continue to move in the right directions even when they've overrun the map or otherwise find themselves outside of charted waters and temporarily out of radio contact with you. Most people operate inside the plan as much as possible. But there are times when they're called upon to improvise for any number of unforeseen reasons. That's when it's especially important for you to recognize and reward their right thinking and right behavior.

Operating off plan because of lagging discipline (or the notion that plans are for morons) isn't going to fall under the rubric of good *habits,* *skills, attitudes,* and *activities.* Being a Zig Ziglar-style good finder will be helpful either way. To find people doing good things, you need to pay attention. If you pay attention, you'll also pick up on deviations from the plan. A major benefit of constructive confrontation is to never be very far from progress on the plan or lack thereof. Therefore, you'll always be in position to engage in congratulations, compliments, or in course corrections — which are the two sides of the same constructive confrontation coin.

WHO TO CELEBRATE

Anyone involved in the execution of the covenant should be recognized. Your priority is to recognize and reward the effort and successful behavior of people reporting directly to you. Beyond that you should encourage your team members to recognize and encourage the people helping them. Francine, the researcher wiz, for example, should make it a practice to thank the sales division executives helping her execute her covenant, especially Marvin, her helper from the sales division.

The best way to learn something is to teach it. Teach your team members to recognize and reward the people important to their success. Teach them also about appropriateness and proportion. You're not going to pick up the tab for Marvin to vacation in Aruba just because he helped Francine, particularly if Francine requests a trip for two. You should, however, routinely ask if Francine has appropriately thanked those helping her. Make that question part of your regular constructive confrontations.

If recognizing and rewarding people in the workplace doesn't occur naturally to you, what makes you think it occurs naturally to anybody else? By deliberately bringing up the issue of recognition and reward to your team members, you invite a discussion, perhaps some coaching on your part, about the best way to go about it. You can sense from the amount of attention being paid to celebration that it should become as much a part of your organizational culture as regular and meaningful communication. The fact is that celebration is an integral component of meaningful communication.

What to Celebrate

Displacement theory suggests that a negative thought or behavior can't occupy the same space and time in the universe as a positive thought or behavior. You want positive and productive behaviors to fill the spaces and times that negative or counterproductive behaviors would otherwise occupy. So anything positive is reason to celebrate. But if every effort and minor success is recognized equally, the value and benefit of recognition will be diluted.

What constitutes a positive thought or behavior is ultimately up to you because you know the type of thinking and behavior that will benefit your organization the most. "Good to see you're whittling away at that phone list," is a way of recognizing prospecting efforts with no reference to the success of the prospecting. Recognizing the basic but essential tasks requires only that you notice and acknowledge. A nonverbal thumbs up is a recognition and reinforcement, so long as your team member understands *why* you're offering the gesture.

- Finishing should be celebrated.
- Finishing on time should be celebrated more.
- Finishing on time and on target should be a regular hootenanny.
- Exceeding documented expectations is a behavior you want to see repeated often.

When targets are not met, that doesn't mean you stop encouraging. When a team member seeks out training and development of *habits, skills, attitudes,* and *activities* you want to acknowledge the appropriateness of taking that initiative. You don't want to encourage anyone to hide behind underdeveloped *habits, skills, attitudes,* and *activities.* Once again, your

209

judgment and experience with each team member over time comes into play. As important as it is for you to give feedback on a regular basis as part of your constructive confrontation, it's an unexpected blessing when you have team members who seek evaluation, advice, and guidance.

One of the *greatest* blessings a boss can experience is when a team member reports on a problem she or he came across — and took the initiative to solve — without bringing it back to the boss's feet. That doesn't necessarily mean the team member solved the problem alone. It is often best if he or she doesn't. In the preferred scenario, team members seek out whatever expertise or support that's necessary from their fellow team members or appropriate experts to address and resolve the issue. You've got to love it when that happens. Incentivize cooperative efforts by offering unannounced recognition and rewards when you catch people in great examples of cooperation and collaboration.

Celebrate the fact that your team members stay in priority with their focused efforts and energies. Getting bogged down in minutiae and the resulting organizational inertia can be debilitatingly expensive in terms of lost sales, time, resources, and cash. A classic qualifier of activities is, "Did that [fill in the blank with *pitch, call, letter, visit, etc.*] sell a [fill in the blank with *product, service plan, policy, etc.*]?" If not, where's the priority? What did all that hard work produce? What was it all for? Did we get things done or just look busy doing things? Getting things done is worthy of a celebration.

SCRIPTS: FIND GOOD THEY MIGHT NOT KNOW IS THERE

"Thank you for qualifying your responses and controlling your emotions," you tell an eager team member. It's important for people to act reasonably and keep things in perspective. Words can scarcely describe how much more pleasant appropriate behavior makes your job. Recognize these little things and let your team members know how much you appreciate good attitude.

"The clarity of your writing and speaking make the program much easier to follow," you compliment a particularly good communicator on your staff. "It's part of my job to help everybody on our team speak and communicate more effectively," you confess. "You're a good example of how competent communications translate into more sales."

"Your work is extremely accurate," you point out to another team member. "Accuracy removes the guesswork from what we're doing. I appreciate that." Telling people that you appreciate the accuracy they bring to their work, the quality of their communications, and any other positive attribute you can identify will increase and expand those characteristics. If you notice that a team member is particularly eager to help out other team members (not to the exclusion of his or her own work), recognize and encourage that as well.

Rather than keeping responsibilities on your shoulders for things other people can and should be doing, regularly and deliberately encourage those behaviors and attitudes in your team members. Many team leaders believe that, if they're not carrying their team on their backs, they're stealing their employer's money. Newsflash: carrying team members on your backs means you're *wasting* your employer's money. If you're not encouraging and supporting your team members' efforts to do *everything* within their ever-expanding personal and professional potential, you're overpaying them for the diminished service they are providing. Everything you do to compensate for what they're *not* doing takes you away from exercising constructive confrontation, especially ongoing encouragement, recognition, and celebration.

WHEN TO CELEBRATE

Constantly. As often as anything positive happens, you need to respond to it, even if it's the thumbs up maneuver you've been practicing. Appropriate and proportional celebration needs to take place at the beginning, during the middle, and at the end of each constructive confrontation cycle. Timing is important in order to make sure your team members receive the full effect of your recognition and encouragement. Calling

Harry on his cellular phone while he's in the middle of a face-to-face client presentation is not good timing, even if you're calling to say, "Keep it up, Harry. You're doing a great job."

The beginning of a face-to-face encounter with a team member, the beginning of an e-mail, or any form of contact for that matter is a great time to offer encouragement. "Let me begin by saying the numbers I saw on your report are encouraging." Chances are, with an opening like that, your team member will keep listening. "To wrap this up, let me repeat that the numbers I saw on your report are encouraging." Leaving your team member on an up note with a little positive reinforcement can save you and your team member all that time he or she would otherwise spend licking his or her wounds and kvetching to anyone who will listen about what a crap-head boss you are.

Team meetings or any other time a team member has an audience, like your rehearsed and premeditated impromptu encounter with Fred in the hallway among his peers, are great times to spread recognition and encouragement. Two primary purposes are served by public displays of appreciation (PDAs). First, a public accolade is sincere. To praise people in private and then roll your eyes as soon as the person leaves your office reeks of disingenuousness. To praise a person privately first, then follow it up with public praise is killer.

Second, public praise for behavior you want to see amplified and expanded in your organization sends an undeniable message to those who need some prodding to get on the bandwagon. There should never be any doubt as to the values and principles you espouse and, more importantly, *practice.* The most effective way for leaders to practice the principles they espouse is not to do everyone's work for them but to use their bully pulpit to recognize and reward adherence to those values and principles. Constant reinforcement of the underlying principles behind how business is conducted in your organization should never cease. Beginning, middle, end, new beginning, around the clock, 24/7, whatever — celebration cements the belief systems that form the rails on which your organization rolls.

Don't freak out just because it says previously that celebration should be constant and you're now being told it should also be intermittent. The same type of celebrations about the same achievements can become so redundant that people can set their watches by them. At that point they lose much of their effectiveness. Intermittent reinforcement doesn't mean that you should celebrate positive things some of the time and not others. It means that you should vary the intensity and scope of the celebration. Research indicates that intermittent reinforcement is more powerful than constant reinforcement. So mix it up some.

WHERE TO CELEBRATE

At parties, of course. When a party is appropriate, that is. Celebrations need to be both appropriate and proportionate. Just as *when to celebrate* is dependent on the most appropriate time to maximize the impact and positive potential in the celebration, *where to celebrate* needs to meet similar criteria. A thumbs up can be delivered right at the spot of good work being done. The importance and value of celebrating the right things can be diminished if the timing and location of the celebration don't resonate with the person(s) being recognized and rewarded. All of these factors should be considered when choosing the celebration location. Holding a company-wide picnic to announce that Frank turned in his forecasts on time is overkill. Announcing that Amy is national salesperson of the year for the fifth straight year with a box of Krispy Kreme donuts left next to the coffee maker with a post-it note is a missed opportunity.

The following is a true story about appropriateness and proportion from a world-famous family entertainment corporation: There was a department head who had his secretary run around the office a few days before Christmas handing out company Christmas cards to his staff members. The company and the executive shall remain nameless to spare him the embarrassment of such a profoundly insensitive gesture, the secretary the shame of complicity in the scheme, and a lawsuit for the authors. They were the same Christmas cards the staff was sending to their clients and vendors. In other words, there was a case of them in the office supply closet. Not only did the cards the department head's secretary was handing out *not* bear a personalized message, they weren't even addressed or signed. Blank envelope, blank card — perfect for recycling if you didn't want to make that long walk to the supply closet. There *was* one of the department head's business cards inside each one, which was the same business card every staff member had, except for the name and title.

The staff members were speechless. They just opened the cards and stared at each other in wide-eyed amazement. Not that Christmas is a celebration of anyone's progress or productivity, but the clumsy insensitivity made the boss look foolish and made the team members wonder if *any* compliment they received was sincere. If he had walked around, looked people in the eye, gave them a thumbs up, and said, "Merry Christmas," it would have been infinitely more appreciated.

Behaving in such an unspeakably impersonal manner was a missed opportunity for the executive. A note from a boss to a team member is very powerful and can pay huge motivational dividends, if it is handwritten. It's even more powerful if it refers specifically to items and issues related to the team member's emotional purpose. If a note to Harry said, "Hope you and Brenda and the kids are enjoying the holidays," it would remind Harry that you paid attention and remembered what he's working for.

Symbols of emotional purpose are more powerful yet. If one of your team members described part of his or her emotional purpose is to own a 60-foot sailboat in the Caribbean, cutting a picture of a big sailboat out of a magazine and including it in the note is a killer move. The pièce de résistance would be to get your hands on a sailboat model and award that to your team member to keep in his or her office. These tributes to emotional purpose, no matter how small or inexpensive, keep your connection to that person hot. Having symbols of emotional purpose in an office or cubicle make the office or the cubicle a place of celebration.

The place you choose for celebration says a lot about you as a leader.

If nothing else, it tells your team members that you care enough to think about what's most appropriate and significant for them. Even better is the boss who facilitates a team discussion on appropriate celebration. Celebration is no more left to chance than a solid commitment, written covenant, and consistent confrontation.

Talking about and planning celebrations is not a frivolous waste of time. It helps keep the ongoing efforts of team members in perspective, not only for their own ability to successfully fulfill the circle of confrontation, but also how each team member's circle of confrontation plays out in the context of the organization's ongoing success. Like conversations around commitment and confrontation, the what, when, and where of celebration is worthy of serious consideration.

WHY TO CELEBRATE

Celebrations are a time of coming together, from you and an individual team member to an organization-wide shindig. Depending on the size, location, and timing of the celebration, you can give others above you on the organizational food chain a chance to rub elbows with your team members and vice versa. You can give upper management a chance to participate in your success by including them in your celebrations. You can give them credit for supporting your success, whether or not they deserve it. An opportunity is an opportunity.

Celebrations are also opportunities to recognize people outside of your immediate sphere of influence. Francine, for example, can include Marvin in the festivities, in addition to others from his division. Recognizing efforts and accomplishments across departmental or divisional boundaries warms any CEO's heart. If you're throwing an interdisciplinary soiree, don't miss the opportunity to invite the brass. At the very least, make them aware of what's going on. Invite your corporate media to make even more noise about it.

GIVE THANKS FOR SURRENDER

Surrendering to the system does not mean becoming a lemming. It means buying into the principles, practices, purpose, and protocol of the organization that pays you. If you're not on board with those things, revisit the stealing money thing. Individual goals and ambitions are important. That's why they're intentionally and thoroughly covered in the conversation about emotional purpose leading to the covenant. It's critical that your team members' emotional purposes resonate with the overreaching agenda of the organization. How else will you be assured they will be acting in the best interests of the organization when nobody's looking?

It's no small deal for someone to truly surrender to the system. When someone throws in with your organizational agenda and works with the program, rather than butting up against it, recognize them for the cooperative attitude. Let them know their attitude is appreciated. Towing the company line is a good thing if you're dedicated to the goals, objectives, and overriding principles of the organization that pays you. If you're not dedicated to the goals, objectives, and overriding principles of the organization that pays you, we're back to that stealing money thing . . . again.

SCRIPTS: GIVING CREDIT TO THEM

There are few motivational maneuvers more powerful than giving credit where credit is due. There is no substitute for giving credit and attribution where they've been earned. Don't single out people if the credit truly belongs to the team as a whole. Don't give credit to the team as a whole if the credit belongs to one person alone. The smart and savvy leader gives credit to the team and specific individuals who "represent the spirit and dedication of the whole team." Individual ego versus the group conscience is a delicate tight rope. It's better to include more rather than too few when passing out the accolades. Most important, make sure you're being specific about what the accolades are for.

"Your contribution to the heart and soul of this project has helped me in a number of ways," you tell your loyal team member. "For one thing,

I'm free to confront people and problems that threaten the objectives we've identified. Any autonomous, self-directed contribution you make has a multiplier effect."

"Some covenants have been troublesome, but yours has been delightful and trouble free," you gush to an exuberant team member. "I love it when that happens."

"Your reliability has saved me untold anxiety," you tell another. "I look forward to attacking more obstacles and threats to our organization with you, using constructive confrontation."

"*You* are mostly responsible for us working so well together with this system. It takes follow through and that's been you to a 'T'."

"We got off to a rocky start because the process was unfamiliar to both of us. Since then you've adapted quickly and made this system your own."

"You've helped me stay on course. I'm paid to be the leader here. But I don't mind telling you that you've been the one setting the direction for the most part." (Notice the clever use of "but" followed by a *positive* stroke?)

"You've stayed on task. That's helped keep *me* on task."

"I don't know if you've noticed, but the more we work this constructive confrontation business, the sharper your *habits, skills, attitudes,* and *activities* become."

"You're willing to do the uncomfortable things that less successful people refuse to do. It's no wonder you're making this kind of progress."

The *third-party compliment* made famous by Danny Cox in his book *Leadership When the Heat's On* (New York: McGraw-Hill, 2002) comes into play often with constructive confrontation. "I told [fill in the blank with anyone important and influential in your team member's career] about the success you're having and she [or he] wants to hear more about your progress. Please add them to your progress report distribution." People become immensely more cooperative and collaborative when they believe other people care and are paying attention. You're the one who can stir up attention for your team members and let them know you've done it.

217

HOW TO CELEBRATE

Tremendous guidance in the field of employee recognition can be found in a body of work by Bob Nelson, Ph.D. His flagship document is a book titled *1001 Ways to Reward Employees* (New York: Workman Publishing, 1994). Dr. Nelson sites examples by the thousand of different ways various companies effectively reward their employees. As a field of endeavor, employee recognition is championed by the National Association for Employee Recognition. They can be visited and studied at www.recognition.org.

The overriding principle Dr. Nelson operates from is the need for a culture of recognition in all work environments. He's not singing "Kumby-ya," either. He links employee recognition to motivation, productivity, and performance. Acknowledging that recognition is a multitiered issue, he even offers on-line assessments to create a baseline for developing and sustaining a culture of recognition. Check him out at www.nelson-motivation.com. It's great stuff and can help you make important decisions about the most appropriate acts of recognition and reward. "But where," you ask ever so brilliantly, "does the criterion for recognition and rewards come from in the first place?" That's why you bought *this* book.

CELEBRATION MUST BE SPECIFIC

Returning to Ken Blanchard's Shamu example, there is more to be learned from the killer whale than building trust and diminishing a sense of threat every day before training begins. When Shamu, or anyone else, is rewarded for positive and productive behavior, the recognition must be recognizable to the whale. The person being recognized must understand *why* he or she is receiving the attention. Otherwise, the recognition is wasted for the most part. The specificity comes from all the components in the circle of constructive confrontation.

It might feel warm and fuzzy to thank team members for being all-around nice folks and great employees. Never let it be said that you were discouraged from doing so by reading this book. What this book strongly *encourages* you to do is to be specific about what a team member is being recognized for. The point of recognition and celebration is not to make your team members feel good about you. The point of recognition and celebration is to make your team members feel good about themselves and what they accomplish.

Properly executed, constructive confrontation removes all ambiguity about *who, what, when, where, why,* and *how.* Expectations are never left to chance or assumption. With experts like Dr. Nelson, the focus is on the need and benefits of recognition, with lots of specific suggestions. The focus here is more on the *concept* of celebration as it relates to the constructive confrontation process.

Dr. Nelson might not mention close-action rewards, which are carrots you can hang out to encourage swift resolution of unexpected problems. Problems that hadn't surfaced at the time you constructed the covenant can be written into a revision of the covenant or dispatched with a short-term and narrowly defined incentive program associated specifically with the immediate problem. The quicker the problem can be resolved, the lower the threat to, or need to alter, the covenant. Gift certificates are effective rewards for short-term challenges and don't call for company time to be spent in celebration. Buying dinner for team members and their significant others at a nice restaurant puts the celebrating on *their* time, while preserving the powerful impact of your appreciation. You don't even need to be there. Perhaps it's better that you're not.

Think about saying "Thank you" in a number of different ways, as Dr. Nelson suggests. But thank you for what? Remember the "you're a good person" stuff won't be very meaningful in terms of modifying behavior until the recognition and rewards are tied to specific *habits, skills, attitudes,* and *activities* that you want to improve and increase. The exact nature and substance of the celebration shouldn't be defined in the original covenant lest it becomes an expectation and your team members start acting like Pavlov's dog every time you ring the bell. The element of surprise heightens the sense of reward. Use celebration wisely and strategically.

CHAPTER 9 SUMMARY

Chapter 9 lists appropriate ways to monitor and encourage the critical components of achievement, no matter how small. Key elements of using celebration as a strategic component of the constructive confrontation process include the following:

- Avoid the common mistake made in business of taking small accomplishments for granted. Organizations have become accustomed to celebrating only extraordinary achievements. The circle of confrontation process involves celebrating the devotion to daily effort as quantified in the covenant.

- When loyalty and adherence to the process are sufficiently encouraged, the major results will happen. If the deliberate, daily activities required to achieve larger results are not encouraged and dwindle as a result, the larger outcomes will be jeopardized and probably not be realized, except by coincidence.

- When targets are not hit and goals are not reached, the leader and the team member suffer, although not necessarily in that order. Constructive confrontation is a well-engineered process that breaks down what needs to be done, how it needs to be done, and how often it needs to be done in order to produce higher-profile results. With each step comes a prescribed level of recognition.

- Just as success over time builds confidence, appropriate recognition for every level of effort builds goodwill and the desire to meet and exceed expectations the next time around. Anticipating that good effort will be recognized, even on a small scale, is strong motivation. Anticipating that good effort will go unrecognized breeds cynicism.

- Make celebrations intermittent, somewhat unsuspected, and as much of a surprise as possible. Recognition shouldn't come like clockwork. Rewards and encouragement must resonate with the receivers to maximize effectiveness. Your timing should be premeditated and strategic. In other words, recognition and reward are your most powerful motivational tools. Make them count.

Celebration can't be an afterthought. Building the powerful, behavior-modifying potential of celebration into your constructive confrontation plans from the beginning makes perfect sense. After all, you want your team members to develop increasingly proficient *habits, skills, attitudes,* and *activities.* In order to accomplish that, they must receive constant feedback on their performance and experience a celebration of the things they do right, even the smallest tasks. In Chapter 10 you'll learn more about dealing with the grand-slam home runs.

Plan for the Peaks

Like Chapter 9, this chapter isn't about listing all of the possible types of celebrations you can plan. We leave that type of detail to experts like Dr. Nelson or the National Association for Employee Recognition. This chapter is more about the psychological issues underpinning the concept of celebration. Even though celebration of the small, incremental tasks that lead to the accomplishments of large initiatives was emphasized in Chapter 9, there's more to the celebration story. An enormous accomplishment, when broken down, is an aggregation of smaller efforts, less impressive on face value. Consider the mountains.

Mountains are made from rock, specifically a lot of rocks. With the exception of a few isolated pockets of igneous (formerly molten) rocks, the Canadian Rockies are composed exclusively of layered sedimentary rocks like limestone, dolomite, sandstone, and shale, among others. Rock is made from smaller elements. Without the rocks and the particles that comprise them there would be no Canadian Rockies, no Colorado Rockies, and no Sierra Nevada. Skiing would be limited to volcanic aftermath like the cascades of California, Oregon, and Washington State.

Celebration, as it relates to constructive confrontation is a matter of perspective. The lure of the mountaintop is important to your motivation scheme. Yet if all you look at is the mountain peak, you probably won't understand or appreciate the particles that make it up. This is a lesson you need to teach your team members: The mountaintops are only mountaintops because a lot of smaller mountain parts are piled up underneath them.

By the same token, the Grand Canyon is only a spectacular hole in the ground because of the enormous amount of rock particles that have been washed away. Whether you stand and gaze up at the mountain peaks in wonder or on the rim of the Grand Canyon looking down, what impresses you is the *difference* between where you are standing and the top of the mountain or bottom of the canyon. It's about what's there or not there. The most impressive accomplishments in organizational life are measured in the *difference* between where you are now and where you finish.

Why is running a 100-yard dash considered less of an accomplishment than running a 26-mile marathon? A finish line is a finish line, right? A starting line is a starting line, right? Right and right. One accomplishment feels different from the other accomplishment not because of where they begin or end. The experiences differ because of the differing distances between where they begin and where they end.

DOUBLE VISION

Acknowledgment and encouragement of small, incremental accomplishments could be called micro-celebrations. Rewards and recognition for the really big stuff could be called macrocelebrations. Large or small, constructive confrontation celebrations are always a function of the organizational agenda. As you're now aware, constructive confrontation begins with conversations and commitments based on personal and professional emotional purposes and organizational needs. The smaller, incremental tasks are broken out of the grand scheme.

The double vision occurs when you keep one eye on the grand scheme, the big picture, the ultimate goal, and so on and the other eye on the immediate task necessary to reach the final destination. The incentive to focus on and accomplish the less spectacular small stuff is the promise of a big payoff. The challenge is to keep the big payoff in mind while not forgetting the importance of the less spectacular small stuff along the way. True success requires attention to both, which is another reason why constructive confrontation deliberately deals with specific long-range goals and equally specific intermediate tasks.

At the beginning of every football season in the United States, coaches in locker rooms in every NFL city remind their players and staffs that their goal is not merely getting to the Super Bowl. Their goal is to *win* the Super Bowl. Everything required to reach that goal must be backed out of the overall achievement. The same is true of becoming a world champion ice skater or tennis player. Winning the Olympic Gold or a world championship requires seemingly endless practice, drilling, and attention to subtleties in technique and conditioning . . . all of that and enormous natural athletic ability, of course.

Climbers who assault Mount Everest have double vision. They begin with the summit in mind. However, they plan and prepare diligently for every detail of the journey. If details of the organizational effort are planned, prepared for, monitored, and celebrated as they occur, arriving at the summit won't be a surprise. Although planning and preparation reduce the element of surprise, they enhance the sense of accomplishment and make reaching the milestone that much more gratifying. Anyone who has reached an elusive or difficult-to-achieve goal knows that the sense of accomplishment is based less on the pinnacle itself than on everything required to reach it.

A natural and expected component of every macrocelebration is recognition of the overriding achievement. Recognition that the overriding achievement was made possible only by the execution of daily, weekly, monthly, and quarterly tasks and initiatives reinforces the holistic concept of complete effort. Larger celebrations mark the high-water points that future covenants will be based upon. This is why they are designed into the circle of confrontation process. The more visible the achievement, the easier it is to hold up as an example of highly regarded behavior and accomplishment. The peaks in performance serve a good purpose as building blocks for future accomplishment.

INDIVIDUAL VERSUS GROUP CELEBRATION

One of the primary differences between microcelebrations and macrocelebrations is individual effort versus group effort. Covenants are difficult to forge and enforce with teams because responsibility will naturally shift and flex within the group and between team members. The inherent variabilities in human nature are too unpredictable to make team accountability practical. True accountability must be monitored and enforced from individual to individual. That's why covenants are individual agreements.

However, larger organizational accomplishments are team efforts. The team efforts, being an aggregate of individually accountable efforts, constitute the peaks. Microcelebrations, from a thumbs up to dinner and a movie on the company to a juicy bonus, are rewards that recognize individual effort and accomplishment. Company- or department-wide parties, picnics, and even group trips recognize the collective efforts of everybody involved in major initiatives.

Either way, celebrations must promote the ongoing organizational agenda. There are varying points of view as to whether individual effort should be rewarded more than collective effort. Although there are cases to be made on either side of the issue, it's ultimately your call. The decisions you make should reflect the best way for you to promote the ongoing organizational agenda.

POLISH THE STONE, DIM THE DIAMOND

Lowering the bar so more people can win doesn't advance the organizational agenda, unless the organizational agenda is to make everybody feel warm and fuzzy. Unfortunately, that's becoming an increasingly popular approach to education. The phrase "Polish the Stone, Dim the Diamond" came from a report on education. One of the quantifiable results of lowered expectations in the classroom is less learning. The mantra of education officials more concerned with self-esteem than functional knowledge seems to be that lowering the bar lowers the need for us, and thereby the students, to perform. We all wiggle off the hook together.

The result of this reasoning in the workplace is similar to the result in the school system. Individual accomplishment is discouraged when individual accomplishment is minimized so as not to offend the less accomplished. This doesn't necessarily make the less accomplished feel better. It simply makes them feel less convicted by the comparison. If warm and fuzzy feelings are what you're after, (1) don't beat anybody up emotionally, and (2) don't give anyone an excuse to beat themselves up emotionally.

At the end of the day, individuals, as well as the organization as a whole, are less capable, less skilled, and less eager to tackle the tasks required to achieve great things. All of this is okay if you're not concerned with accomplishing great things. As always, your ultimate goals and objectives are your decision, or they're imposed on you by those higher on the organizational food chain.

In the best of all possible worlds, you can achieve resonance between both. Where attaining organizational excellence runs afoul of individual feelings of self-worth, you need to step up to the leadership plate and manage the variances or cash in on the excellence. It's your job as a leader to get the self-esteem issues dealt with effectively and out of the way. In many cases, that can simply mean removing self-esteem issues from the equation and setting and enforcing appropriate and consistent boundaries about what range of emotional baggage will be tolerated at work and what won't. Constructive confrontation will help do that.

POLISH BOTH DIAMOND AND STONE

All leaders have a variety of talent, enthusiasm, and commitment levels to deal with. Most will tell you they want to get the best out of everyone. Getting the best out of everyone is a far cry from lowering expectations and performance demands to a level anyone and everyone can attain. At the extreme low end of talent and ability, your organization — hope-fully — won't employ people completely incapable of contributing any-thing. In reality, you have something to work with in everyone reporting to you.

The constructive confrontation process allows you to tailor your ex-pectations to a variety of abilities by individualizing *habits, skills, attitudes,* and *activities*. Your expert application of the constructive confrontation process establishes an environment in which every individual in your sphere of influence can achieve all that she or he is capable of. You es-sentially polish your diamonds *and* your stones.

There are those who will say, "Polish the diamonds and screw the stones." Such put-all-your-eggs-in-one-basket thinkers fail to acknowl-edge that although 20 percent of the work is done by 80 percent of your people, that's 20 percent productivity you don't want to do without. Ob-viously, you want to be particularly vigilant to support and encourage the 20 percent who produce 80 percent of your results, which can be an adventure all its own.

The 20 percent that produce 80 percent of your results are often the most high-strung racehorses in your stable. They require special hand-ling and an extra measure of patience and tolerance. It's handling these folks that makes constructive confrontation, with all its built-in encour-agement and accountability, so valuable. Ergo, the need for effective in-dividual reward and recognition systems is paramount in organizational success, regardless of the igneous or crystalline origins of your team members.

ENCOURAGE COLLABORATION

Despite the disparity in talent levels you have to deal with, it's always in your interest to invoke synergy as much and as often as possible. Opti-mists say, "No one of us is as smart as all of us." Pessimists say, "No one of us is as dumb as all of us." Both are true depending upon which lens you're peering through. Team efforts can bring out the best in everybody involved and produce results that are greater than the sum of their parts. Team efforts, improperly led, can lead to groupthink and groupstink.

The difference is determined by whether your leadership is coaxing out the best in human nature or the worst. Everything you do to lead and inspire the group efforts of your team members should be intentionally designed to motivate the most confident and enlightened thinking and behavior of which your people are capable. Whenever possible, set up a *combination* of individual and team rewards that guide and motivate everyone toward a common objective that contributes to the organizational agenda.

Every time you construct a covenant, consider the overarching organizational goals and objectives. Every time you compose individual rewards and recognition, bear in mind what will most encourage each individual to cooperate and collaborate with the rest of the team. This way you'll encourage and maximize individual energy, *and* you're encouraging and maximizing team synergy.

GOLD SHIPS/TIN SHIPS

Talk to people who *get it* and turn them loose to move as fast and as far as they can. At the same time, encourage the less enlightened to follow in the vapor trail of the more enlightened. With everyone's efforts moving in the same direction, no matter how fast one individual is moving versus another, you can expect better results. Instead of focusing exclusively on guiding your ships with cargos of gold, contrive a strategy to get your entire fleet to the proper destination, even if most ships carry tin.

Planning for the peaks can involve making a big deal out of navigating your entire fleet to the proper port. Some will arrive with precious cargo, and some will arrive with less than precious cargo. The best you can hope for and work toward is for all to arrive with the most valuable cargo they're capable of carrying. *That's* making the most out of what you have to work with.

Obviously, your prime energies should be invested in those who will generate a prime return. But abandoning the group effort because it's easier to focus all of your energy on the top producers is an automatic loss of that 20 percent. Some leaders find those eccentric thoroughbreds too much to handle, so they focus all of their attention on the lower-producing 80 percent, which puts the 80 percent of the results the race-horses can account for in jeopardy. The most effective leaders devise ways to accommodate both.

All organizational leaders face this dilemma: On a scale of one through ten, there are very few eights, nines, and tens. Sad, but true. Great leaders know that a secret to growth and expansion of organizational productivity comes from guiding fives to become sevens, sixes to become eights, and so on. The eights, nines, and tens don't usually have that much headroom to grow before you've burned them out. Knowing how much time, energy, and skill it requires for leaders to engender growth and development of anyone on their teams, why would you hire a one, two, three, four, or a five? True growth calls for appropriate attention to everyone.

If the department's reward for making or exceeding plans is to take a fancy trip to a resort destination, everybody goes. If the plan is not met, nobody goes. Climbing to the summit involves everybody. Whether in a support capacity or blazing the trail, everyone's efforts must be encouraged and rewarded. Individual expectations and rewards are dealt with between you and the team members with whom you have covenants. Group effort needs to involve everyone. Everybody sinks or swims together. If the team succeeds together, they celebrate together. The biggest celebrations, like the peak performances, should be team experiences.

EFFORT AND RESULTS

Good effort should be congratulated. Results must be rewarded. If you hand out the same accolades and prizes for effort that you hand out for results, you'll soon have all of the former and none of the latter. Make sure that all else is equal so effort is a wash. If people are not putting forth adequate effort to get anything done, revisit your commitment and covenant. It might be that you've miscast them, asked them to do something of which they're not capable, or they're flat out thumbing their nose at you. A boss who doesn't care enough to confront consistently and constructively can form an unholy alliance with team members who care even less. Constructive confrontation is a terrific system within which you can quickly diagnose and correct misalignment and miscasting. Employees that refuse to buy in, no matter what you do, might simply call for a good old-fashioned termination.

Sometimes certain team members can produce high results without much effort. That's great, as long as they don't corrupt those around them. Ridding an organization of cancer is extremely difficult if the cancer is talented and producing. If a talented high producer is negatively impacting the performance of others, chances are that the high producer's megaproductivity does not make up for the lost productivity he or she causes. That's when it's time to part ways. Some very high producers are also extremely talented manipulators, dare it be said—liars. Sticking religiously to the components of constructive confrontation give even marginally talented managers an agenda and structure with which to address the gamesmanship and manipulative abilities of the organizational infections. Rewarding results must be done with the complete picture in mind.

You have just cause to expect a similar amount of effort across the board from your team if you've even-handedly applied the principles of constructive confrontation. The results will vary because the natural talent and ability level of different individuals will vary. Making their best effort is what your people are essentially paid for. If they're properly cast and equipped, their best efforts should produce positive results. Varying amounts of individual reward and compensation should be based on results achieved minus liabilities encountered.

Straight commission is the purest form of fair compensation. Wouldn't it be great if the concept of straight commission could be applied across the board for every position in your organization? Compensation directly proportionate to contribution—what a concept. Unfortunately, that would require an incredible, almost unimaginable, amount of consistent leadership talent to quantify everybody's performance and put a price tag on it. Instead, what most organizations do is set a range of compensation based on what people are supposed to be doing and how enthusiastically they ostensibly do it. These assumptions are based on what a function is supposed to be worth to an organization's bottom line.

You need to do the best you can to champion what your people earn within the parameters of your organization's policies and procedures. Guided by the principle of encouraging the best from everyone, compensation needs to be consistent with contribution. Recognition on the other hand, is much more available to dispense. Wisdom and prudence dictate that you don't waste the opportunities for behavior modification that recognition provides. If you recognize Person A in the same way you recognize Person B for radically different performances, one of them is going to feel cheated. Unfortunately, the most deserving of the two will feel the sting of injustice.

SYMBOLISM IS YOUR FRIEND

Valid execution of the covenant calls for recognition if the covenant represents something meaningful to the individual and to the organization. The objective or hoped-for outcome of the covenant must symbolize something, like the model of the sailboat or picture of the fancy home mentioned in Chapter 9. What are the symbols of success in your organization? Market share? Profits to brag about in the annual report? Regional or global expansion? The Malcolm Baldrich Award?

The celebration, whether for the whole team or an individual accomplishment, for reaching the peak or one step along the way, must symbolize the nature of the quest. If your organization's goal is to produce a spacecraft capable of interplanetary passenger travel, images of that, perhaps even an enormous model of the ship, should be in front of people's noses everywhere they turn.

Whether you're staging a kick-off meeting for a new initiative or a victory celebration, releasing accolades about progress or success on a project to the organizational or public media (newspapers, magazines, web sites, etc.), the specific nature and *who, what, when, where, why,* and *how* details of the objective or initiative should be clearly articulated along with the *habits, skills, attitudes,* and *activities* that have become worthy of celebration. An important part of celebration is to brand the constructive confrontation process. Each time the cycle of constructive confrontation leads to both a tangible and symbolic victory, it becomes easier to sell the next time out.

Celebration is a time of special recognition and rewards and is usually self-explanatory. However, it never hurts to help people connect the dots. Making sure the celebration is appropriate in scale and proportion to what's been accomplished is important, just like engineering the symbolism to psychologically represent the nature of the effort. These are some of the most fundamental components of constructive confrontation: ensuring that people understand exactly what's expected of them so they can fully and completely comprehend the feedback they receive.

CHAPTER 10 SUMMARY

It's important for your team members to make the distinction between what is the aggregate effort of the team — the effort that reaches the peaks — and the individual *skills, habits, attitudes,* and *activities* that, taken together with everyone else's *skills, habits, attitudes,* and *activities,* make up the mountain. This means tying celebration of the peaks to collaborative performance that's distinctly different in scope and detail from individual effort. Celebrating the overall victory might mean a lot more noise, pops, bangs, whistles, and champagne. There might be a lot of effort on your part to keep the team's collective mind around the ultimate goal. But everything continues to be tempered with individual effort. Through the aggressive use of constructive confrontation, all roads lead to the organizational objectives and the biggest possible payoff for everyone involved.

Chapter 10 is the celebration planning guide that describes the nature and point of celebrations that are appropriate and best suited to promote the ongoing organizational agenda. Some of the major issues involved with planning for the peaks include the following:

- Help your team understand how the tallest mountain peaks are made up of the smallest rock particles. Where enough rocks are assembled in masterful plan, enormous mountains rise above the plains and valleys. If your organization is in a valley, or even on a flat plain, the peaks can appear impossible to reach. Constructive confrontation will break down the mountains into their component parts and make building them seem much less daunting.

- At the beginning of every football season, coaches in locker rooms in every NFL city remind their players and staffs that their goal is not getting to the Super Bowl. Their goal is to *win* the Super Bowl. Everything required to reach that goal can be backed out of the overall achievement. The same is true of the intricate conditioning and endless practice required to become a champion tennis player of figure skater. The little things make up the great things, as long as you plan on the big things. Celebrate the little things *and* the big things.

- Climbers who assault Mount Everest begin with the summit in mind. However, they plan and prepare diligently for every detail of the journey. If details of the organizational effort are planned, prepared for, monitored, and celebrated as they occur, arriving at the summit won't be a surprise. Neither will the anticipated problems and difficulties along the way. Although planning and preparation reduce the element of surprise, they enhance the sense of accomplishment and make reaching the milestone that much more gratifying.

- A natural and expected component of every major celebration is recognition of the overriding achievement. Recognition that the overriding achievement was made possible only by the execution of daily, weekly, monthly, and quarterly tasks and initiatives reinforces the holistic concept of complete effort. Celebrating the team's arrival at the mountaintop is big stuff. Celebrating the individual efforts required to get there should be an equally powerful, if not more subdued, experience.

- Larger celebrations mark the high-water points that future covenants will be based upon. This is why they are designed into the circle of confrontation process. The more visible the achievement, the easier it is to hold up as an example of highly regarded behavior and accomplishment. The peaks in performance serve a good purpose as building blocks for future accomplishment.

- The more the celebrations symbolize the true nature of what has been accomplished, the more they set the stage for future buy-in. Good coordination and alignment between the language and symbols of the project or initiative and the substance of the project or initiative serve to brand the whole concept of constructive confrontation. The organizational agenda and the way it's operationalized become etched into your team members' consciousness.

Celebrating the right things and planning for the peaks involve understanding the difference between individual and collaborative team effort. They work together but should never be confused or commingled. As long as individual responsibility remains individual responsibility, the collective interests of the team and the organization as a whole will be served. It all starts with a strong understanding and appreciation of the role of celebration when the initial commitment conversations are taking place. Just as the *habits, skills, attitudes,* and *activities* of your team members must resonate with the organizational agenda and the individual's emotional purpose, the recognition and rewards for their efforts and accomplishments must resonate with who these people are. That's where the conversation about celebration goes next.

Rewards that Resonate

Chapters 10 and 11 have contained references to rewards that resonate. The issue of resonant rewards should seem pretty obvious when it comes to making rewards meaningful. What good is celebrating anything, large *or* small, if the celebration holds no appeal to the celebrant? Recognition becomes a mockery if it doesn't ring genuine or if it ignores the essential nature of the person of accomplishment.

You'll find a culture of celebration behind virtually any successful and positive organization. No culture can be sustained if its premise is false. To be an organization that thrives on celebration — more specifically, the accomplishments that call for celebration — the style and content of recognition and reward must be aligned with the emotional purposes of the people you rely on to get the work done.

The underlying agenda of celebration in the circle of confrontation is to build motivation for the next phase of the operation. The next phase of the operation is simply whatever is in the organization's best interest to do next. Anything worth doing is worth being motivated for. If you look at the end of a circle of confrontation, you're also looking at the beginning of the next. If you're celebrating the successful completion of a small task, you're foreshadowing the successful completion of the next one. The celebration that takes place at the successful completion of a major initiative is the launch platform for what follows.

CELEBRATION AND EMOTIONAL PURPOSE

To identify the most appropriate style and content of recognition and reward, revisit your original commitment conversations about emotional purpose. Make it a loosely scripted part of your early conversations to ask about what motivates your team member the most. Then make a note of it and pay attention over time to see if what your team member told you is consistent with his or her behavior. "What have been some of the greatest victories in your life?" is a good question; the answer will tell you a great deal about how your team member sees him- or herself in the world and where and how he or she feels the most competent, confident, and competitive.

"Tell me about the best prizes you've ever won," is another purposefully leading question. Write down the answers. This isn't just idle chat. Remember that you need this data for future reference. Note that the question didn't ask, "What are the biggest prizes you've ever won?" The biggest prizes might not be those that resonated most. Asking about "the best" invites a description of those rewards and types of recognition that appeal to your team member's core motivations and emotional purposes.

Harry's lifestyle with Brenda is an issue for him. He wants to provide his wife with the type of home she wants, in a neighborhood of their choosing, and so on. It's family stuff for Harry. If you need to choose rewards for Harry, time off with the fam will be a good choice. A gift certificate to a home-decorating or home appliance center won't be bad. If Harry hits an incredible home run, worthy of a megaperk, how about paying his kids' private school tuition for a year? Maybe you could spend the same amount on that minivan that Brenda has had her eye on, the one with the DVD player in the back for the Sponge Bob movies?

In other words, reward Harry in a way that resonates with his emotional purpose for working: providing for his family. As you do so, watch to see if the rewards are working, even in small ways. Does he light up to receive them or does he nod, mumble some sort of gratuitous gratitude, and then never use the gift certificate? If your rewards and style of recognition aren't resonating with your team members, you need course correction in understanding their emotional purposes, or aligning rewards and recognition with their emotional purposes, or both. In either case, you need to go back to that part of your conversations and get it straight. As long as you're out of alignment or miscalibrated on the rewards and recognition thing, you're missing enormous opportunities to create buy-in, develop loyalty, and build enthusiasm for your organizational agenda.

If someone's emotional purpose for working is to receive public recognition, there are ways to scratch that itch. Issue news releases to the local media to extol his or her accomplishments, promotions, and so on. Depending on the size and complexity of your organization, you might need the cooperation of the public relations department for that. You have numerous media opportunities closer to home to exploit. You can use department bulletin boards, intranet sites, newsletters, announcements, and presentations at staff and sales meetings.

Francine likes to conduct research. She's a curious person by nature. Her emotional purpose is to exercise that curiosity. A resonant reward or way to recognize Francine might be to award her a sabbatical to conduct research outside the company or attend a long seminar on organizational growth opportunities. Pay for seminars and educational opportunities for her to become even more effective eyes for the organization as you try to navigate your way through the fog and murky waters of the future. Going back to school is some people's lifelong ambition, but it takes time and money. Perhaps that's where you can help and motivate at the same time.

Many people dream of travel. But they can't seem to pull the trigger, pick up the phone, and call a travel agent. You can pull the trigger for them by prepaying a trip, anything from a weekend at the Kampground of America (KOA) to a week at a casino anywhere in the world, depending on what's appropriate. Even if everyone in the department is going on the same trip because the travel is a reward for a group effort, the amount of spending money can vary as well as the level of accommodations, or the way the bar is stocked; use your imagination. Make sure you send a camera with them if they don't have their own. You want pictures of the trip around the office as constant reminders of the reward and recognition you provided.

INDIVIDUALIZE

The trap many leaders fall into is assuming that their team members will respond to the same emotional purpose triggers that they do. Your team members' emotional purposes might differ from yours a great deal. That's normal and even advantageous. To recognize the differences between you and your team members illustrates how many opportunities you have to use their strengths where you are not so strong.

Don't settle for the strictly money approach just because that's what you're in it for, *if* that's what you're in it for. Money might seem like its own reward, but unless people stuff their mattresses with it, bury it in the backyard, or hoard it in the bank, they'll likely buy something with it. That something is your clue to their emotional purpose, a purpose they might not realize they have. If financial security is the motivation, there are ways to help encourage that. You can reward your team member with estate planning services or seminars and learning materials on financial security.

By not automatically defaulting to monetary rewards as the best choice of reward or team member recognition, you're not necessarily becoming Ebenezer Scrooge. You are becoming a more enlightened motivator, learning to get more mileage for whatever it costs your organization than mere dollars, pounds, franks, yen, rubles, or deutschmarks. There is a psychological agenda around money that you need to be aware of. If people use money that you give them to pay bills, they might inadvertently diminish much, if not all, of the motivational power of the reward. They might feel some relief from the bills that get paid, but they won't feel the uplift from the home improvement, the sabbatical, the trip, the tuition, or whatever else you might scheme to provide.

It might become a conspiracy between you and your team member, if that's what will motivate him or her the most. "Honey, they forced me to accept the big-screen television," Harry explains when the Electronic Express truck shows up at his house and Brenda demands an explanation. "It was that or a golf weekend for me and the sales team at Hilton Head . . . no spouses." Suddenly, Brenda is thinking how good *Law and Order, Desperate Housewives,* or *Sex in the City* reruns will look on a 60-inch plasma screen. Of course, where Harry is concerned, adding a few days to the end of his family vacation might be a huge morale booster. A gift certificate to Toys-R-Us could work well, too. The gift certificate is taxable. The added vacation is not. Just something to think about.

You might not know why a team member won't indulge him- or herself with certain things that you can indulge him or her with. Their hesitation might be psychological. They might not believe they are worthy of the indulgence. When you become the vessel to grant the indulgence, he or she is relieved of the burden to indulge self. Not only will he or she get to have something or do something he or she wouldn't spend the money to do for him- or herself, he or she will enjoy it more with you picking up the tab. For antiquers or crafters, a trip to Savannah or Vermont. For football fanatics, playoff tickets in the city of their choice. Resonance, resonance, resonance.

Francine might want to spruce up her wardrobe, but she won't prioritize her budget to accommodate the pipe dream. You learn these things by talking to your people and asking deliberate questions. A fat gift certificate to St. John's or Anne Klein will do much more than the $2,500 in cash — especially if Francine's husband wants to spend her bonus on a new bass boat motor. Bass boat motor or St. John's knits? St. John's knits or a bass boat motor? If you send Francine home with $2,500 in cash, chances of her psychologically connecting the reward with her accomplishment are diminishing by the moment. If the reward for her accomplishment winds up being a bass boat motor, you just punted your motivational opportunity away.

Rewards and recognition are an opportunity for you to become your team member's advocate and help him or her promote a personal agenda.

There's nothing wrong with that. You're not the judge of what motivates them the most or how appropriate (within reason) their desires are. Your job is to reward and recognize accomplishment that begets more accomplishment. To do that, the rewards and recognition must resonate with your team members' hearts' desires. You're not nearly as concerned with your team member's spouse's or mother's emotional purpose as you are concerned with your team member's emotional purpose — unless, of course, your team member's spouse or mother is coming in to do his or her work for her.

Speaking of Scrooge, Christmas bonuses (when there were such things) also exacerbated this singular approach to recognition and reward. Staying with money as the end-all motivator is merely transferring the problem elsewhere. But rewarding people at holiday time misses the point. Is it a holiday because of some effort exerted on your team member's part? No. It's the holiday season for everyone, no matter what they've done or left undone. Wish them happy holidays, but don't reward them for it. You can distribute a reward or make some sort of recognition at holiday time as long as the accomplishment or series of accomplishments are still tied directly to the recognition or reward — and you are absolutely, positively certain that your team member makes the connection.

SCALABILITY

Besides seeking resonance between the reward or type of recognition and your team members' emotional purposes, appropriateness involves matching the size of the prize with the results achieved. If you establish a rewards rotation of varying sizes, you can match them to varying results. You can set up a $250 category and increase it in increments of $250 up to $25,000 or whatever you choose depending on what's at stake and what there is to gain. You can start at $100 if you're tight.

Beware of giving away cash. As you're already aware, people tend to spend cash either too frivolously, and thereby regret or quickly forget about the experience, or spend it on mundane things like paying bills, thereby not enjoying the unexpected opportunity. The perks you provide should follow a scale of monetary value to be appropriate for the size and scope of the accomplishment. They still need to be things people wouldn't necessarily purchase for themselves. That way you're giving them a guilt-free bonus. What a great boss you are.

The risk is always present that you can provide something they don't want. In that case, who cares how much you spent on it? The money is wasted, and you proved that you don't pay attention to your team members' clues and direct answers. That's why a *selection* of things out of any given monetary tier on your prize table is a good idea. This requires that you spend a little time and effort planning the celebration phase of the constructive confrontation cycle. The temptation is to blow this off because of all the pressure you feel for performance results. That's why many leaders just give cash bonuses. It's easier and requires little thought.

Your team members know that a cash bonus, while nice, is not a gregarious gesture on your part. It's not your money, after all. You've also blown an excellent opportunity to demonstrate that you pay attention to what's important in your team members' lives, not to mention a blown opportunity to get your overworked team member to take a little more time off or go somewhere exotic on his or her vacation. Remember what Stephen Littlejohn said: We're never *not* communicating. Setting up a creative passel of perks and then scaling them to match the appropriate amount of effort and accomplishment shows you're interested and involved in your team members' lives and paying attention.

Stock ownership is a great perk. It's a favorite among executives. If it's not possible to offer options to your team members, remember the nature of the motivation you receive vis-à-vis *your* stock options and set up your team member's perks packages to deliver the same type of feeling. One of the benefits of stock ownership, as far as the organization is concerned, is emotional and practical investment in the success of the whole. Make sure any effort that is rewarded, and thereby repeated, is tied directly into the success of the organization. Don't assume people can figure that out for themselves. Preach it from the mountaintops, paint arrows on the pavement, run ribbons down the hallways, everything leading to the utterly inescapable conclusion that team members rewards and recognition is all about the marriage of individual emotional purpose *and* organizational needs.

MOTIVATION REDUX

Because celebration is a conjunctive activity that links recent success to future success, it's not hard to see how the skilled use of celebration establishes a positive expectation of success. Nothing motivates human beings to invest in future success more than recent success. Leaving recent success uncelebrated is a missed opportunity to motivate.

As you've already been reminded, it's not about hitting grand-slam home runs. Twelve dimes add up to more than a dollar bill. Don't waste your money on trying to motivate your people to hit grand slams or make it all the way to end of the marathon in one step. Motivate them to take one step at a time. Your energies and resources are best invested in motivating your team members to do the next right thing, and then the next, and so on.

Yes, a major celebration is a reloading for the next major initiative. But every minor thumbs-up recognition is an important reloading for the next right step. Your use of rewards and recognition in constructive confrontation celebrations is intended to reinforce the things you and your team members have found that work. Encourage your people to pull those things out of their tool box or arsenal and use them again and again, as long as they keep working. It's easy to see how the constant flow of information created by the constructive confrontation process keeps positive and productive thinking in motion.

TIME TO SETTLE

You've heard it said that "timing is everything." That's also true about how quickly you follow a victory celebration with a kick-off celebration. Make sure you don't blur the distinction between endings and beginnings for your team members. If they don't have a clear sense of when one effort ends and another begins, everything will start to look and feel like an endless spiral. They will feel as if they go down into the mine and never come out. That's an invitation for them to settle into the holes they dig and to never think outside the ditch.

Ending is separate from beginning. People shouldn't be made to feel like pack mules. Don't make the mistake of using a time of celebration to merely burden your people for the next trek. That's on your calendar and will come soon enough. Give your team members enough *time* to revel in their accomplishment before shifting gears to the next initiative. You must make those decisions based on the length of time it took to accomplish what's being celebrated and the size and scope of the effort. Once again, it's a matter of scale. A thumbs up can immediately precede discussion of the next small step. A big blow out in a hotel ballroom might kick off a few days or a weekend of kicking back before the kick-off meeting for the next round.

Reloading too quickly can diminish the emotional impact you're seeking from your celebration. People won't care how much money you're spending on a party if they leave feeling like beasts of burden. The time frame around various-sized celebrations within your culture of celebration must match the intentional pentameter or rhythm of your organization. As a matter of work process design and structure you need to be aware of your team members' adaptiveness and overall metabolism for execution. These things are also determined by trial and error, conversations with your people, triangulated data gathering and analysis, and general observation over time.

PRECIOUS TIME

Tie rewards to time. If you plan to put a permanent or semipermanent reward system in place over and above traditional compensation packages, make sure it's time sensitive. It's a little like playing three-dimensional chess. The level of accomplishment determines the value of the reward or the magnitude of the recognition. But time is money as far as organizational results are concerned. The meter never shuts off — even when the income does. It takes a lot to feed an insatiable organizational monster.

Just because you're having a bad quarter doesn't mean the monster isn't still hungry.

Unfortunately, without effective, anticipatory planning and execution, like the kind constructive confrontation provides, resources start drying up long before the monster notices. By the time you finally announce to the organizational monster that it's belt-tightening time, he looks at you as if, "that's your problem . . . you didn't plan properly." More unfortunately, even being honest seldom helps at that point.

"True, the leadership of this organization was lax in anticipating and planning," you confess. "Now the wolf is at the door, and there is no choice but to right-size. I have a handful of pink slips to hand out and, looky there, my name's not on any of them." Once again, the (mostly) innocent suffer for the sins of the leadership or lack thereof. If you want to lose credibility fast as a leader, let your people take the fall for your poor planning and failure to confront. If anyone challenges why you're so sold on constructive confrontation, explain how much better it is than the alternative.

By the time most organizations realize things have gotten out of hand, they have long since been out of hand. In such cases there is far too little accountability and much too much blaming going on. Use your reward systems to emphasize that time is important. If the target is reached on time, the reward is X. If the target is hit a month late, the reward is X–1. If the target is hit two months late, the reward is X–2, and so on. Of course, if the target is hit early, the reward should be X+1. Reward, recognition, and celebration, in general, are tremendous opportunities to both guide and encourage your team members along the road to success. Don't miss the opportunity to accelerate the schedule as well.

CHAPTER 11 SUMMARY

Celebration, with its resonant rewards and recognitions, psychologically and symbolically brings the cycle of success full circle and begins the cycle anew. Regardless of the specifics around the rewards and types of recognition you extend to your team members, celebration is a time to motivate, to teach, and to make a meaningful demonstration of the degree to which you want to see them succeed. Some of the major issues to bear in mind while planning for celebration include the following:

- Celebrations, large and small, must be meaningful to your team members if they are to support and encourage ongoing loyalty to the circle of confrontation. The most meaningful rewards resonate with the emotional purpose upon which the team member's personal and professional agendas are based.
- Circles of confrontation vary, depending on the depth and scope of the achievements being sought. Matching the style of recognition to the style of the team member is important if the recognition is to promote future buy-in. Knowing what motivates various team members is part of a team leader's preparation for celebration.
- Daily, weekly, monthly, quarterly, and annual celebrations, based on successful adherence to the covenant, must be consistent with the covenant in terms of scope and scale. Celebrations that resonate with the team member must also match the effort and, more importantly, results. This lends perspective to the various tasks and subtasks being accomplished.
- The true resonance of rewards with the team member's emotional purpose should be constantly monitored and adjusted if necessary. Sometimes team members find greater satisfaction from types of recognition they hadn't considered before. A catered team lunch in honor of a particular accomplishment might mean more than lunch with the boss in the executive dining room. Reward and recognition practices should remain flexible.
- Don't perpetuate the dysfunction that a team member might already be dealing with around money by giving them more. Give them meaningful, appropriate, properly scaled noncash gifts. Communicate the level and depth of your commitment to them by helping them get things they wouldn't get on their own. Help them work their agenda at home if it comes to that.
- Trash the trinkets. People really don't want more swag like coffee

mugs, sweatshirts, and ink pens. They are not motivated and don't feel rewarded by any expensive minutiae cluttering up their offices. They want their home lives enhanced, their love lives intensified, and their family's futures secured. You can help do all of those things and spend no more money than you would on cash bonuses.

- Teach them how to play by giving the gift of relaxation and recreation. Many people would never take a cruise except for the fact that you gave them one. This helps them elude the feelings of guilt and extravagance that they still carry from their parent's frugalness. Keeping the scope and expense under control, you can provide perks that bear exponentially more meaning than cash awards. Plus, experiences have much longer-lasting results.

Celebration is a huge opportunity to promote the organizational agenda and move it forward. The type of recognition you deliver and the nature, quality, and meaningfulness of the rewards you award are among the most powerful tools of attraction you can use. But even the best tools are more valuable in skilled hands. There is a craft to celebration; learn it, sharpen it, and never stop getting better at it. The most profound results you will realize from the skilled, intentional, and deliberate use of celebration will be the satisfaction of watching the growth and development of your team members. That's why the last chapter in this book deals with exactly that — building others.

CHAPTER 12

Building Others

No matter what you accomplish in your personal or professional lives, that cynic mentioned in Chapter 1 will still be lurking in the shadows ready to say, "If you want to know how much difference you make in the grand scheme of things, put your hand in a bucket of water, pull it out, and see the impression you leave behind." If constructive confrontation weren't such a high-road endeavor, you might consider inserting the cynic's head into said bucket of water. A better way to prove the cynics wrong is to leave an indelible impression on the people who look to you for leadership, and nothing will do that more than practicing the principles of constructive confrontation.

The reason to salt discussions of constructive confrontation with language like "personal *and* professional" is to remind you that the two are connected. You can't authentically act to increase accountability and decrease conflict in your professional life while disregarding those things in your personal life. You can act like it, but the truth will be revealed in time. You can't be the real deal until you practice what you preach everywhere, all the time. Acting sincere in professional situations and insincere in personal situations (or vice versa) disqualifies the sincere performance, wherever it is.

As you've already seen, constructive confrontation, when properly executed, increases accountability and minimizes conflict wherever it's applied. It will also give people the best possible opportunity to grow and develop personally and professionally. There is no more rewarding payoff to the inevitable hardships and long suffering that true leadership requires than the knowledge that you played a key role in the personal and professional success of another human being. As you also learned in Chapter 1, history is replete with evidence of how successful people invariably attribute their success to the help, encouragement, and guidance of leaders in their lives.

Building people up is not the primary purpose of constructive confrontation. Yet it is one of the natural consequences of continuous conversations, commitments, covenants, and celebrations. When conversations, commitments, covenants, and celebrations are synchronized and focused like a laser beam, constructive confrontation gives structure and method to the core elements of people building — personal responsibility for self, the good of others, and choosing guiding principles to live by.

Merely executing the basics of constructive confrontation places a performance demand on leadership. In turn, demonstrating competent and sincere leadership places a performance demand on everyone reporting to you. It's impossible to lead someone where you won't go yourself. If you take the risks and expose yourself to possible failure, you give permission to others to take the same risks.

If you perceive failure as an opportunity and obligation to learn, your team members will have permission to do the same. They will refuse to surrender to defeat as long as you do. They might show a natural inclination to accept failure too easily, but your refusal to do so will convict that notion in them and, hopefully, impeach it. If you genuinely redefine failure as *learning*, your team members will redefine failure in their minds as well.

A man should never be ashamed to own he has been
wrong, which is but saying, in other words, that he is
wiser today then he was yesterday.
— ALEXANDER POPE

THE MOTIONS ARE GOOD ENOUGH

Personal and professional development must be sincere and genuine.
This doesn't mean that you and the leaders throughout your organization
need to experience some transformational epiphany. Constructive confrontation is a road map, not a religion. It can't help you change your
heart, but it can give you a system to follow that employs the right practices for the right reasons. If, perchance, executing the system makes a
believer out of you, it can do the same for your people. But you must
surrender to the system first. It's all about learning. Everything is about
learning. As long as you're open to that, the results you and your team
members achieve will continuously improve.

Perhaps the most essential element of a covenant is the promise to act
right before you feel right. Growing is usually uncomfortable. But *habits,
skills, attitudes,* and *activities* pull you through.

If you wait until you're completely sold in your heart before you begin
executing the system, you'll probably never begin. Action comes before
feeling. If you don't adopt constructive confrontation, how is it ever going to help any of the people relying on you for leadership? Even after
you've become a semiexperienced purveyor of constructive confrontation, there will be rough edges to sand off and marginal techniques to improve. It will never be perfect. But it will make much more sense than any
alternative.

OPPOSITE MOTIONS

To drive the point home, consider advocating the inverse application of
the constructive confrontation principles. How would it go down if you
stand up at the next staff meeting or sit in your next performance review

and say, "I think I'll stop talking to my team members?" Even if you soften that to "I'll talk to my team members, but only *after* they screw something up so bad that the conversation will be reduced to nothing more than threats of discipline up to and possibly including dismissal." That won't win you friends or positively influence those looking to you for leadership.

"I don't feel like securing a commitment from my team members to do any of the things that they're being paid to do," you continue as long as you're on a roll in front of your boss. "In fact, I don't feel like committing in any sort of formal way to doing what *I'm* being paid to do. I mean, somehow we all manage to muddle through and get things done one way or another, don't we?"

Keep it up. You're making your case nicely — a case for your own termination, of course. "To actually commit to a specific course of action, with specific *habits, skills, attitudes,* and *activities* places an enormous monkey on everybody's back," you reason. "People don't work well under that kind of pressure." This will all be recorded in the minutes of the meeting. Who said honesty is not the best policy?

"And to write the specifics of the commitment down and sign off on it," you say incredulously. "What are we? A bunch of Boy Scouts and Girl Scouts? We might as well stand and say the Pledge of Allegiance to the flag every morning. Look at what that antiquated practice did to education in this country." Your fellow executives and managers are shifting nervously in their seats. The fact that they don't engage in constructive confrontation on a regular schedule is true enough, but they don't want to be associated with *your* reasons.

In the end, the reasons don't matter. If everybody operates under their own set of governing principles, on their own schedule, producing whatever outcome will get them by without losing their jobs, does it matter why you're not following a systematic, purposeful program designed to produce the best possible performance in human beings? If your organizational celebrations are confined to holidays and birthdays and have no connection to productivity, they're just more missed opportunities. So what?

It's doubtful that you would actually come out publicly to advocate *not* doing the things that constructive confrontation calls for. That would be impossible to justify. It's hard to imagine that not practicing constructive confrontation principles will help you groom your replacement, either; unless he or she will be expected to fly by the seat of his or her swivel chair. It's even harder to imagine the following:

... *not* talking to people in a premeditated, deliberate, consistent manner

... *not* defining the emotional purposes behind why your people work where they do

... *not* securing a clear commitment to organizational objectives and methods for producing them

... *not* writing down the essential elements of the plan and its execution and signing off on them

... *not* regularly confronting progress on the plan

... *not* recognizing that rewarding and (thereby) reinforcing best practices through appropriate celebration will help anybody grow and develop one iota in their personal or professional lives.

If it happens without any organized and deliberate intervention on your part, it is pure coincidence and you didn't have anything to do with it. You might as well try to make a living by playing the lottery. That knowledge won't produce any warm and fuzzy feelings as you drift off to sleep.

YOUR COVENANT

What better way to practice what you preach than to construct a covenant that reflects your personal commitment to the growth and development of everyone on your team. Carrying out the constructive confrontation cycle yourself is your first step toward sealing your own credibility. If you are one of the lucky ones with a tremendous boss who is committed to your personal and professional growth and development, then he or she will gladly confront you constructively about your commitment to and progress toward the personal and professional growth and development of your team members.

To: Your Name (Title and Name of Organization)
From: Your Name (or your Boss's Name)
Date: (Today is the first day of the rest of your career.)
Subject: Covenant: To practice the principles of constructive confrontation in order to increase accountability among my team members, minimize negativity and conflict in the workplace I'm responsible for, and to encourage the personal and professional growth and development of the people reporting to me.

Who:
1. This covenant is first and foremost my written responsibility to myself.
2. This covenant also chronicles my obligation to the organization that pays me.
3. This covenant is written evidence of my commitment to those who report to me within our organizational design and structure.
4. This covenant is also my written commitment to those in my personal life who appropriately depend on me for emotional and physical resources.
5. This covenant reflects my public commitment to be an ongoing source of solutions and encouragement for my team members and this organization's strategic partners and affiliated organizations.

What:
1. I'm committed to leading the principles of constructive confrontation by example in continuous efforts to increase accountability (beginning with my own) and decrease conflict in all my personal and professional affairs.
2. I'm committed to doing everything within my power to promote the growth and development of the people who report to me by providing the best possible leadership guidance, encouragement, support, learning and growth opportunities, and resources.
3. I plan to fulfill my chosen and accepted obligations to people in my professional and personal lives by practicing the principles of constructive confrontation.

---

4. I will solicit regular and comprehensive feedback on my performance as a participant in, and leader of, constructive confrontation.
5. if at any time it is brought to my attention that I need to make behavioral or emotional adjustments to improve my effectiveness as a leader or business associate, I'll make course corrections enthusiastically in the most enlightened and best-informed manner possible.

When:
1. Leading constructive confrontation by example will be a nonstop activity for me.
2. I'll solicit feedback from those who report to me every time we have scheduled confrontations, more often if necessary.
3. I'll schedule weekly feedback sessions with (your Boss's Name).
4. I'll revisit this covenant weekly to reinforce my continuous effort to improve and expand upon it.
5. I'll remain open and receptive to feedback in any form, received through any media, processing and acting upon it as quickly as possible.

Where:
1. I'll employ the methods and techniques of constructive confrontation wherever people are willing to engage in the practice.
2. I'll personally practice the principles of constructive confrontation everywhere, regardless of the behavior or beliefs of others.
3. I'll consider and identify the geographical implications of *habits, skills, attitudes,* and *activities* with everyone I lead through the constructive confrontation process.

Why:
1. The principles of constructive confrontation are consistent with my belief that anything worth doing is worth doing through a thoughtful, systematic, and responsible approach.
2. The principles of constructive confrontation are consistent with my belief that people never fail in personal or professional endeavors because they are too skilled as communicators.
3. The principles of constructive confrontation are consistent with my belief that writing down and signing off on agreements helps to clarify intent and purpose of the commitment.
4. The principles of constructive confrontation are consistent with my belief that checking-in and confronting progress on any project or proposed behavior, in a constructive way, helps keep everyone's efforts

(continued)

on track, producing maximum effectiveness and accountability and minimizes potential for conflict.

5. The principles of constructive confrontation are consistent with my belief that recognition and reward for every positive effort and result, through the most appropriate celebration, will reinforce the best *habits, skills, attitudes,* and *behaviors.*

How:

1. I will lead the principles of constructive confrontation by engaging my team members, and anyone else for whom the constructive confrontation process is appropriate, in commitment conversations about personal and professional emotional purposes and how those purposes resonate with the needs of the organization.

2. I will guide my team members, and anyone else for whom the constructive confrontation process is appropriate, in the drafting and refinement of written covenants to record our mutual commitment to the effort and resources required to achieve specified goals and objectives, quantified as accurately, realistically, and reasonably as possible.

3. I will constructively confront my team members, and anyone else for whom the constructive confrontation process is appropriate, on a mutually agreed-upon schedule as recorded in the covenant.

4. I will further solicit and provide feedback on an accelerated schedule if necessary to keep the program on track. If corrections or alterations on the covenant are called for and mutually agreed upon, I'll facilitate those changes and keep things moving forward.

5. I will engage in regular recognition and reward for each team member in appropriate scale, scope, and significance as to best resonate with the effort and results produced.

6. If at any time it is brought to my attention that I need to make behavioral or emotional adjustments to improve my effectiveness as a leader or business associate, I'll do so without delay in the most enlightened and best-informed manner possible.

Other Notes:

1. I will at all times choose principles over personalities.

2. I will at all times be conscious and loyal to the constructive confrontation guiding principle of taking the best possible actions to produce the best possible results for everyone involved.

3. I will always practice the principle that correct actions will lead to correct thinking. It's always preferable to act my way out of difficulty

> or confusion than to dwell on my feelings and let emotions guide my actions.
> 4. I will do my best at all times to promote the personal and professional growth and development of my team members and anyone else for whom the constructive confrontation process is appropriate.
> 5. I will do my best at all times to represent myself and the organization that pays me in the most constructive, productive, and profitable manner in the long-term interests of my team members and anyone else for whom the constructive confrontation process is appropriate.

If you're wondering how such a covenant written by, for, and about you will lead to the personal and professional growth of your team members, and anyone else for whom the constructive confrontation process is appropriate, wonder no more. There is nothing more you can possibly do for your team members and anyone else for whom the constructive confrontation process is appropriate. Practicing the principles of constructive confrontation to the best of your ability will produce the greatest amount of support, encouragement, and resources possible to your team members and anyone else within your sphere of influence. There is no better way to facilitate their personal and professional growth and development than to facilitate your own.

THE TOUGH STUFF

You can be successful without constructive confrontation. However, it's difficult to repeat. Many companies become successful but can't sustain their success. Salespeople have good years followed by bad years. One of the greatest benefits of constructive confrontation is consistency. Practicing the principles of constructive confrontation will become easier over time as you and your team members become more familiar with the process. It will never become effortless. Doing the things that other people refuse to do is never *easy* because, if it was, everybody would be doing it. The most outstanding performances, the greatest successes, and the most outstanding accomplishments are not found in the main stream; they're found in the margins.

By leading constructive confrontation by example, you're giving your team members, and anyone else for whom the constructive confrontation process is appropriate, the opportunity to operate in the margins — at the top end of the bell curve. This is special because the vast majority of people never operate in the margins where the greatest successes are realized, the grandest achievements are accomplished, and full potential is exercised. That's not why you adopt the principles of constructive confrontation, though, at least not initially.

There are immediate needs for increasing accountability and reducing conflict. When you adopt a highly principled, organized, premeditated, and systematic approach to improve organizational productivity and performance, you automatically put people on track to succeed. All of those difficult, disciplined things that successful people do (and unsuccessful people don't do) are built into the constructive confrontation system. You could say that people will succeed by default, except that sounds as if they can execute the constructive confrontation process without effort. Well-directed effort, however, is much more likely to produce compliance.

HABITS

Just to develop healthy, productive habits around skilled use of time, effective communication techniques, and productive work practices is something people exiting motivational seminars are sworn to do but forget about within 48 hours (if it takes that long). The secret to the success that everyone covets is simply the persistence and tireless dedication to doing the next right thing, then the next, and the next, and so on . . . and everybody knows it. Ergo, it's no secret.

That doesn't stop people from *believing* that there is a secret method known only to the rich and famous. To admit that the only difference between ordinary pedestrians and successful people is the amount and consistency of effort is to confess one's laziness or impatience. Let the one who is truly operating at 100 percent and has realized his or her full potential cast the first stone. The rest are guilty as charged.

Habits are formed by doing, not wishing. *Doing* is much more likely if there is a clear agenda to follow, supported by regular and constructive confrontation. Proper execution of all the constructive confrontation components results in habit formation and skill enhancement. Without a conscious or deliberate decision to seek large scale professional or personal success, anyone actively involved in constructive confrontation will be nonetheless engaged in the exact sort of disciplined behavior that ultimately produces success.

SKILLS

Like habits, skill development doesn't occur by sitting around and thinking about how things should be done. Skills are enhanced every time they are used. Constructive confrontation intentionally designates the types of skills to be exploited in pursuit of the goals and objectives to be reached. There is always room to include new and unanticipated skills. But, generally speaking, the skills necessary to achieve the desired outcomes are discussed thoroughly during commitment conversations.

If for no other reason, skills are part of early and ongoing conversations because some sort of formalized learning and skill enhancement might need to be designed into the process. In a true learning organization, the learning never stops. This applies to organized, formalized learning as well as the greater oceans of learning that take place informally through day-to-day experiences. Habits and skills are built faster, with longer-lasting results, when formal learning supports, distills, and synthesizes informal learning. It's one thing to chop vegetables with a table knife. It's altogether different to chop vegetables with a super-sharp kitchen knife. Saying "A knife is a knife" fails to encompass that distinction.

ATTITUDES

Attitudes are determined to a large degree by expectations. Expectations can emerge from an individual's imagination or be based on rational and reasonable thinking and experience. When expectations are not realistic or reasonable, they are invariably unfulfilled and unrealized. The result is cynicism. Cynicism, pessimism, and generally negative attitudes are partners in crime. They can destroy all the good things you want to accomplish in your organization.

Actively engaging in an organized, systematic, and purposeful program like constructive confrontation will diminish or remove altogether the role of wild imaginings or catastrophic thinking when it comes to work process design. Imagination should be encouraged and even nurtured for the sake of creativity. But, like emotions, there are parameters as to how much it should be allowed to influence prudent decision making. There should always be reality checks when formulating plans.

The positive attitudes you desperately want your people to develop and sustain will come as a direct result of achieving positive results from their organized and systematic efforts, results for which they will be grateful. Once again, people building results from properly practicing constructive confrontation principles. It's easy to say that negative attitudes won't produce the kind of effort or results you're looking for. True enough. But without a displacing alternative to negative attitudes, what's going to hold back the tide? It's just as accurate to say that producing the results you're looking for will result in increased confidence and increasingly positive attitudes.

ACTIVITIES

Aside from the occasional lottery winner or professional athlete it's the small stuff that makes people rich. The day-in and day-out grinding efforts others are not willing to do lead to any kind of long-term success. If you have a crystal ball, you wouldn't use it to determine which small things you need attended to in order to achieve long-term success. You'd use your crystal ball to pick your lottery numbers. So it's just as well there are no crystal balls.

Rephrasing the words of Theodore Roosevelt, tennis great Arthur Ashe said, "Start where you are. Use what you have. Do what you can." In real terms, both men are saying, "Get out of your imagination because imagination is the only place where you can start from somewhere other than where you are." "Use what you have" follows the same common sense logic. What else are you going to use, at least in this moment? "Do what you can" opens up an entirely new realm of possibilities.

Considering where you and your team members want to end up is not the same as pretending you're already there or riding a magic carpet to your final destination. Defining the desired outcome to the best of your ability is how you begin the process of breaking down what it will take to get there, both in terms of necessary resources and activities. Successful people will quietly, systematically, and methodically execute the unglamorous and often tedious activities without complaint, while the unsuccessful waste precious time and energy complaining.

There is no better way to build people than to lead them through a structured process of habit development, skill enhancement, attitude elevation, and activity accomplishment. That's why successful people in all walks of life rarely say, "I did it all on my own." Even when they do say such things, it's just as rarely the case. This book opened with successful people giving credit and proper attribution to those who guided them through the maze of confusion life can often be. Successful people don't credit their success to people who did it for them. They credit those who gave them structure, guidance, hope, and the belief that it could be done. That's the gift you can pass on to those who look to you for leadership.

CHAPTER 12 SUMMARY

Chapter 12 is the gospel of growing the organization through the marriage of human capital and organizational needs. In the midst of that noble cause are certain profound but ancillary benefits. High among them is the opportunity to help others within your sphere of influence grow and develop personally and professionally.

- The greatest fulfillment in the cycle of success is to pass on the learning to others and prepare them to move up. This should be a highly promoted priority for team leaders. Top performers should pass on the experience to others. When the team member begins to mentor other team members, the way he or she has been mentored, the circle of confrontation becomes an upward spiral.
- The circle of confrontation process is the training ground for succession. If the leader keeps his or her promise to confront team members in a positive, constructive, and consistent manner, new leaders will emerge, not necessarily new leaders with natural charisma, but leaders who know, understand, and respect the system that made them successful.
- Constructive confrontation is a blueprint for legacy building. An organization can make commitment, confrontation, and celebration an enterprise-wide cycle of success. Building on each successful cycle, the organization can reinvent its own culture. The process is like slow-drying glue, but the bond is strong.
- Alignment of team member's wants and needs with the organization's wants and needs is at the heart of constructive confrontation. As the individual is built up and strengthened through constructive confrontation, the organization's pilings are sunk deeper into the bedrock of strong and positive traditions. Celebrations at all levels become the rituals that continually reinforce those new traditions and the growth and development of your people.

The cycle of conversation, commitment, covenant, confrontation, and celebration never ends in a successful organization. People don't just talk to one another now and then; they constantly keep getting better at it. Commitment becomes synonymous with anything worth doing and cleans the slate of anything not worth doing. "Is it worth drafting a covenant for?" you ask. If the answer is, "No, it's not that important," then why are time, energy, and resources being spent on it? Small, seemingly insignificant activities need to be tied to a significant effort and desired outcome. If they can't be, that's your cue to dispatch them and liberate your team members from unnecessary burdens.

Drafting covenant documents makes structured commitment a way of life in organizational culture, further cleansing the organizational agenda of inertia-producing minutiae. Regular constructive confrontation of progress on the covenant propels the agenda forward and keeps it on course. Vectoring to the right or the left wastes time, energy, and resources. Constructive confrontation creates the closest thing to a straight line between where you are now and where you want to be.

Anything that keeps you or your team members' efforts along that path deserves to be recognized and rewarded to encourage such behavior to be repeated. Teaching people to set goals and break the goals down into doable components builds character and capability. Encouraging people to take the right steps, and to keep stepping, builds character and capacity. Teaching people the value and purpose of celebration can open up new vistas in their ability to do for others what you've done for them. That, in a nutshell, is the future you want for your organization: character, capability, and capacity — with an attitude of gratitude.

Index

1001 Ways to Reward Employees, 218

Activities, 260–262
  commitment and, documented, 68, 104, 114
  complex covenants and, 99
  framing solutions, 135–136, 141, 151
  imbalances in, 160
  impromptu conversations and, 30
  individualizing, 228, 235
  listening and, 193
  means of execution and, 76
  openness and, 128
  personal and professional development, 251,
      252, 255
  positivity and, 150, 151
  progress, focusing on, 151
  rewarding behavior, 205–206, 209, 219, 221
  scripted conversation and, 179–182
    expressing concern, 200
    giving credit, 217
  symbolic victory, 233
    attentiveness, 207–208
Accountability, ix, x, 6, 16, 24, 62, 258
  authority and, 198
  continuous, 177
  covenant for, importance of, 99, 113, 226, 254,
      256
  face-to-face meetings, importance of, 127
  feedback and, 42
  leadership skills and, xvi
  monitoring, 226
  personal development and, 249, 250
  promotability and, 20, 113
  realistic expectations for, 42, 60, 226
  resonance and willing, 61
  rewards and recognition, 228
    time and, 246
  trust and bonding, as a means of building, 186
Ad hoc confrontations, positivity and, 164
Adair, Red, 155
Adams, John, 13
Agreement, reaching:
  compromise, 48–49
  consensus, 49
  expertise, 48
  majority rule, 49
  minority rule, 49

Akroyd, Dan, 37
Apathy:
  dishonesty and, 189
  resentment of confrontations and 15
Ashe, Arthur, 261
Attentiveness, celebrating the right things and,
      207–208
Attitudes:
  commitment and, documented, 68, 104, 114
  complex covenants and, 99
  expectations and, 260
  framing solutions, 135–136, 141, 151
  imbalances in, 160
  impromptu conversations and, 30
  individualizing, 228, 235
  listening and, 193
  means of execution and, 76
  negative, 198, 199
  openness and, 128
  personal and professional development, 251,
      252, 255
  positivity and, 150, 151
  progress, focusing on, 151
  rewarding behavior, 205–206, 209, 219, 221
  scripted conversation and, 179–182
    expressing concern, 200
    giving credit, 217
  symbolic victory, 233
    attentiveness, 207–208
Authority:
  institutional
    appearance of interest, 27–28
    benefits and compensation, 66
    candor, encouraging, 35
    commitment
      leader and team member, 64, 80
      specificity and, 47–48, 68–70
    courtesy, modeling, 32–34
    flexibility and, 178, 183
    information sharing and, 28–29
    vs. majority rule, 49
    minority self-image and, 41
    organizational power and, 185
    positivity and, 151
    unreasonable confrontations, 146
    who to confront, 122
  popular

Authority (continued)
    candor, encouraging, 35
    courtesy, modeling and, 34
    positivity and, 151
    promotions and, 27
    self-image and, 41

Backbiting, negativity and, 161
Blanchard, Ken:
    creating a safety zone and 46, 218
    consistent recognition and, 207, 218
Blitzer, Wolf, 155
Blowfish syndrome, 153
Bonding:
    honesty, 188–191
    listening, 191–194
    overview, 185–186, 200–202
    scripts, 194–196
        expressing concern, 198–200
        getting to know team members, 196–198
    trust and, 186–188
Brain hemispheres, 156
Bryant, Kobe, 15
Burnout, dishonesty and, 189

Cable News Network (CNN), 154, 155
Celebration:
    macrocelebrations, 224–226
    microcelebrations, 224–226
    personal and professional development
        activities, 260–261
        attitudes, 260
        covenant, 253–257
        habits, 258–259
        motions, 251–253
        overview, 249–250, 261–263
        skills, 259
    planning for peaks
        collaboration, encouraging, 228–230
        double vision, 224–226
        effort and results, 230–232
        individual vs. group, 226–228
        overview, 223–224, 233–235
        symbolism, 232–233
    the right things
        how, 218–219
        overview, 205–206, 220
        what, 206–208, 209–211
        when, 211–213
        where, 213–215
        who, 208–209
        why, 215–217
    underlying agenda of, 237–238

Changes and challenges:
    flexibility, 178
    overview, 169–175, 182–184
    scripting, 179–182
    time management, 175–177
Christianity, confrontation and, 11
Christmas cards, toxic, 213–214
Churchill, Winston, 29
Collaboration 48, 173, 188, 210, 228
Collins, Jim, 26
Commitment:
    benefits and compensation, 65–67
    forming a, 68–70
    job satisfaction, 67–68
    leadership and, 64–65
    overview, 63–64, 79–81
    scripts, 70–71
        how, 76–78
        what, 72
        when, 73–74
        where, 74
        who, 71
        why, 74–76
    summing up the conversation, 78–79
    See also Confrontation; Conversation; Covenant
Communication, nonverbal, 38
Compliments, 157, 217
Conflict, ix, x, xiv, 62
    ambiguity, 177
    covenants, 99, 114, 254–256
    dishonesty, 24
    negative confrontations, 6
    outlining conversations, 50–51
    personal development, 141, 249–250
    personal and professional responsibilities, 141
    positivity, 149
        compliments and, 157
    procrastination and ineffective communication, 29, 54
    promotability, 20
    trust and bonding, 186
    unrealized expectations, 19, 60
    Wooden comments on, 16
Confrontation:
    career success and, 14
    as compressed therapy, 10
    courage and, 11–12
    defined, 5
    expectations and, 19
    habits, skills, attitudes, activities, and, 135–146
    historical, 12–13
    honesty and, 120–122
    how to confront, 128–129

misunderstandings about, 4–5
negative, 5–7
overview, 3–4, 20–21, 119–120, 146–148
planning and preparation, importance of, 7–10
scripted, 129–135
talent and, refining raw, 15–16
wasted effort, reducing, 16–17
what to confront, 124–125
when to confront, 125–126
where to confront, 126–127
  open vs. private, 127–128
who to confront, 122–124
written commitments, importance of, 17–19
See also Bonding; Changes and challenges;
     Positivity
Conversation:
beginning, 46
  agreement, reaching, 48–49
  specificity, 47–48
critical components, 28–29
  courtesy and timing, 31–34
  location, 34–35
  no surprises, 30–31
  what to cover, 36
  when, 29–30
MBWA
  lost, 24–26
  reborn, 26–28
outlining, 49–51
  how, 57–60
  what, 53–54
  when, 54–55
  where, 55–56
  who, 52–53
  why, 56–57
overview, 23–24, 60–62
triangulating information, 36–46
Corporate counsel, 40
Course correction, viii, xiv
catastrophizing and, 154
emotional purpose and, 239
expectation and, 19
timeliness and, 125
Covenant:
CEO, role of, 86–88
  responding to the first draft, 89–90
  item-by-item, 90–98
  success, 98–99
complex, 99–100
double usage, 84–85
obligations and opportunities, 111–113
overview, 83–84, 113–115
sales director, role of, 100–102

commitment and, 102–107
  sample covenant, 107–111
Cox, Danny, 217
CNN, 154–155
Cynicism, xiv
making an impression, 3, 21
positivity and, 149, 260
failing to acknowledge progress and, 165, 206,
     220
organizational power and, 185
dishonesty and, 189

Data collection, 44. *See also* Observations
Desperate Housewives, 241
Displacement theory, 156–158, 167
celebration and, 209
Double usage, 84–85
Double vision, 224–226
Douglas, Will, 25

Effort, rewarding, 230–232
Emerson, Ralph Waldo, ix
Emotion, absence of, 156
Emotional Purpose, xi
celebration and, 238–240
  individualization, 240–242
  scalability, 242–244
foundation for commitment, 64
understanding, 239
Encouragement:
appreciation and finding employee strengths,
     210–211
leadership and, 152–153
Expectations, importance of realistic, 19

Feedback, gathering from others, 41–42
Five Whys test, 75–76
Franklin, Benjamin 13

Gandhi, Mahatma, 13
Goals, ultimate:
double vision, 224
self-esteem issues and, 227
Goldilocks theory, 55, 58
Gossip, negativity and, 161
Guidance, organizational productivity and, 229–
     230

Habits, 258–259
commitment and, documented, 68, 104, 114
complex covenants and, 99
framing solutions, 135–136, 141, 151
imbalances in, 160

Habits (continued)
  impromptu conversations and, 30
  individualizing, 228, 235
  listening and, 193
  means of execution and, 76
  openness and, 128
  personal and professional development, 251,
    252, 255
  positivity and, 150, 151
  progress, focusing on, 151
  rewarding behavior, 205–206, 209, 219, 221
  scripted conversation and, 179–182
    expressing concern, 200
    giving credit, 217
  symbolic victory, 233
  attentiveness, 207–208
Hierarchical organization, 185–188, 190
Hewlett, Bill, 23, 26
Hewlett-Packard, MBWA and, 23, 24, 26, 27
Honesty:
  bonds and, forming, 188–191
  brutal, problems with, 158–159, 189, 252
  clearly stated goals and, 54
  efficacy and, 120–122
  trust and, 186–188
  vs. truth, 120
Hoover, John, 46

Individualization:
  rewards and, 240–242
  triangulation and direct conversations, 42–43
Inter-hemisphere data transfer, 156
Intermittent Recognition. See Recognition, inter-
    mittent
International Organization for Standardization
    (ISO), 24

Jefferson, Thomas, 13
Joy. See Emotional purpose, foundation for com-
    mitment
Judgment:
  attentiveness, 207
  change, dealing with, 169, 176
  consideration of team member moods, 46
  decreasing tension in confrontations and, 128
  feedback and, 210
  lack of trust and, 126
  reaching agreement and, 49
  successful execution and, 97, 111, 132, 139,
    175
  timing trade-offs and, 73
Justification, 98, 109, 137, 253

Kampground of America (KOA), 239
Keller, Helen, 12, 13, 21
King, Martin Luther, Jr., 13
Klein, Anne, 241
Kvetching, 161

Law and Order, 241
Leadership:
  commitment, 64
  servant, 186
Leadership When the Heat's On, 217
Littlejohn, Stephen, 243
Lynne, Carol, 25

Management by Walking Around (MBWA):
  confrontation location and, 127
  covenants and, 83
  defined, 23–24
  leadership commitment and, 64
  lost, 24–25
    style, lack of, 25
    support, lack of, 26
    time, lack of, 25–26
  reborn, 26–28
  who, what, when, where, why, and how rou-
    tine, 51
Management by Writing it Down, 83
Masters of business administration (MBA)
    programs:
  absence of confrontation instruction in, xvi
  commitment and, 64–65
  MBWA and, 25
McGraw, Phil, 10
Mendacity, 189
Microcelebrations. See Celebrations, micro-
    celebrations
Micromanaging:
  vs. constructive confrontation, 150, 166
  employee version of, 68–69
Misrepresentation, xiv
Motivation redux, 244–245
Mt. Everest, double vision and climbing, 225, 234
Murphy, Eddie, 37

National Association for Employee Recognition,
    218, 223
National Basketball Association (NBA), 15, 71
National Broadcasting Company (NBC), 29–30
National Football League (NFL), 71, 225, 234
Negativity. See Positivity
Nelson, Bob, 218–219, 223
Nicholson, Robert, 25

Obligations, 111–113
Observations from afar, 37–40, 44
Opportunities, 111
Opposing motions, 251–253
Ostrich effect, 190

Packard, Dave, 23, 26
Parcells, Bill, 16–17, 21
Peale, Norman Vincent, 46, 201
Peer reviews, 44
Performance, assessing and confronting:
 data and, 43–44
Peters, Tom, 23, 27
Plan for the Peaks 223
Pope, Alexander, 251
Positivity:
 catastrophizing, avoid, 153–154
 confidence building and, 159–160
 displacement theory and, 156–158
 encouragement, 152–153
 honesty and, 158–159
 in leadership roles, 160–161
  celebrations, 165
  commitments, 162–163
  confrontations, 164–165
  conversations, 161–162
  covenants, 163–164
 overview, 149–151, 166–167
 progress, focus on, 151–152
 solutions, importance of offering, 154–156
Powers, Austin, 159
Privacy, confrontations and, 128
Progress:
 assessing and confronting
  data and, 43–44
 focus on, 151–152
Public displays of appreciation (PDAs), 212
Public service announcements, 23–24

Qualifications:
 flexibility and 178, 182
 leadership, 65
Quid pro quo, 17, 101
Quitting, prematurely, xvi–xvii
Quotas:
 motivation and, 105, 110, 138
 realistic expectations and, 102, 105

Recognition:
 continuous, 213, 220
 intermittent, 213, 220
 overview, 44–46

See also Celebration
Respect, timing and, 30–31
Results, rewarding, 230–232
Rewards, 44–46
 behavior and, xiv, 205
 that resonate, 237–238, 246–248
  emotional purpose and, 238–244
  formula X, 246
  motivation and, 244–245
  time and, 245–246
Roosevelt, Theodore, 190, 261

St. John's, 241
Sanger, Margaret, 13
Scalability, rewards and, 242–244
Scheduled confrontations, ad hoc vs., 164
Schlessinger, Dr. Laura, 10
Scouts, Boy/Girl, 8, 252
Scripts:
 giving credit, specificity and, 216–217
 recognizing team member strengths, 210–211
 structuring, 49–51, 70–71
  how, 57–60, 76–78
  what, 53–54, 72
  when, 54–55, 73–74
  where, 55–56, 74
  who, 52–53, 71
  why, 56–57, 74–76
In Search of Excellence, 23
Self-image, 41
Sequoia National Forest, 154, 155
Servant leadership. See Leadership, servant
Sex and the City, 241
Shamu, 46, 207, 218
Six Sigma, 24
Skills, 259
 commitment and, documented, 68, 104, 114
 complex covenants and, 99
 framing solutions, 135–136, 141, 151
 imbalances in, 160
 impromptu conversations and, 30
 individualizing, 228, 235
 listening and, 193
 means of execution and, 76
 openness and, 128
 personal and professional development, 251,
  252, 255
 positivity and, 150, 151
 progress, focusing on, 151
 rewarding behavior, 205–206, 209, 219, 221
 scripted conversation and, 179–182
  expressing concern, 200

Skills (continued)
  giving credit, 217
  symbolic victory, 233
  attentiveness, 207–208
Solutions, importance of offering, 154–156
Specificity:
  celebrations and, 218–219
  commitment and, 47–48
Stand-up boss, 34, 38, 61
Subordinates' revenge, 68
Sullivan, Annie, 12–13
Summations, conversation, 78–79
Surrender to the system, 64, 80, 250, 251
  giving thanks for, 216
Symbolism, celebrations and, 213–214, 232–233

Talk shows, 10
Third-party compliments, 217
Time, rewards and:
  completed tasks, 244–245
  course correction and, 125
  MBWA and lack of, 25–26
  tying the two together, 245–246
Toys-R-Us, 241
Trading Places, 37
Triangulating information, 36–37
  achievements, recognizing/rewarding, 44–46
  direct conversations, 42–43
  feedback from others, 41–42
  observations, 37–40
  progress and performance, assessing/con-
    fronting, 43–44
Total Quality Management (TQM), 24
Truth:
  efficiency and, 120–122
  See also Honesty
Trust:
  in the abilities of team members, 126

bonds and, creating, 185–188, 200–201, 218
defensive behavior and, 38
honesty and, 121–122
information sharing and, 43, 56
motivation and, 56, 182, 184

University of California, Los Angeles (UCLA),
    15, 38
Unleashing Leadership: Aligning What People Do Best
    with What Organizations Need Most, 185–186

Validity, issues with changes and challenges,
    169, 182
Victory:
  symbolism and, 232–233
  timing celebrations of, 244
Vulnerability:
  confrontations and, 35
  unrealized expectations and, 19

Walton, Bill, 15–16, 21
Waterman, Robert, 23
Western Electric Hawthorne Plant studies, 27–
    28, 125, 147
What's in it for Me? (WIFM), 66
Wiggle room:
  fears of micromanagement, 76
  fluidity misinterpreted as, 178, 183
  unrealized expectations and, 123, 126, 129,
    160
  underperformance and, 160, 169
Women's National Basketball Association
    (WNBA), 71
Wooden, John, 15–16
World Trade Center, 25

Zering, George, 23, 26, 27
Ziglar, Zig, 206, 208